Demons of the
Body and Mind

This book is due on the last date stamped below.
Failure to return books on the date due may result
in assessment of overdue fees.

Fines : $.50 per day

ALSO OF INTEREST

*Horrifying Sex: Essays on Sexual
Difference in Gothic Literature*
(edited by Ruth Bienstock Anolik; McFarland, 2007)

*The Gothic Other: Racial and Social Constructions
in the Literary Imagination* (edited by Ruth Bienstock Anolik
and Douglas L. Howard; McFarland, 2004)

Demons of the Body and Mind

Essays on Disability in Gothic Literature

Edited by
RUTH BIENSTOCK ANOLIK

McFarland & Company, Inc., Publishers
Jefferson, North Carolina, and London

LIBRARY OF CONGRESS CATALOGUING-IN-PUBLICATION DATA

Demons of the body and mind : essays on disability in
gothic literature / edited by Ruth Bienstock Anolik.
    p.   cm.
Includes bibliographical references and index.

ISBN 978-0-7864-3322-3
softcover : 50# alkaline paper

   1. Gothic fiction (Literary genre), English — History and
criticism. 2. Horror tales, English — History and
criticism. 3. People with disabilities in literature.
4. Mental illness in literature. 5. Mind and body in
literature. I. Anolik, Ruth Bienstock, 1952–
PR830.T3D46   2010
823'.0829093527 — dc22   2010013309

British Library cataloguing data are available

Cover images 2010 Shutterstock

Manufactured in the United States of America

*McFarland & Company, Inc., Publishers
 Box 611, Jefferson, North Carolina 28640
  www.mcfarlandpub.com*

To my dear friends Cecily and
Warren Carel, lights in my darkness.

To my life-long friend Dorene Hirsch,
the only possible substitute for June.

To Bob, anti–Gothic exemplar:
good husband and benevolent physician.

With much love.

Acknowledgments

I extend well-deserved gratitude to the patient contributors to this collection whose essays reflect an impressively wide range of scholarship. As always I am grateful to my wonderful children, Jonathan, Rachel and Sarah, for the inspiration they provide; I am glad that they have found alternative sources of nutrition since the publication of the first collection. I continue to be in debt to my great friends and erstwhile colleagues Vince Hausmann, Bill di Canzio and Kate Henry for their brilliant ideas and insight, and for allowing me to laugh at the absurdities of the world we inhabit. I am also constantly thankful for a wonderful group of friends whose support and love keep me grounded and keep me laughing: Gwen Borowsky and David Camp; Eric and Esmé Faerber; Debby and Joe Foster; Carol Gantman; Gerry and Lila Margolis; Carole and Dan Monahan; Barbie Zelizer; Fred Baurer; Carol Bernstein, for her lasting influence, and especially, Sharon Pollak, for her kind understanding of the exigencies of proof-reading.

Table of Contents

Introduction: Diagnosing Demons: Creating and Disabling the Discourse of Difference in the Gothic Text

Ruth Bienstock Anolik

The Gothic mode of narrative is the "hideous progeny" (*pace* Mary Shelley[1]) of Enlightenment faith in the powers of the rational mind to apprehend the world. In her Introduction to *The Female Thermometer* Terry Castle demonstrates how Enlightenment ideologies re-contextualize the unnatural (and supernatural) so that their unexplained appearance in a reasonable world evokes the troubled sense of the uncanny, the unsettling identification of the unfamiliar within the familiar:

> [T]he Freudian uncanny is a function of *enlightenment*: it is that which confronts us, paradoxically after a certain *light* has been cast. Freud quotes repeatedly (and famously) from the late eighteenth-century philosopher Schelling: everything is uncanny "which ought to have remained hidden but has come to light" [7].

Thus, as Castle suggests, without reason and realism, the unnatural and the supernatural are not particularly troubling; they fit comfortably in a world which is based upon superstition and magical thinking. The Enlightenment assumption of a rational world is what makes the appearance of the inexplicable troubling. The light of the Enlightenment is thus necessary to create the shadowed space of uncontrollable irrationality in which the Gothic lurks.

Terry Castle and Michel Foucault both note the Enlightenment tendency to transform the world into the known world through the creation of defining and confining categories. Castle notes "the distinctively eighteenth-century impulse to systematize and regulate, to bureaucratize the world of knowledge" (9). The eighteenth-century impulse to achieve knowledge by

1

creating conceptual categories of definition lies at the root of Foucault's assertion that heightened control in the eighteenth century was effected through
the development of new conceptual categories.[2]

The emergence of the Gothic mode as a direct counter to Enlightenment approaches works in two complementary ways. The Gothic avoids the
rational light of the Enlightenment by hiding in the shadows of its own
unknowable and irrational world. Additionally, the Gothic resists the Enlightenment impulse to construct defining conceptual categories, buttressed by
material barriers. The breaching of the walls of church and state (the abbey
and the castle) is echoed by the Gothic tendency to subvert conceptual boundaries as well. Most assiduously, the Gothic interrogates the central category
of thought identified by Foucault, the category of "man,"[3] the Enlightenment
category that is narrowly defined as orderly, rational, healthy, white and male.
The effect of this rational and scientific category was to consign all those who
did not fit the standard definition to shadowy exile. On the social level that
Foucault observes, human beings who did not fit squarely within these categories were deposited in newly created spaces of imprisonment: the prison,
the hospital, the madhouse.[4] To this list might be added the domestic sphere
of the home. On the cultural level, the non-normative human, excluded from
the category of the human, becomes the human Other, as mysterious and
unknowable, as inhuman, as any ghost or monster lurking in the darkness.[5]

The Gothic mode emerges as a response and a counter to the impulse
of the Enlightenment to repress darkness, unreason, the unknown, the Other.
The locus of the Gothic is the shadowy, mysterious and unknowable space
inhabited by the inhumanly unknowable Other — supernatural or human.
The Gothic adventure is the journey of the normative, enlightened Self as it
encounters the unknown. In its repressive aspect, the Gothic reflects the exclusionary categorization of the Enlightenment, figuring human difference as
monstrosity. In its more progressive moments the Gothic recognizes that the
monster also has a subjective existence, that the figuring of the human Other
as inhuman is itself a monstrous act. Thus in its considerations of the human
Other of the Enlightenment — inhuman, unknowable, dangerously uncontrollable — the Gothic presents human difference as monstrous, and then, paradoxically, subverts the categories of exclusion to argue for the humanity of
the monster. The Gothic investigation of the mysterious human Other who
deviates from the normative standards for race, religion, ethnicity and social
class was the focus of my earlier collection of essays, *The Gothic Other*. The
Gothic investigation of the human Other who deviates from Enlightenment
norms for gender and sexual identity was at the center of my second collection, *Horrifying Sex*. This collection of essays concentrates on the human
Other who is exiled from the category of the human because of deviations

from standards set by Enlightenment medicine for the healthy human body and mind.

The Horror of Physical and Mental Difference

The essays in *Demons of the Body and Mind* focus on the response of Gothic texts to human beings who are figured as inhuman because they do not align with the physical or mental standards of their society: the "other Other" (to borrow from Catherine Kudlick 557), who like "women, Jews, queers, people of color" (557) have been marginalized by societies and demonized by texts. In fact, Leslie argues for the primacy of this category of otherness:

> I found that the archetypal outsider was figured not by the woman, the homosexual, the Jew, the Red Man, and the Black, as it often has been in classic American literature. Instead, I discovered that the strangely formed body has represented absolute Otherness in all times and places since human history began [xiii].

The Gothic by its nature is drawn to all types of mysterious difference; however, David Punter notes the particular affinity of the Gothic for otherness figured as physical difference: "the Gothic knows the body (and thus the animal) well. It knows about physical fragility, about vulnerability" (*Gothic Pathologies* 9). As Punter further observes, the Gothic also knows about deviant monstrosity and about people who seem to be dangerously unknowable because "the empathies [of the normative subject] are blocked by the deformed body" ("A Foot" 45). That is, the social and psychological empathy that links people through a sense of shared humanity disappears in the face of a deviation that seems to remove the sufferer completely from the human and thus from human intercourse.

Kudlick observes the impact of Enlightenment ideology on this particular "deviant" group:

> The parallels between disabled people and other outcasts can ... be found in how each was pathologized.... It was only after the Enlightenment and the subsequent development of medicine as a respected field of social intervention that human characteristics such as minority, female or queer sexuality, and physical or mental handicap came to be perceived as problems in need of professional management. This medicalization of society affected virtually every marginal group. However, it had a particularly large impact on those deemed physically and mentally anomalous, who found themselves categorized, institutionalized, and often made targets for sterilization justified by medical science [559].

The impulse of Western culture to define the human norm by the physical ideal and to construe the non-normative as dangerously close to the non-human actually predates the Enlightenment by millennia,[6] as does the tendency to prioritize the norm and ignore the non-normative. Quayson demonstrates the early-Renaissance tendency to ignore important distinctions among the non-normative: "With the progressive collapse of the medieval social structure," it was not uncommon for "lepers and lunatics as well as epileptics and sometimes the sick poor to share an asylum" (Quayson 7). The various essays in this collection, while recognizing distinctions, will address the full spectrum of human difference, including physical disability and disease, sense disability, mental disability and disease, and physical difference. In the discussion that follows the term "disability" is applied to any condition within this spectrum that presents physical or mental challenges to fully developed function.

What unites the texts examined in the essays of this collection is that each illustrates the Gothic tendency to reflect the Enlightenment delineation of a boundary between the known and the unknown, and to cast the figure of human difference into the frightening territory of the unknown,[7] safely apart from the normative thinking and writing subject. In the case of the texts discussed in this collection, then, the classic Gothic binary — Self-human-known-Good / Other-inhuman-unknown-Evil — is repackaged as the binary of Enlightenment medicine: health/pathology, with pathology as the code for otherness and all it represents. As Sander Gilman notes, the essential separation of the Self from the Other is also built into this binary, as the boundary is drawn between the "'healthy' observer, physician or layperson, and the 'patient'" (4). The premise of Gilman's observation is that social distribution of power determines and perpetuates the definition of the healthy, observing, defining Self, the representative of the powerful norm who is empowered to diagnose deviation: "the act of seeing is the act of the creation of historically determined (and therefore socially acceptable) images that permit a distinction to be made between the [healthy] observer and the [diseased] Other" (Gilman 7). Punter points out the illogic that underlies the idea of this binary given "the illusion of a perfected wholeness, a body sound in every limb, a perfectly distributed figure of fantasy" ("A Foot Is What Fits the Shoe" 40). That is, in absolute terms, all bodies and minds are imperfect, and thus deviating in some way from the ideal norm; the binary thus collapses into itself.

The Binary and the Spectrum

The illogical artificiality of the health/pathology binary is of understandable concern to activists in the disabilities rights movement, who see first-hand the limiting and dehumanizing power of the defining categories. The response of the disability rights movement is the creation of the term TAB — Temporarily Abled-Body — which connotes that the abled body might, at any random moment, become disabled. This notion interrogates the rigid binaries of abled/disabled and health/pathology and replaces it with a new paradigm: the spectrum of ability, in which each person occupies a random and temporary position. Susan Sontag presents this concept a bit more poetically in the opening lines of *Illness as Metaphor*: "Everyone who is born holds dual citizenship in the kingdom of the well and in the kingdom of the sick. Although we all prefer to use only the good passport, sooner or later each of us is obliged, at least for a spell, to identify ourselves as citizens of that other place" (3). The term TAB recognizes the impermanence of identity based on the condition of the body (or the mind), and goes beyond Sontag in indicating that there is, in fact, no border between the kingdom of the well and the kingdom of the sick.

The concept of TAB, the identity that subverts fixed boundaries, is anticipated by the deconstructive Gothic tendency to destroy the same boundaries that it establishes. Just as the Gothic text almost always ends with the destruction of the walls of the castle and monastery that imprison the Gothic self, so does the text end with the disorienting suggestion that conceptual barriers have also been breached. The Gothic project to resist limiting boundaries and defining categories thus aligns with the project of those engaged with the disability rights movement: "Many with disabilities have come to equate breaking free of medical definitions as a form of liberation and a way to contest historically contingent ideas of normality" (Kudlick 559). As the essays in this collection reveal, the always-ludic, always-transgressive Gothic is readily available to contest limiting categories of identity. All of the texts discussed in this collection work at some level to undermine the very binaries of the human that they establish: normal/non-normative; healthy/sick; able/disabled; human/inhuman; Self/Other. As Punter observes, these paradoxes and reversals lie at the center of the Gothic, "the history of ... dealings with the disabled body runs throughout the history of the Gothic, a history of invasion and resistance, of the enemy within, of bodies torn and tortured, or else rendered miraculously, or sometimes catastrophically, whole ... the obvious example ... *Frankenstein*" (40) — indeed, Shelley's text is discussed twice in this collection, and in the essays of Andy Scahill and Martyn Colebrook, we will encounter two other characters who are tellingly named "Frank."

Thus, while some of the horror in these texts reflects the shocked response of the "dominant culture [that] assumes an able body" (Crutchfield and Epstein 7), much of the textual horror derives from the cruel social practice of defining human identity based on a fixed standard, and demonizing difference. As the following essays reveal, Gothic texts that categorize human disability as a frighteningly inhuman deviance, tend conversely to interrogate cultural preoccupations with definition and categorization — in other words, with diagnosis. The essays in this collection reflect a doubled and conflicted set of anxieties: fear of the non-normative human Other; fear of social authority that excludes human difference. Figures of authority — often, but not always, physicians — draw upon their social power to create and replicate categories that contain and exclude others who do not fit into rationally and scientifically constructed notions of what is healthy, and thereby human.[8] Punter notes that the focus on the consequences of social power and social marginalization is also a typically Gothic concern: "the Gothic is, in any reading, about power ... The question of disability and power, is, of course, all around us" ("A Foot" 47). Figures of authority are thus empowered to determine (diagnose) human identity on the basis of socially/politically/aesthetically/medically mandated criteria. In a society that dehumanizes deviation, this diagnosis amounts to diagnosing deviance as inhuman, as monstrous. The non-normative human is thus transformed (through the process of diagnosis) into a demon.

The pieces here thus work to highlight the Gothic distrust of confining categories and boundaries and of the powerful authorities who create them, a distrust that is revealed by many of the texts discussed in this collection. This approach suggests that the demons are, in fact, the physicians and other figures of authority who define human difference as dangerous pathology, thereby exiling a category of people from the world of the human. In his book, *Gothic Pathologies*, Punter identifies the dangers of legal power that can establish social norms to exclude deviance, especially considering that humanly created laws and standards are subjective and flawed: "the law is not absolute, it is a way of seeing things" (*Pathologies* 3). In fact, "the voice of absolute authority ... is simultaneously the voice of a caprice" (43). Punter makes an additional observation: "there is little to distinguish the lawyer from the criminal in much eighteenth-century fiction" (*Pathologies* 38) — thus there is a link between those who arbitrarily enforce the erratic and harmful rules[9] and those who break them. This collection points to the slippage between the demons who are diagnosed and the demonically powerful and even evil physicians who do the diagnosing. These medical demons — and others socially empowered to diagnose deviance and exclude the human — make dangerous assumptions and decisions that destroy the lives of non-normative human. Authorities so empowered are, then, demons who diagnose.

The tendency of the texts discussed in this collection to dislodge the identifying term "demon" from the non-normative object to the diagnosing subject illustrates the Gothic mistrust of defining categories and fixed identities. This facet of the Gothic explains the subversive Gothic inclination to empathize with the Other, the non-normative, transgressive figure who troubles the category of the norm and transgresses the boundaries necessary to create the norm: the monster. The Gothic is drawn to "startling bodies whose curious lineaments ... confuse comforting distinctions between what is human and what is not" (Rosemary Garland Thomson 1). As we shall see, the Gothic is also drawn to startling minds that direct behavior which also troubles the definition of the human. The image of the Gothic monster as the fearful and yet liberating emblem of difference and deviance is thus central to many of the essays in this collection. Judith Halberstam's discussion of the monster highlights the relationship between monstrosity and human difference. The monster is "embodied horror" (2–3). As Halberstam recognizes, monstrosity can be ambiguous and over-determined: "monsters always combine the markings of a plurality of differences even if certain forms of difference are eclipsed momentarily by others" (5–6). Yet to her, the overarching difference emblematized by the monster is sexual difference. This reading exemplifies a critical tendency to see the diseased or disabled body as the code for "another Other," gesturing to differences of race, class, gender. A number of texts discussed in this collection do conflate the otherness of disability with racial, ethnic and gendered difference,[10] and a number of the essays suggest that the otherness of disability acts to distract the reader from some other inhumanly dangerous deviation. Yet, it is crucially important to keep sight of textual depictions of disability as representing very real human disability, and not merely as metaphor. As Michael Davidson puts it: "there are cases in which a prosthesis is *still* a prosthesis" (120); that is, in some cases "disability is not a metaphor" for something else but a reflection of "a lived reality" (120). In fact, the critical displacement of the disabled or diseased body reflects the invisibility of disability in "polite" society. Seeing the non-normative body as representing itself renders that body visable and accessible to the kind of analysis that appears in the essays in this collection.

Invisible and Visible

As I have worked on this collection, I have been inspired by the scholarship of the writers who have contributed to this volume, and I am grateful for what I have learned from them on the way. In the early stages of this collection, I considered that I might be able to draw upon the term "invisible disability" as I attempted to categorize the essays — ceding to academic and Enlightenment imperatives for classification that admittedly violate all Gothic principles.[11] The idea of invisible disability, deployed by the disability rights movement, seems at first glance to set up yet another limiting binary: invisible disability/visible disability. But in fact the term, like TAB, opens up and destroys the limiting categories of disability and disease. The concept of invisible disability suggests that most, and even all, people have some physical or mental challenge; some are just more visible than others. As articulated by the web site of The Invisible Disabilities Advocate, an "organization that reaches around the world to people touched by chronic illness, pain, injury and disabilities":

> A person can have an *Invisible Disability* whether or not they have a "visible" impairment or use an assistive device like a wheelchair, walker, cane, etc. For example, whether or not a person utilizes an assistive device, if they are debilitated by such symptoms as extreme pain, fatigue, cognitive dysfunctions and dizziness, they have invisible disabilities.

The organization is very precise in its use of language; it should be since language is the tool of diagnosis and exclusion. The web site asserts that:

> just because a person has a disability, does not mean they are "disabled." Many living with physical or mental challenges are still able to be active in their hobbies, work and be active in sports....The term *Invisible Disabilities* refers to a person's symptoms such as extreme fatigue, dizziness, pain, weakness, cognitive impairments, etc. that are sometimes or always debilitating. These symptoms can occur due to chronic illness, chronic pain, injury, birth disorders, etc. and *are not always obvious to the onlooker* [italics mine]. <http://www.invisibledisabilities.org/ids.htm>

I was initially drawn to the concept of invisible disability and the implied concept of visible disability because the two seem to line up with a set of terms that can be useful in distinguishing between two types of Gothic fear: terror and horror. Ann Radcliff sets up this influential distinction in "On the Supernatural in Poetry" (1826):

> Terror and horror are so far opposite, that the first expands the soul and awakens the faculties to a high degree of life; the other contracts, freezes, and nearly annihilates them ... and where lies the great difference between horror and terror, but in the uncertainty and obscurity, that accompany the first, respecting the dreaded evil? [168].

Horror thus depends on the visible spectacle, the realized experience, to provide fear. The iconic figure of horror is the monster. Terror, on the other hand is the *frisson* that is provoked by the invisible, by what lurks unseen in the dark. Therefore, I reasoned that the texts would likely provoke horror in response to visible disabilities like bodily deformity, and terror in response to invisible disabilities like sense disabilities and infection. Of course the application of reason to Gothic studies seldom works.

One explanation for the deconstruction of my supposed categories is the paradoxical social tendency to render all disease and disability, however spectacularly horrifying, as invisible. Ato Quayson begins his book, *Aesthetic Nervousness*, with a poster showing a man with cerebal palsy, who, unnervingly, has an empty space where his face should be. The words on the poster read: "I'm disabled. Not someone to look straight through. Please don't see me as the invisible man ... See me for who I am ... and treat me as an equal." The use of the phrase "the invisible man" sets up a fascinating chain of allusions. H.G. Wells's *The Invisible Man* (1897) tells the story of a scientist who discovers how to make his body invisible. Ralph Ellison taps into the various layers of meanings to be found in this image in the Prologue to his autobiographical novel, *Invisible Man* (1953): "I am an invisible man. No, I am not a spook like those who haunted Edgar Allan Poe.... I am invisible, understand, because people refuse to see me" (3). Ellison's words anticipate the statement of the man on the poster: those who are different — physically, mentally, racially — are blocked out by a society that insists that only the norm exists. Mitchell and Snyder note that members of marginalized groups are also invisible in that their social needs are ignored: "Disabled writers and scholars of disability have consistently agreed upon one point: the neglect of people with disabilities has resulted in their preeminent social invisibility" (11).

The social paradox of the visible made invisible is countered by the paradoxical Gothic impulse to render invisible difference as horrifying spectacle. In *Freaks*, his seminal work on human monsters, Leslie Fiedler explains the essential connection between the visible and the monstrous when he discusses the origins of the word "monster": "The etymology of the word is obscure ... it derives [either] from *moneo*, meaning to warn, or *monstro*, meaning to show forth" (20). In either case, the purpose of warning or of showing depends upon the visibility of the creature. And despite Ann Radcliffe's protests, the mode of the horrifying spectacle is the mode that dominates the Gothic — even her own works depend on the spectacular, the sight of the dead body, the pool of blood. While Radcliffe ultimately provides a comforting rational explanation for the spectacle, she does not eject it entirely from her texts.

The Gothic tendency to make the invisible visible can be explained in a number of ways. As the irrational counter to the rational Enlightenment, the intellectual movement whose categories remove the emotional and the irrational from the norm of human experience, the Gothic is committed to externalizing the internal and invisible human responses repressed by Enlightenment notions of human subjectivity. Thus, for example, the affinity of the Gothic for what John Ruskin calls the Pathetic Fallacy, the tendency to project invisible emotion upon visible natural phenomena, resulting in the dark and stormy nights that mirror the dark nights of the Gothic soul. This tendency thus illustrates the Gothic movement toward liberation, exhibiting the realm of human experience that the Enlightenment attempts to repress.

Yet, the wall-breaching progressive Gothic exists side by side with the monster-creating conservative and even repressive Gothic, the Gothic that often closes with a seeming restoration of old structures. This aspect of the Gothic is also revealed in the inclination to render invisible difference as visible. Along with visibility comes the attribution of malevolence, serving to warn the reader away from the monstrously different human Other. I came upon an egregious example of this nasty tendency while writing about the human monster, Svengali the Jew, the villain of George Du Maurier's *Trilby* (1894). I discovered that Du Maurier's representation of the visibly evil Jew is an anxious response to fears of an invasion of English society by invisible assimilated Jews. The dangerous and supernatural power of Svengali is neutralized by the text because he is the spectacular, unmistakable Jewish monster, who uses his inhuman — both animalistic and Satanic — powers to take possession of the title character, a young Christian woman. A number of texts in this collection illustrate this process; indeed no pathology remains invisible, as the essays will reveal: madness, infection, sense disability — all appear as visible threats.[12]

Visible and Invisible Disabilities

Since my plan to categorize the essays that follow by the modes of representation was subverted by the transgressiveness of the Gothic text, in representing all "deviant" conditions as visible spectacle, I have divided essays of the collection into two sections determined by the visual status of the original condition. Thus "Part II: Visible Specters: Horrifying Representations of Invisible Pathology" features discussions of texts in which invisible pathology is rendered as spectacular monstrosity. The essays in Part I "Monstrous Deformity: The Horrifying Spectacle of Difference" discuss texts that paint visible physical difference with the garish colors of the Gothic brush. Some of the differences depicted are functionally challenging to the sufferer, others may challenge only the aesthetic standards of the norm; some are challenging to both sufferer and observer. In each text, the deviation from the norm is marked upon the body, recalling Halberstam's comment that "the emergence of the monster within Gothic fiction marks a peculiarly modern emphasis upon the horror of particular kinds of bodies" (Halberstam 2–3). In each case of external deviation, monstrosity is interpreted as representing interior, moral monstrosity at some level.

The collection fittingly opens with the iconic figure of horrifying physical difference: Frankenstein's monster.[13] In "A Space, a Place: Visions of a Disabled Community in Mary Shelley's *Frankenstein* and *The Last Man*," Paul Marchbanks moves beyond the standard argument that the horror of the monster illustrates the horror projected onto the human figure who does not fit cultural aesthetic norms. Reading Shelley's two novels, Marchbanks discovers an overarching critique of the social tendency to judge people by a superficial glance, judging inner worth by external appearance. In fact, Marchbanks asserts that Shelley defines the normative sense of vision as a deficit since it leads the observer to make incorrect judgments based only on superficial phenomena.[14] Marchbanks also asserts that in both novels Shelley presents a fleeting possibility of an inclusive utopia structured on the inner worth of the individual rather than on arbitrary definitions set by visually-determined normative categories.

Cynthia Hall's essay, "'Colossal Vices' and 'Terrible Deformities' in George Lippard's Gothic Nightmare," examines a nineteenth-century American novel that connects physical and social dysfunction in a gothicized American setting. Hall, like Marchbanks, notes that her author works to undermine the dependability of decisions based on superficial judgment of aesthetic difference. Lippard's rich and beautiful characters are as corrupt as the ugly poor, whose twisted morality is reflected by their twisted spines. Hall contextualizes the representation of the humped back of the lower-class criminal and the Jewish criminal as a sign of immorality within nineteenth-century discourse about the upright spine, the signifier of the human.[15]

In "Ominous Signs or False Clues? Difference and Deformity in Wilkie Collins's Sensation Novels," Tamara S. Wagner argues that Collins taps into the aesthetic prejudices of his readers to heighten the suspense regarding the identity of his villains. Thus Fosco, the obese villain in *The Woman in White*, confounds Victorian expectation of the jolly and benevolent fat man; *The Law and the Lady* confounds expectations that physical deformity always indicates villainy; *The Mark of Cain* confirms that criminal tendencies cannot be readily ascertained by external evidence.[16]

Elizabeth Hale turns to a different type of villainous difference in "The Dangerous Mr. Casaubon: Gothic Husband and Gothic Monster in *Middlemarch*." Hale argues that Eliot draws on Gothic tropes in her representation of Casaubon as an example of the sickly scholar, whose body is depleted because of his focus on his studies. In fact, Eliot delineates Casaubon as both Gothic husband and Gothic monster, physically repulsive, subjectively empty, dwelling in realms of death. Hale argues that once Casaubon is exorcised from the text, *Middlemarch* transforms from Gothic to *Bildungsroman*, as Dorothea's restored agency allows her to embark on her life's journey.[17]

In "Folk Medicine, Cunning-Men and Superstition in Thomas Hardy's

'The Withered Arm,'" Simon J. White identifies the struggle between scientific and superstitious modes of diagnosing and treating disability. White argues that Hardy, writing about the early nineteenth century from the perspective of the century's end, expresses the fear that an educated and scientific mind can slide back from the ideas of the Enlightenment toward dangerous supernatural thinking.

Catherine Delyfer's essay, "Lucas Malet's Subversive Late-Gothic: Humanizing the Monster in *The History of Sir Richard Calmady*" moves back to the kind of spectacular disability discussed in the earlier essays of Hall and Wagner. The title character of Malet's novel is at least as monstrous as Lippard's hunchbacks, and Collins's Miserrimus Dexter. Yet as Delyfer asserts, Malet completely rejects the stereotypes that inform the earlier novels. While Richard's monstrous disability is a throwback — the result of a typical Gothic curse — the hero is no Gothic creature. He is humanly multi-faceted, both physically and psychologically, and his humanity ultimately redeems him and breaks the curse. Since Richard is certainly not the monster of the novel, Delyfer argues that he acts as a textual distraction from the real monster, the deviant New Woman whose threat to social structures exceeds that of any Gothic creature.

Tara Surry's "Encounters with the Monster: Self-Haunting in Virginia Woolf's 'Street Haunting,'" demonstrates that the Modernism of the early twentieth century draws from the Gothic rather than opposing it. Surry reveals that the speaker in the essay, who begins a typical twentieth-century search for a commodity, stumbles upon a Gothic journey —first an encounter with the monstrous Other, and then an inward journey to the monstrous Self. As the narrator encounters non-normative ghosts and monsters on the street, she comes to realize that she, like all human beings, deviates from the normative ideal.

Part II, "Visible Specters: Horrifying Representations of Invisible Pathology," moves from the figure who illustrates explicit, spectacular deformity, easily diagnosed, and misdiagnosed, to the even more troubling figure, whose non-normative pathology is invisible until rendered as spectacle by the Gothic text. In each of the texts discussed in this section, a condition that would be invisible if presented in realistic terms, is presented as a spectacular and readily identifiable danger to the normative subject. A number of the texts discussed adopt the typical Gothic strategy of figuring madness and other invisible mental conditions as externally and visibly dangerous. Moments in which madness is spectacularized are considered in the essays of Melissa Wehler, Lisa M. Hermsen, Carla T. Kungl and Martyn Colebrook. Together, these essays suggest that the ultimate place of Gothic mystery and horror is the invisible inner space of the human mind. Other essays in this section also demonstrate the Gothic tendency to expose and reveal secretly invisible conditions and to render them as spectacular monstrosity: Carolyn D. Williams and Christine M. Crockett consider the pathologizing and demonizing of those who engage in "deviant" sexual practices, conducted behind closed doors; my essay considers the horrifying allegorical representations of invisible disease and its victims; Maria Purves demonstrates textual associations between sense disabilities in women, and monstrously dangerous power; Andy Scahill considers horror films that peer into the private inner space of the womb to reveal the dangerous deformed fetus. These essays thus consider textual moments in which secret and private conditions are exposed as monstrous, serving to warn the audience of the invisible dangers lurking within the unknown. They also illustrate the source of the reactionary Gothic fear of invisible, undetectable difference.

Melissa Wehler's essay, "Revising Ophelia: Representing Madwomen in Baillie's *Orra* and *Witchcraft*," examines the difference between Shakespeare's representation of the mad Ophelia and Baillie's dramatic representation of madwomen. Wehler argues that in appropriating Shakespeare's character for her plays, Baillie transforms the properly contained Renaissance madwoman into the frighteningly unbound madwoman of the Gothic.

Carolyn D. Williams also considers the pathologization and demonization of female power in "The Case of the Malnourished Vampyre: The Perils of Passion in John Clelands's *Memoirs of a Coxcomb*," a text that repackages female sexual appetite (a deviation from medical and social norms) as vampirism. In locating the origins of this vampiric theory of female sexuality in Aristotle's influential theories of medicine, Williams shows how accepted scientific approaches can have more in common with Gothic iconography than with rational science.

With Christine M. Crockett's essay, "'The Monster Vice': Masturbation, Malady, and Monstrosity in *Frankenstein*," we turn once again to Shelley's creature. While the monster is certainly a visible figure of monstrosity, Crockett argues that he also encodes eighteenth- and nineteenth-century medical assessments of the private practice of masturbation. Crockett shows that medical discourse, influenced by the Enlightenment insistence on standardized behavior, draws upon Gothic imagery to expose the horrifyingly deteriorating body of the masturbator, using this monstrous figure to warn practitioners about straying from the norm. The body of the masturbating monster of medical discourse thus appears to anticipate that of Shelley's creature. Yet, as Crockett shows, the ultimate masturbating monster of *Frankenstein* is the doctor himself; the major threat posed by the monster is that he reveals the confining limitations of Enlightenment standards.

My contribution to the collection, "Invasion and Contagion: The Spectacle of the Diseased Indian in Poe's 'The Masque of the Red Death,'" focuses on an invisible source of danger, infectious disease, represented as monstrous specter in Poe's text. In fact, Poe's story visualizes two invisible threats to his world: smallpox bacteria and the disappearing Native American. By reading Poe's story in conjunction with a Native American legend about the movement of an allegorical figure of smallpox from the east, I argue that Poe's ambiguous plague may be diagnosed as smallpox, and that the figure of the Red Death stands in for the disease as well as for the diseased Native American.

Lisa M. Hermsen reveals more anxieties of young America in her essay "*Knights of the Seal*: Mad Doctors and Maniacs in A.J.H. Duganne's Romance of Reform." Duganne's novel presents the typical Gothic madhouse in order to interrogate the application of asylum reform in a young democracy. Hermsen asserts that Duganne articulates a mistrust of any inequitable distribution of power in any American institution, including the mental hospital. While the people confined in the madhouse seem to be the monsters of the novel, they are ultimately represented as victims of the demonic physician who has abused the power of diagnosis by marginalizing and imprisoning those who deviate from the normative ideal of mental health.

Carla T. Kungl addresses the difficulty of identifying invisibly ambiguous insanity and epilepsy in "'The Secret of My Mother's Madness': Mary Elizabeth Braddon and Gothic Instability." Kungl considers two Sensation novels by Braddon, each of which reveals anxiety regarding the mysterious inner mental state of the title character. Kungl argues that invisible and ambiguous madness, the secret of the title character of *Lady Audley's Secret*, is figured as a danger in the novel because it allows her to covertly subvert social boundaries, including the standard that prohibits ladies from committing murder. Similarly Brandon Mountford's epilepsy is diagnosed as dangerous within *Thou Art the Man* because it supposedly leads him to commit murder. Ultimately, Kungl argues that the actual danger posed by both characters is that they transgress gender categories as a consequence of their non-normative mental states.

In "'Don't Look Now': Disguised Danger and Disabled Women in Daphne du Maurier's Macabre Tales," Maria Purves identifies a pattern of dangerous disabled women in Du Maurier's stories and then concentrates on the figures of malevolently powerful women who are blind or deaf. Purves demonstrates that in the stories, the power of the women is as invisible as their disability, rendering them particularly dangerous.

In "Deviled Eggs: Teratogenesis and the Gynecological Gothic in the Cinema of Monstrous Birth," Andy Scahill turns to another set of texts that demonize invisible difference: horror films of the 1970s which transform defective fetuses into monsters. Scahill provides the cultural context for the power of these films: the emerging notion of the independent fetus. The idea of the fetus as a separate individual, possibly hostile to the mother and to her society, arose as a consequence of new medical technology that could observe the development of the fetus in the womb, as well as of the rhetoric of the anti-abortion movement which also figured the fetus as an independent being. Scahill asserts that the idea of an angry deformed fetus also revealed cultural anxieties regarding the toxic environment, and the mother who transmitted environmental toxins to her unborn child.

The collection ends with the last essay on the dangers of invisible madness, Martyn Colebrook's "'Journeys into Lands of Silence': *The Wasp Factory* and Mental Disorder." Colebrook locates Iain Banks's novel in the tradition of the Scottish Gothic, in which the interest in marginalization and doubling reflects the cultural relationship of Scotland to England. The unreliable narrator of the novel, Frank, tells the reader of his institutionalized brother, who Frank suggests is criminally insane. As the novel unfolds the reader comes to realize that Frank is, in fact, the insanely homicidal brother of the pair. Colebrook asserts that the novel thus emphasizes the danger posed to normative society by the invisible and undiagnoseable nature of insanity.

Frank also illustrates, as do many of the "deviants" represented in this collection, the paradoxically liberating nature of disability in a society structured upon the power and the presence of the norm. We will see a number of moments in which both visible and invisible disability is overlooked by a society that attends to the normative human. Although invisibility can be demeaning, it can also be empowering; invisibility releases the "object" from the controlling surveillance of society. The invisibility of the disabled discussed in this collection allows them to create all sorts of joyously transgressive havoc because no one notices their existence. Punter notes this transgressiveness is the ultimate goal of the Gothic: "Gothic is able, because of its freedom from the law, to play" (12); "Gothic is therefore all about supersession, about the will to transcend, and about the fate of the body as we [the subject] strive for a fantasy of total control, or better, total exemption — from the rule of law" (17). This is certainly the goal of the progressive Gothic; yet, as the essays reveal, the responses of the texts to the transgressions of the disabled characters run the gamut from shock to delight, often within the same text. The Gothic text thus celebrates the joyful liberation of the monster while simultaneously recoiling in fear. This ambiguous response to its own monsters results in the continuing debate regarding the politics of the Gothic: Does the demonization of the human Other indicate repressive tendencies? Does the liberation of the monster indicate progressive tendencies? Or, is the repressive/progressive political binary implied by these questions yet another binary that is deconstructed by the Gothic text?

NOTES

1. "I bid my hideous progeny go forth and prosper" (Mary Shelley. Introduction *Frankenstein* 173).

2. Michel Foucault observes that the new categories are based upon confining scientific definitions of the norm. These newly created definitions lead to new categories of deviance, thus providing opportunities for greater social control. Foucault presents variations of this argument throughout his work. In *Madness and Civilization* he argues that the newly defined category of social danger defined as madness called for a new means of containment: confinement within the walls of the madhouse. Similarly, in *Discipline and Punish* Foucault asserts that the new category of the criminal called into being by the increase in consumer commodities — that is by property in need of greater protection than the old form of real estate — was contained within the walls of the penitentiary.

3. Foucault argues in *The Order of Things* that the concept of "man" as an object of study was also developed in the eighteenth century through the construction of the linguistic and epistemological barriers of new discourses in order to place man at the center of intellectual scrutiny and thereby as the cynosure of social control. Foucault asserts, "Before the end of the eighteenth century, *man* did not exist.... He is a quite recent creature" (308), that is, as an object of study. As Foucault also notes, "man is only a recent invention, a figure not yet two centuries old, a new wrinkle in our knowledge, and ... he will disappear again as soon as that knowledge has discovered a new form" (xxiii). In fact, as the essays in this collection demonstrate, the rapidly disappearing figure of the normative "man," as the representative of the human, has long been the target of the Gothic critique.

4. Foucault says, "the history of madness would be the history of the Other — of that which, for a given culture, is at once interior and foreign, therefore to be excluded (so as to exorcize the interior danger) but by being shut away (in order to reduce its otherness)" (*The Order of Things* xxiv).

5. Leslie Fiedler observes that this new form of monster, the human monster, is a recent formulation. He notes that early Gothic writers tend toward the old ideas of monstrosity. William Beckford, Matthew Lewis, Clara Reeve and Ann Radcliffe implanted fear into their novels through "grotesques: vestiges of medieval superstition ... physiological abnormalities appear nowhere" (262–263). Fiedler asserts that it was Mary Shelley who introduced "a new kind of Freak into the new genre" (263), in her account of modern technology creating a monster unknown in nature. Indeed, it was not only modern technology that allowed Shelley to create her monster; the notion of human monstrosity promoted by the ideologies of the Enlightenment also led to his creation.

6. The Torah demands physical perfection of priests who approach God through the Temple sacrifices; imperfect members of the priestly family are abjected (Lev. 21:17–23). (My thanks to Rabbi Edward Feld for directing my attention to these verses.) Quayson points to the development of this attitude in an early Medieval text: a "taxonomy of monstrosity in which the disabled take their place beside monsters" (6). Disease is also figured as a source of transgressive danger and a cause for human exclusion by the Torah. The Torah presents leprosy (Hansen's disease) as a mark of sin and divine displeasure, thus legitimating the exclusion of the leper from the community (Lev.13; Num.12). The New Testament quite literally demonizes mental disease; Jesus heals the Gerasene demoniac, who demonstrates symptoms of mental illness, by casting out the possessing evil spirits (Mark 5:1–20; Matt. 8:28–34; Luke 8:26–39).

7. Although the demonization of human difference — social, sexual, or medical — is clearly an irrational process — hence the deployment of this strategy in the always-irrational Gothic text — Susan Sontag provides an explanation, if not a rationale for the impulse. In "AIDS and Its Metaphors," Sontag explains the slippage by which fear of the illness (or disability) translates into fear of the ill (or disabled) person; the victim thus replaces the condition, becoming the figure of mystery and murder. Thus the "stigmatization of certain illnesses" leads "by extension" to the stigmatization of "those who are ill" (99). Of course, the Gothic mode possesses all the apparatus to present such a human, yet inhuman, monster.

8. Conversely, some of the texts discussed in this collection present moments in which the failure of modern medicine results in a relapse into superstitious and supernatural thinking.

9. Punter associates the dangerous power of creating rules and standards with lawyers and the law; the texts discussed in this collection, often identify the physician as the source of the exclusionary and confining diagnosis.

10. Quayson notes that "The colonial encounter and the series of migrations that it triggered in its wake served to displace the discourse of disability onto a discourse of otherness that was correlated to racial difference" (10).

11. As illustrated by the disdain for scholars demonstrated by George Eliot and Daphne du Maurier.

12. I would like to mention the work of two colleagues on the topic of visualizing human difference as monstrous spectacle. Katherine Henry, a contributor to *The Gothic Other* and to *Horrifying Sex*, and the author of *Liberalism and the Culture of Security: The Nineteenth-Century Rhetoric of Reform and Reaction* (U of Alabama P, forthcoming), identifies this trope in *Rebecca* by Daphne du Maurier, co-incidentally a granddaughter of George Du Maurier. Henry focuses on the invisible internal pathology of the title character: her infertility. Henry argues that this invisible physical defect, representing a failure to serve the patriarchy, is the secret evil that lurks within the monstrous Rebecca. Henry is particularly interested in the intersection of the politics of the norm with the representation of female infertility as a deviation, the result of a physical deformity, and as the source of villainy in an otherwise typical Gothic villainous, unchaste and sexually insatiable. The question Henry raises: how does Rebecca's barrenness influence our reading of her as the monstrous Gothic Other of the novel? Andrew Scahill (a contributor to *Horrifying Sex*, whose essay on filmic representations of deformed fetuses appears in this collection) would entitle his work on infectious disease in film, "I Am Lethal: Contagion as Spectacle in the Contemporary Pathogen Thriller." He is interested in the externalized and demonized representation of invisible pathology that occurs in the various plague movies of the last decades: *I Am Legend*; *28 Days Later*; *28 Weeks Later*; the *Resident Evil* series, *Quarantine*; *Dawn of the Dead*; *Land of the Dead*; *Cabin Fever*; *Splinter*; *Planet Terror*. As Scahill observes, these films suggest that the consequence, the symptom, of (invisible) contagious illness is the demonization of the victim. While these films certainly tap into the public hysteria generated by such "plagues" as AIDS, SARS, avian flu, the threat of biological warfare, and now Swine Flu, they also work within the ongoing Gothic project to visualize difference in a spectacular way, a project that is certainly reflected in the conventions of cinematic horror.

13. As Punter suggests, "*Frankenstein* is a text which crucially, is about the body ... that is beyond the law" (*Pathologies* 50).

14. Further discussion of the limiting and liberating aspects of blindness is to be found in Purves's essay on Daphne du Maurier.

15. Lippard is one of the several representatives of the Philadelphia Gothic featured in this collection. Other members of this not-very-illustrious group discussed in this collection are Poe, Lippard and Duganne. Charles Brockden Brown, an important member

of the group does not appear in this collection, although his novel, *Arthur Mervyn*, is of interest as a delirious and hallucinatory account of the yellow fever epidemic in Philadelphia in 1793. A recent exhibit at the Library Company of America in Philadelphia highlighted these native sons. From the informative website of the exhibit:

> Philadelphia Gothic illuminates this stunning paradox: Perhaps the most enlightened, genteel, urbane, and humane of American cities in the first half of the 19th century, Philadelphia spawned a literary tradition of Lurid Crime, Weird Hallucination, and the Brooding Supernatural. By the 1840s, "The Quaker City" had become a byword for sheer horror! This was the work of three largely forgotten Philadelphia novelists: Charles Brockden Brown, Robert Montgomery Bird, and George Lippard. This exhibition resuscitates these writers, through first editions of their major works and oil portraits that have never before been exhibited, and puts them in the company of Edgar Allan Poe, who absorbed their Gothic themes and obsessions while he lived in Philadelphia, the birthplace of the Gothic tradition in American literature. <http://www.library company.org/gothic/>

16. Collins is one of three Sensation novelists discussed in this collection. As Wagner observes, the non-normative body and mind were a recurring source for the sensational effects that impelled this genre as it interrogated Victorian standards and certainties. The other Sensation writers discussed in this collection are Lucas Malet and Mary Elizabeth Braddon.

17. In her discussion of Daphne du Maurier's "Not After Midnight," Purves notes another instance of aversion to scholars. Casaubon clearly represents the kind of defining and limiting Enlightenment scholarship that offends the transgressive sensibilities of the Gothic.

WORKS CITED

Anolik, Ruth Bienstock, ed. *Horrifying Sex: Essays on Sexual Difference in Gothic Literature.* Jefferson, NC: McFarland, 2007.

_____, and Douglas L. Howard, eds. *The Gothic Other: Racial and Social Constructions in the Literary Imagination.* Jefferson, NC: McFarland, 2004

Castle, Terry. Introduction. *The Female Thermometer: Eighteenth Century Culture and the Invention of the Uncanny.* New York: Oxford University Press, 1995.

Crutchfield, Susan, and Marcy Epstein. Introduction. *Points of Contact, Disability, Art, and Culture.* Ann Arbor: University of Michigan Press, 2000.

Davidson, Michael. "Universal Design: The Work of Disability in an Age of Globalization." *The Disability Studies Reader.* 2nd ed. Edited by Lennard J. Davis. New York: Routledge, 2006.

Ellison, Ralph. *Invisible Man.* New York: Vintage, 1995.

Fiedler, Leslie. Foreword. *Freakery: Cultural Spectacles of the Extraordinary Body.* Ed. Rosemarie Garland Thomson. New York: New York University Press, 1996.

_____. *Freaks: Myths and Images of the Secret Self.* New York: Simon and Schuster, 1978.

Foucault, Michel. *The Order of Things: An Archaeology of the Human Sciences.* 1966. New York: Vintage Books, 1973.

Gilman, Sander L. *Disease and Representation: Images of Illness from Madness to AIDS.* Ithaca: Cornell University Press, 1988.

Halberstam, Judith. *Skin Shows: Gothic Horror and the Technology of Monsters.* Durham: Duke University Press, 2000.

Kudlick, Catherine J. "Disability History, Power and Rethinking the Idea of 'the Other.'" *PMLA* 120. 2 (Mar 2005): 557–61.

Mitchell, David T. and Sharon L. Snyder. Introduction. *The Body and Physical Difference*. Ann Arbor: University of Michigan Press, 1997.

Punter, David. "A Foot Is What Fits the Shoe: Disability, the Gothic and Prosthesis." *Gothic Studies*. 2.1 (2000): 49–49.

_____. *Gothic Pathologies: The Text, the Body and the Law*. New York: St. Martin's, 1998.

Quayson, Ato. *Aesthetic Nervousness: Disability and the Crisis of Representation*. New York: Columbia University Press, 2007.

Radcliffe, Ann. "On the Supernatural in Poetry." *Gothic Documents: A Sourcebook, 1700–1820*. Ed. E.J. Clery and Robert Miles. Manchester: Manchester University Press, 2000.

Shelley, Mary. Introduction. *Frankenstein*. 3rd edition. 1831. *Frankenstein*. Ed. Paul Hunter. New York: Norton, 1996.

Sontag, Susan. *Illness as Metaphor and AIDS and Its Metaphors*. New York: Anchor Books, 1990.

Thomson, Rosemarie Garland. "Introduction; From Wonder to Error — A Geneology of Freak Discourse in Modernity." *Freakery: Cultural Spectacles of the Extraordinary Body*. New York: New York University Press, 1996.

PART I

Monstrous Deformity:
The Horrifying Spectacle
of Difference

A Space, a Place: Visions of a Disabled Community in Mary Shelley's *Frankenstein* and *The Last Man*

PAUL MARCHBANKS

Mary Shelley came of age in the early nineteenth century, a period enthralled with reading texts, reading nature's landscapes, and reading personality in the contours of another's countenance. Public literacy grew as swiftly as the popular practice of aesthetic categorization which led Shelley and her contemporaries to evaluate every landscape as sublime or picturesque, and every individual's face as a map of character. This last fad, echoing the neo–Socratic notion of *kalokagathia* which had long equated good looks with moral character — and disfigurement with depravity — resonated loudly in the works of Percy Shelley, who declared that God valued beauty above all else.[1] Mary Shelley's travel journals reveal that she is willing to objectify and dismiss as "monstrous" those fellow tourists whose "shapeless" and "horrid" features offend her eyes (History 35; Journals 20–21), and readers of her novels and short fiction frequently find her heroines' future courage and nobility telegraphed by lovely faces and lithesome limbs. At times, however, Shelley resists the cultural impulse to link physiognomy and psychology, particularly when constructing differently enabled characters. Her interrogation of the objectifying male gaze in the novella *Matilda* (unpublished until 1959) complements Rosemary Garland Thomson's critique of *the stare*, the "gaze intensified," which works to "sculpt the disabled subject into a grotesque spectacle" (26). Shelley also interrogates that Gothic literary tradition which deploys the chronically ill and differently formed character to signal malignant personality or intent. In doing so, she questions the social practice of wresting subjectivity away from the disabled human being, reducing the person to a two-dimensional cipher. Additionally, she provokes readerly suspicion about the many, structurally important acts of perception performed by her novel's characters. Evidence of this two-pronged exploration of the reliability of vision to ascertain character, and of the physiognomic prejudices of able-bodied majority appears in Shelley's novel *Valperga* (1823) and in her short stories "The Evil Eye" (1829) and "Transformation" (1830). Each of these undercuts society's mistaken reliance on visual markers to decode character. In both *Frankenstein; or The Modern Prometheus* (1818, 1831) and the dystopic *The Last Man* (1826), Shelley creates a sustained dismantling of society's ocular and physiognomic apparatus. Both novels also poignantly present visions of community that might welcome instead of expelling the disabled.

The Monster-Making Instincts of a Vision-Enabled, Aesthetically Myopic Multitude

In the two centuries since a Shakespeare–citing critic for the *Quarterly Review* excoriated *Frankenstein* as stupid and confusing — "'a tale / Told by an ideot [*sic*], full of sound and fury, / Signifying nothing'" (*Quarterly Review* 385) — critics have harvested a rich crop of heterogeneous *somethings* from the novel. Sandra M. Gilbert and Susan Gubar's feminist reading of the creature as a disguised representation of monstrous womanhood in *The Madwoman in the Attic* (1979) has in recent years sparked other, equally provocative readings of Frankenstein's nemesis. These range from the sociopsychological reading — the creature is a battered child become battered parent (Mellor 43) — to the assertion that he acts as therapeutic container for the exorcised, primal emotions of "the primitive Mary Shelley: her guilt at being her mother's killer-reincarnation, her rage that her father abandoned her, and her resentment of her half brother, William" (Sunstein 131).

Shelley's novel has also been praised for its critique of western society's preoccupation with narrowly defined standards of beauty.[2] This preoccupation, which disenfranchises the physically disabled and the disfigured today as it did in Shelley's era, is paralleled by the isolation and disempowerment of vision-impaired individuals who remain ever the object — rarely the subject and source — of the delimiting stare. The social tendency to position the normative as the gazing subject also marginalizes those intellectually disabled individuals whose behavioral and linguistic distinctiveness is often compounded by visible bodily difference. Thus, while concerned most directly with disfigured individuals, *Frankenstein* also questions those cultural values that circumscribe and devalue other differently enabled populations.

Over the course of Shelley's novel, charged stares fly at the creature from everyone with eyes to trace his abnormal features, followed closely by equally pitiless action that is implicitly critiqued by the text. There is no kind or comforting compensation for the many who flee or the few who assail, for little William who curses, beloved Felix who strikes, and the ungrateful man who shoots the creature for his pains in rescuing a drowning girl. We have no proof that what the creature says to Frankenstein of the "multitude of mankind" does not indeed generalize to everyone with eyes to see: "If [they] knew of my existence, they would do as you do, and arm themselves for my destruction" (75). If by some chance the beholder does *not* attack when facing this abomination, only fleeing or fainting are viable alternatives. Even the creature's designer, who temporarily bows to his creation's compelling logic and allows himself to empathize with the creature's situation, ultimately fails to see beyond his strange appearance. As Frankenstein admits, "I compassionated him, and sometimes felt a wish to console him; but when I looked upon him, when I saw the filthy mass that moved and talked, my heart sickened, and my feelings were altered to those of horror and hatred" (109–10). The creature sees matters quite clearly when he asserts that there can be no communion between himself and an aesthetically prejudiced majority unwilling to look beyond his abnormal appearance, for "'the human senses are insurmountable barriers to our union'" (108).

The humans whom the creature encounters react with horror to his presence in part because both his features and (temporarily) his behavior resemble those of the despised "idiot," an association suggested by the psychologist Burton Blatt's comparison of the creature with "retarded" individuals (Blatt 304–5).[3] Though Blatt's own reflections never venture beyond the realm of analogy, Mary Shelley provides ample evidence that popular pseudo-medical and physiognomic notions concerning the idiot did inform her construction of the creature, especially as it appears in its early, developmental stages. Medical historian Jonathan Andrews notes that such gigantic stature and enormous features as those sported by the creature have retained strong associations with mental retardation in the popular imagination ever since Aristotle's *Remarks on Physiognomy*, a text consistently reprinted throughout the eighteenth and nineteenth centuries (Andrews 194). Andrews asserts that the creature's "convulsive motion" brings to mind the species of seizure that often plagues such individuals, and that his yellow and watery eyes in their "dunwhite sockets" (40) recall the "vacant expressions ... [and] bulging eyes" which form part of the popular taxonomy (Andrews 184). The description of the monster, as sketched by the horrified scientist who awakens from a nightmare to find the creature staring at him, evokes contemporary descriptions of the idiot. The monster exhibits an "'imbecilic expression,' 'unmeaning grimace,' and the 'fixed and unmeaning stare'" (Wright 287), as well as the gaping mouth and capacity "to articulate only a few syllables or words to which [he] seem[s] to attach no meaning" (Morison 217). Frankenstein relates: "He held up the curtain of the bed; and his eyes, if eyes they may be called, were fixed on me. His jaws opened, and he muttered some inarticulate sounds, while a grin wrinkled his cheeks" (40). The creature's early tendency to perceive and yet not (initially) differentiate amongst the data gathered by his five senses recalls the limitations of an individual with a severe intellectual disability: "No distinct ideas occupied my mind; all was confused. I felt light, and hunger, and thirst, and darkness; innumerable sounds rung in my ears" (77).[4] His awkward mobility from the moment of his "birth" similarly suggests the functioning of an individual with the intellectual level of a newborn. This observation helps resolve the apparent incongruity between his mental youth and his motor skills, a discrepancy complained of by at least one of Shelley's contemporaries.[5] Additionally, the pleasure the creature takes in the mysterious moon's radiance recalls that experienced by the hero of Wordsworth's "The Idiot Boy" (1798). The creature's delight in the song of the birds — the first sound he is able to recognize and enjoy — aligns him with the series of idiots and imbeciles whom the nineteenth-century physician Alexander Morison "interpreted," some of whom were similarly able to enjoy music but little else (Morison 223, 245).

Yet the creature's capacity ultimately surpasses that of a developmentally disabled individual. In fact, his surprising transformation into an articulate intellectual and agile athlete dramatizes (and, admittedly, exaggerates) the new optimism of Shelley's medical contemporaries concerning the potential of the "idiot" (Andrews 67, Rix 161). The monster's capacity for mental growth destabilizes common assumptions concerning the link between non-normative appearance and mental disability, and disables the unmerited linkage between non-normative appearance and limited intelligence. Similarly, Shelley traces the moral growth of the creature, initially as innocent as a child, despite his appearance. Only when the monster's inner worth is ignored and he is cast out because of his appearance, does he become the stereotypically Gothic monster, ugly inside and out.

Shelley's Destabilization of Her Ocular Architecture

Shelley's extended critique of physiognomic prejudices based on visual perception is the more effective because *Frankenstein* relies so heavily on optical motion and metaphor, a preoccupation highlighted by the 1831 frontispiece which frames a triangular network of intersecting gazes issuing from horrified creator, befuddled creature, and the hollow eye socks of a supine skeleton on the laboratory floor. The narrative's inquiry into the reliability of vision becomes an interrogation of its own rhetorical structure, in which acts of perception provide an unmistakable framework for character communication and plot action. The opening of a "dull yellow eye" signals the creature's very first movement, while the wateriness of the orbs in their "dun-white sockets" provides what the aesthetically biased Frankenstein considers a most horrible contrast with the creature's pearly teeth and luxurious hair (39–40). When the creature peers through the frightened scientist's bed-curtain only hours later, he effectively reverses this dynamic between spectator and spectacle with his own gaze, a gaping look which torments Frankenstein throughout the rest of the novel, lingering even when the increasingly dangerous creature is nowhere to be seen (40, 140). Only with his own death does this menacing image fade from Frankenstein's mind, replaced by the reader's image of the remorseful creature, standing over the body and articulating his plan to follow his creator's example, ending sight and life with one act.

The strange phrase the monster uses to describe his impending suicide is notable. He longs "for the moment when these hands will meet my eyes." These words underscore one of the novel's implied lessons, that the blessing of vision — and knowledge — can become a curse (169). Similarly, in one of his most poetic moments, the creature describes his entry into the world and his approaching exit in terms of changing access to compelling *images*: "I shall no longer see the sun or stars.... Some years ago, when the images which this world affords first opened upon me ... I should have wept to die; now it is my only consolation" (170). This linking of loss of sight with loss of life is given further meaning by an observation of Martha Stoddard Holmes in *Fictions of Affliction*: medical practitioners in the nineteenth century not only treated blindness as an emblem for disease, they often equated vision impairment with death itself (63–64). Mary Shelley thus works to disrupt the formula of blindness as death, which her creature so pathetically adopts. Additionally she works to dismantle the blind/sighted binary that dictates two mutually exclusive states, aligning blindness with the non-normative half of the binary. Frankenstein describes a blinding burst of light reflected off a lake's surface and into his eyes: "Vivid flashes of lightning dazzled my eyes, illuminating the lake, making it appear like a vast sheet of fire; then for an instant everything seemed of a pitchy darkness, until the eye recovered itself from the preceding flash" (54). Frankenstein's explanation of the temporary vision loss and recovery interrogates the experiential boundary dividing sight-enabled from sight-impaired individuals. Shelley also probes this line of demarcation in metaphorical terms. Reliving his past horrors, Frankenstein, describes his long ignorance of the creature's murderous plans as a kind of blindness

(146–47). He also likens an ostensible moment of clairvoyance — in which he imagines the creature and his future mate wreaking havoc on the world — to the removal of a film that has blocked his vision: "I, for the first time, saw clearly" (132). Thus Shelley suggests that, certainly on the metaphorical level, a single person can be located on both sides of the blind/sighted paradigm, and that it is more a spectrum than a binary.

Blind Opportunities

Shelley goes even further in contesting the idea that blindness is inferior to normative sight, suggesting advantages to blindness. While many passages from the scientist's narrative rehearse the accepted wisdom that blindness — real or figurative — denotes an unhealthy ignorance of important knowledge, the climax in the creature's own tale actually pairs vision impairment with a valuable, if rare, fair-mindedness. Just before the creature assigns himself the indelible stamp of "monster," we see a surprisingly hopeful confrontation between the creature and the elder De Lacey, the hideous outcast and the blind man whose very deficiency holds the promise of real communion.

To the despondent and isolated creature who, in the position of specta-tor, observes the De Laceys through a crack in their cottage wall, the fam-ily's visually impaired patriarch betokens a final opportunity for human connection. The education in language and social customs the creature acquires from his momentary position as powerful subject, provides him with the tools he needs to request what he desires even more than a means of com-munication: an emotional connection and a friend. In many ways, the eld-erly musician seems a likely conduit between the creature and the society that has hitherto rejected him. De Lacey's musical skill with the guitar and his disability both suggest a figure accustomed to alternative modes of inter-course. He cannot see the picturesque forests around him, nor the faces of his beloved family. Dispossessed of sight, defined by John Locke as "that most instructive of our senses" (Understanding 214), De Lacey must peer beyond the physiognomic map traced by others and regard the personality hiding behind the visible façade. Unlike the many characters, who depend on a net-work of looks and gazes to navigate social space, he "reads" his companions by listening closely to the cadence and intonation of their voices as much as to their words, discerning the emotion hiding behind their declarations. De Lacey's sensitivity to his children's plight — betrayed on his features only when they leave him alone in the cottage — establishes the power of the vision-impaired paterfamilias to perceive that which might be invisible to the sighted.

Shelley thus reverses the unquestioned rhetorical relationship between the physically disabled object and the gazing, normative subject, which Holmes identifies in much nineteenth-century discourse. Holmes suggests an asymmetrical interpersonal dynamic, "an emotional exchange system," linking the able-bodied with the disabled (29). This relationship designated the disabled individual as the impotent receiver of the strong healthy observer's sympathy. Shelley flips this assumed power structure on its head by assigning subjectivity, and the power of knowledge, to the blind and exiled De Lacey, setting up a situation where *he* will extend the hand of compassion. It is this power that allows De Lacey to perceive the true, benevolent nature of the creature: he is the only character in the novel who can detect the honesty in the creature's voice.

While the private moments shared by the creature and De Lacey provides a tantalizing glimpse of a disabled community, *Frankenstein* offers no sustainable social networking model for those manifesting physical or cognitive difference. As the ensuing events painfully demonstrate, even the most enlightened sight-enabled individual can be swayed by aesthetic prejudice. The fruitful exchange between De Lacey and the creature ends abruptly when De Lacey's kind son Felix and the cottage's female inhabitants open the door onto this tête-à-tête: physiognomic assumptions precipitate instantaneous judgment, and the newly objectified creature finds himself violently ejected from the family he had hoped to enchant with his goodwill, his hopes dashed and his murderous destiny set in motion by dehumanizing and scrutinizing stares.

Possibilities for Community

The Last Man (1826), Shelley's apocalyptic novel, that tracks the erasure of the entire human race, ironically provides a more stable and sustainable (though equally doomed) space for the infirm and disabled. Nestled between the melodrama of the heavily auto-biographical Book I and the bleak conclusion in which the narrator alone inhabits the planet, we glimpse a society that *could have been*—an organic, inclusive community that assimilates all kinds of embodied and cognitive difference as it adapts to a rapidly changing and equalizing social order.

The society presented in Book I is a rigid hierarchy, seemingly healthy and stable, populated by characters inspired by the people in Shelley's life.[6] In this world, the powerful aristocrats are unsympathetic to untitled and impoverished denizens. Only Adrian opposes the tenets of his own class; he is a progressive aristocrat who wishes to eliminate systems of power inimical to interdependence and community. Adrian's audaciously egalitarian princi-

ples fail to thrive in a political atmosphere that privileges the flamboyant ego-
tism of those like the Byronic war hero Raymond, for whom "self-gratification"
is "paramount object" (38). This kind of leader best suits a government that
prefers the old comfortable class-based structures.

The narcissism of the normative, pre-plague social order discourages
communal solidarity. The passionate marriage of the marginally-tamed Raymond and his lover Perdita ruptures quickly under the pressure of Raymond's
emotional infidelity and politically honed hubris. The narrator, Lionel, also
encounters emotional difficulties. Socially prescribed rules dictating gender
roles and sexual behavior discourage him from acting on his love for an old
male friend, from openly expressing the emotional, and perhaps sexual, tenor
of his thoughts and affections. When the friend returns after months of cap-
tivity, Lionel writes, "happy are women who can weep, and in a passionate
caress disburthen the oppression of their feelings; shame and habitual restraint
hold back a man. I would have given worlds to have acted as in days of boy-
hood, have strained him to my breast, pressed his hand to my lips, and wept
over him" (137).

The death-dealing plague that appears in Volume II rapidly destroys all
the institutional structures that supported the earlier hierarchies and divisions. The dwindling numbers who survive each onslaught of the disease discover that just as they can no longer depend upon the fading institutions of
government and church to define or defend them, they cannot afford the old
luxuries of deceit, selfishness, and emotional evasion which once divided people. National boundaries dissolve under the pressures of mass immigration as
more personal divisions are also erased. The reserved Lionel, for instance,
learns rather quickly how to express himself in a decidedly "unmanly" manner as multitudes die en masse about him, opening himself up to an ongoing process of intense, shared bereavement with a shrinking circle of family
and friends.

The fall of the old order also empowers Adrian. His "frank and unsus-
picious mind," that was a threat to the old order, is now an asset in an increasingly fluid society. His delicate and trusting nature had rendered him unable
to withstand the assaults of his old society. When the fickle Evadne jilted him,
he was sent to an insane asylum for a time: "this ill world" having proven
itself "no clime for [his] gentle spirit" (37). Adrian's former society, seemingly
healthy but morally infirm, pushed him to the periphery. But when the world
becomes *literally* ill the idealistic Adrian finds his place. A civilization in which
the unhealthy political structures are destroyed by a literal disease values
Adrian's flexibility and his compassionate world view which embraces all
despite their previous placement in rigid social categories. Even his arrogant,
class-defined mother comes to agree that love is "the only good of life" (300).

In the face of the ultimate equalizer, the plague that respects no human borders or boundaries, Adrian leads a new, intensely equal community; the new social order values every living being as "a gem" (251) of infinite worth, regardless of physical, mental, or social status:

> There was but one good and one evil in the world — life and death. The pomp of rank, the assumption of power, the possessions of wealth vanished like morning mist. One living beggar had become of more worth than a national peerage of dead lords ... of dead heroes, patriots, or men of genius [229].

The plague also erases the boundaries of nations and nationalism. When his community is threatened by a lawless force of foreign invaders, Adrian proclaims a new transnational brotherhood that will transform any death into an act of fratricide. This ideal strikes a note with the soldiers on both sides: "on either side the bands threw down their arms ... a gush of love and deepest amity filled every heart" (235).

In the new united community that results, each person is valued as an individual, rather than being pre-judged by pre-existing categories. When Lionel, Adrian, and the country's scattered remnants finally leave England for what they hope is a healthier climate, they discard their old, class-minded attachments to property and place and put all their resources into searching the countryside so that they do not "leave behind a single human being" (256–57, 259). The growing nomadic community which coalesces around Adrien abandons the hierarchical codes that privileged the attractive and able-bodied, the educated and entitled — the kind of idealized human that Rosemary Garland Thomson and others have termed the "normate" (8).[7] Thus the old categories of marginalization and exclusion have also been destroyed by the plague.

Conversely, the categories of privilege are meaningless: A "high-born beauty" discovers her appearance has become a curse in the lawless streets of London (250). Young Clara's intelligence, sensibility, and beauty — noted appreciatively by her Uncle Lionel (179, 323) — prove far less valuable than her willingness to nurse and cheer the more despondent members of her family (240–41). Even more substantial attainments lose their meaning: the newly obsolete academic Merrival, an astronomer once absorbed by his work, learns that erudition provides little comfort for the death of loved ones. Consequently, learning and book-reading lose their old valences in the new order: "To read were futile," Lionel reflects, "to write, vanity indeed" (240) — a somber admission for one who once prided himself on being "wedded to literature" 122). In the newly depopulated Europe the only privilege, the only attainment is the possession of life itself. With society level, all the accoutrements of social success that are based on human definitions are revealed as empty constructions. Any living body, "normal" or non-normative, represents a great success on the part of its inhabitant.

Ironically, universal catastrophe has created the conditions necessary for the creation of a social utopia. The complete social leveling that follows in the plague's wake catalyzes a dynamic symbiosis among all who still draw breath. Those once considered expendable or inconsequential discover a new significance in the post-industrial order. Lionel's closely knit band incorporates previously demonized untouchables of all sorts as they move through the countryside: an abused and abandoned charity girl, a rapidly dying man who dances about dressed as a "Black Spectre" (318–19), a number of diseased indigents, and a variety of people with mental illness. Each life is of equal value, equally worthy of the sacrifice of another. The narrator's wife, Idris, dies attempting to save Lionel's friend Lucy and her disabled mother, who have been left behind by their migrating neighbors. Lucy explains that the new order also resists viewing the elderly as dispensable and not quite human. She insists on treating her mother as fully human despite others who "speak carelessly of her. because she is old and infirm, as if we must not all, if we are spared, become so" (250, 274).

Seeing Differently

In the futuristic *The Last Man*, then, Shelley repositions and develops the tantalizing suggestion of the inclusivity glimpsed in *Frankenstein*, turning a ludic moment into the sustained vision of a community ready to enfold and accommodate those non-normates with physical and intellectual disabilities. Neither novel, of course, offers a realistic model for long-term social synergy, and even Shelley's imagination fails to construct the possibility of a level social order that could be achieved without the catalyst of cataclysm.

Yet, while Shelley does not prescribe a true social cure, she does suggest that the cause of many social ills is to be found in flawed social vision, vision based on the evaluative gaze and the immobilizing stare. Shelley suggests that society adapt instead a manner of apperception that recognizes the distinction between corporeal and cognitive difference, accepting both, a vision that values individuals based on subjective truths and not superficial categories. Shelley shows the liberating consequences of the destruction of these social categories and the mode of seeing that insists upon them. The new enlightened social order privileges a new kind of sight that is not based on the physical powers of the eyes. The new powers of sight belong to those who can see the invisible and the intangible and who blind themselves to the superficial categories. In the new intimate community, that privileges storytelling over reading, interdependence over autonomy, and *presence* over *power*, Mary Shelley provocatively envisions a society open to those dealing with any combination of cognitive, physical, and physiognomic differences.

NOTES

1. Mary Shelley affirms this idea in a journal kept while traveling through Europe: "Next to the consciousness of right and honour, God has shown that he loves best beauty and the sense of beauty, since he has endowed the visible universe so richly with the one, and made the other so keen and deep-seated an enjoyment in the hearts of his creatures" (*Rambles* 81).

2. Maurice Hindle, one of the novel's modern adherents, claims that Shelley's first novel provokes her readers to rethink their instinctive, appearance-based reactions to others. Introduction, xxxii.

3. In *The Conquest of Mental Retardation* (1987), psychologist Burton Blatt use the phrases "mental retardation" and "retarded individuals." However, he works hard to remove the negative associations given these words by our culture.

4. David Wright elaborates the distinction between perceptive and comprehensive abilities in The *Certification of Insanity in Nineteenth-Century England and Wales* (285–86).

5. "The author supposes that his hero has the power of communicating *life* to dead matter: but what has the vital principle to do with *habits*, and actions which are dependent on the moral will? If Frankenstein could have endowed his creature with the vital principle of a hundred or a thousand human beings, it would no more have been able to *walk* without having previously acquired *the habit* of doing so, than it would have been to talk, or to reason, or to judge" ("Review of *Frankenstein; or the Modern Prometheus*").

6. Just as *Frankenstein* likely signals Mary Shelley's grief over the death of her infant children, *The Last Man* engages another series of personal tragedies. Mary Shelley's niece, Allegra, had died in 1822, her husband had been killed in a boating accident three months later, and prolonged illness had taken the life of Lord Byron in 1824. Mary Shelley indulges in prolonged, romanticized reminiscing as she works through the treasured lives and recent deaths of friends and family in the first volume of *The Last Man*. The roman à clef lingers tenderly over past interactions with her husband, half-sister, and close friends, creating a most idyllic atmosphere in the most purple of prose styles. The first section also, however, reveals problems, fault lines running underneath the ostensibly healthy society in which the narrator, Lionel Verney, resides. Before Lionel is taken under the wing of Adrian, a character almost identical to Shelley's husband Percy Bysshe Shelley, Lionel lives a criminal lifestyle on the outskirts of his society.

7. That Mary Shelley does not erase *all* sense of position — the well-bred and nobly born Adrian, for instance, proves himself the most able leader for what one companion envisions as a "*patriarchal* brotherhood of love" (326 italics mine) — should not discredit her clear efforts to shape a remarkably egalitarian society.

WORKS CITED

Andrews, Jonathan. "Begging the Question of Idiocy: The Definition and Socio-Cultural Meaning of Idiocy in Early Modern Britain." Part 1. *History of Psychiatry* 9 (1998): 65–95.

_____. "Begging the Question of Idiocy: The Definition and Socio-Cultural Meaning of Idiocy in Early Modern Britain." Part 2. *History of Psychiatry* 9 (1998): 179–200.

Blatt, Burton. *The Conquest of Mental Retardation.* Austin, TX: Pro-Ed, 1987.

Gilbert, Sandra M., and Susan Gubar. *The Madwoman in the Attic: The Woman Writer and the Nineteenth-Century Literary Imagination*. 1979. New Haven: Yale University Press, 2000.

Hindle, Maurice. Introduction. *Frankenstein*. By Mary Shelley. New York: Penguin, 1992.

Holmes, Martha Stoddard. *Fictions of Affliction: Physical Disability in Victorian Culture*. Ann Arbor: University of Michigan Press, 2004.

Locke, John. *An Essay Concerning Human Understanding*. 1693. New York: Prometheus Books, 1995.

Mellor, Anne K. *Mary Shelley: Her Life, Her Fiction, Her Monsters*. New York: Methuen, 1988.

Morison, Alexander. *The Physiognomy of Mental Diseases*. London: Longman, 1838, 1843. New York: Arno, 1976.

"Rev. of *Frankenstein; or the Modern Prometheus.*" *The Literary Panorama and National Register* 8 (June 1818): 411–414.

"Rev. of *Frankenstein; or the Modern Prometheus.*" *Quarterly Review* 18 (January 1818): 379–85.

Rix, Sir Brian. "A Perspective of Mental Handicap." *Journal of the Royal Society of Health* 106.5 (Oct. 1986): 161–65.

Shelley, Mary. "The Evil Eye." 1829. *Mary Shelley: Collected Tales and Stories*. Ed. Charles E. Robinson. Baltimore: Johns Hopkins University Press, 1976.

_____. *Frankenstein; or The Modern Prometheus*. 1818, 1831. *The Novels and Selected Works of Mary Shelley*. Vol. 1. Ed. Nora Crook. London: William Pickering, 1996.

_____. *History of a Six Weeks' Tour*. 1817. *The Novels and Selected Works of Mary Shelley*. Vol. 8. Ed. Nora Crook. London: William Pickering, 1996.

_____. *The Journals of Mary Shelley*. Eds. Paula R. Feldman and Diana Scott-Kilvert. Baltimore: Johns Hopkins University Press, 1987.

_____. *The Last Man*. 1826. *The Novels and Selected Works of Mary Shelley*. Vol. 4. Eds. Jane Blumberg and Nora Crook. London: William Pickering, 1996.

_____. *Matilda*. 1819; first published 1959. *The Novels and Selected Works of Mary Shelley*. Vol. 2. Ed. Pamela Clemit. London: William Pickering, 1996.

_____. *Rambles in Germany and Italy in 1840, 1842, and 1843*. 1844. London: Pickering, 1996. Vol. 8. *The Novels and Selected Works of Mary Shelley*. Ed. Nora Crook, 1996.

_____. "Transformation." 1830. *The Mary Shelley Reader*. Ed. Betty T. Bennett and Charles E. Robinson. New York: Oxford University Press, 1990.

_____. *Valperga: or, the Life and Adventures of Castruccio, Prince of Lucca*. 1823. *The Novels and Selected Works of Mary Shelley*. Vol. 3. Ed. Nora Crook. London: William Pickering, 1996.

Sunstein, Emily W. *Mary Shelley: Romance and Reality*. Boston: Little, Brown, 1989.

Thomson, Rosemary Garland. *Extraordinary Bodies*. New York: Columbia University Press, 1997.

Wright, David. "The Certification of Insanity in Nineteenth-Century England and Wales." *History of Psychiatry* 9 (1998): 267–90.

"Colossal Vices" and "Terrible Deformities" in George Lippard's Gothic Nightmare

Cynthia Hall

> Would to God that the experience of my life had not impressed me so vividly with the colossal vices and the terrible deformities, presented in the social system of this Large City, in the Nineteenth Century [Lippard "Preface" 2].

In the preface to his highly controversial novel, *The Quaker City; or, The Monk's of Monk Hall* (1845), and in the novel itself, George Lippard reinstates a persistent trope for the disabled and deformed: misshapen corporeality as the outward reflection of inner evil.[1] This trope is used by writers from the Bible to Shakespeare and from Montaigne to Melville. What is unique in Lippard's use of the deformed body to condemn Philadelphia's social vices in the late 1840s, is his overarching use of the misshapen body to symbolize the widespread social ills pervading his city: racial and class conflicts; labor struggles; religious hypocrisy; inordinate amounts of perfidious greed. By linking ills of the body politic to ills of the body, Lippard likens moral depravity to a communicable infection, and places himself in the position of healer. Drawing on the medical model of diagnosis and cure, his jeremiad demands that the reader must first "discover" then deter, and finally "reject" and "reject" again, in a twofold purgation of "deformity" and "vice" (Lippard "Preface" 2).

Beautiful Immorality: Interrogating a Convention

As a social reformer and ardent political critic, Lippard watched as a "nightmarish realm of class divisions and economic uncertainty" transformed

Philadelphia from a thriving egalitarian stronghold of republican democracy to an unseemly haven of exploitation and "deceit" (Reynolds xxix). In
response to what he saw as Philadelphia's moral crisis, Lippard unfurled his
scandalous Gothic novel, fully titled *The Quaker City or, The Monks of Monk
Hall: A Romance of Philadelphia Life, Mystery, and Crime.* This sensational
exposé unveiled the licentious debauchery and political misappropriation hidden behind high society's fashionable veneers and upstanding personae. By
combining the "radicalism" of his social commentary with what David
Reynolds calls the "grotesquerie" of the Gothic (xvi), Lippard was able to
present his readers with a horrifying underground world called Monk Hall,
a dark playground overrun by hedonistic cruelty and sadistic sin, where criminal subterfuge and illicit exploits exist as commonplace activities of the
wealthy and elite. With moral insinuations against the rich and privileged,
Quaker City is Lippard's overt and hyperbolic attempt to warn the masses
against automatically assigning moral worth and social respectability to the
upper classes, because, in fact, their outward aesthetics and long-held social
standing allow them the legal and moral rights to ignore human decency and
defy the laws of the land. As a result, the novel amplifies the connection
between indecent and criminal actions, and the elegant and refined appearance of the criminals. Gus Lorrimer, for example presents a "muscular chest,"
"fine manly countenance," and magically "handsome face" (Lippard 6); yet
he is, in fact, a debauched seducer, a cruel libertine whose aesthetic charms
help him to lure the "flower[s]" of Philadelphia's "finest families" down to
their moral ruin (14). Emphasizing the beautifully "bold outline" of Lorrimer's
erectly masculine "form," Lippard points out the folly and emphasizes the danger inherent in assessing morality and merit based solely on a superficial eval-
uation of outward looks. Likewise, when describing the overly ornate
adornment of "corsets" and hip "padding" used to create the "voluptuous
swell" (156) of manly physique in the socially renowned but criminal Colonel Fitz-Cowles, Lippard uncovers the performative nature of both "masculine prowess" and class distinction, suggesting that the showy and elegant
"dandyish aristocrat," as David Anthony describes him, is "all exterior and
no substance" (734). As Lippard's description of Fitz-Cowles's hip "padding"
and "corsets" indicate, the Colonel clings to European aristocratic refinement
instead of adopting America's democratic and rugged manly countenance.
Thus in order to advise that upper-class merit is often garnered from an
impressive veneer, and not from inner worth, Lippard diminishes the semiotic significance of external array. He advises the reader to examine personal
substance and inner worth instead of outer appearance conventionally encoded
as moral.

The Return of a Convention

However, even though Lippard warns his readers against falling prey to quick judgments reliant on visually-induced external criteria, he nonetheless succumbs to the literary and socio-medical conventions of his times. By using an unsightly corporeal shape to heighten the novel's Gothic horror, Lippard categorizes corporeal defects, bodily deformities, and physical difference as monstrous and threatening. In the novel, corporeal deformity incarnates infectious moral corruption. In using bodily deformity as his plot's easily recognizable meaning-making trope, Lippard intensifies the prurient aura of physical deformity, strengthens the monstrous connotations that surround bodily difference, and ultimately marks the economically destitute as being physically as well as morally deviant threats to the physical and moral health of the middle and upper classes.

Lippard's choice of the twisted body as the signifier of communicable degeneracy reflects contemporary scientific belief in the genetic promulgation of all deviance or difference: disease, deformity, insanity, sexual perversion. Lippard fuels his novel's Gothic hyperbole with the fear and loathing generated off the backs of the physically deformed, the profligates most dangerous to American society. In the novel, the crooked and hunched bodies of the poor and outcast reflect the twisted morality of these depraved creatures, re-enforcing the conventional notion that the visible body does indeed reveal internal qualities.

Such blatant use of bodily difference to indicate the threat of social deviance serves, however, to undermine Lippard's own political agenda, his desire to work toward common national goals to elevate *all* citizens. As David S. Reynolds points out Lippard's political sensibilities were ardently "radical" as he valorized early "republican ideals" (xv) of equality. Thus even though *The Quaker City* is a novel deeply invested in exposing what Reynolds describes as the "distance between surface appearances" and actual "reality" (xxix), the overt marking of perniciousness and innate depravity through visible deformity seems merely to re-inscribe the same conventional biases that Lippard's social reform agenda meant to decry.

Lippard carefully establishes a binary between the well-formed bodies of the immoral rich, standing tall and firm, and the deformed bodies of the poor, crouching and crookedly hunched. In relying on the visual aversion and aesthetic horror elicited by crooked or hunched bodies, Lippard leads his readers toward condemning his poor characters, thus leaving his audience with a mixed message: readers should employ skepticism when judging the aesthetically pleasing figures of the upper class, but the reader may be assured that the poor are as ugly within as they are without. Lippard thereby interrogates the "play" of "oppositions" that Fred Botting suggests is indicative of the Gothic genre, oppositions wherein "good depends on evil, light on dark," and "reason on irrationality" (7). In this case the deformity of the poor is reliably intertwined with evil, but, confusingly, so is the health of the rich.

Allowing him to easily point out the text's most fiendish purveyors of immorality and sin, the poor, Lippard does in fact heighten the plot's horror and focus the reader's fear onto specific characters whose grotesque bodily disarray symbolizes inner monstrosity.

The Twisted Spine

Lippard's most villainous characters — Devil Bug, evil proprietor of Monk Hall's iniquitous den and the Jew, greedy master of white-collar thievery — share a specific disability: an overtly visible distortion of their spines. The use of this deformity indicates that each is degenerate and socially outcast: Devil Bug as a member of the lower classes, the Jew as an ethnic and religious outsider. Lippard thus signifies through their spines that they represent the two greatest threats to the insular economic and racial stability of mid-nineteenth century America.[2] Given a mid-century cultural milieu that believed, as R. W. Tamplin articulated in 1846, that crooked spines "generally occur[red] in weak and unhealthy children," those who were "already predisposed, from any slight causality, to diseased action" (204), it is no surprise that Lippard heightens the visual horror of his Gothic plot by providing his novel's most threatening characters with quickly recognizable hunchbacks. Spinal deformity was viewed as an "insidious disease" (Mitchell 4); Dr. John Ellis proclaimed in *The Avoidable Causes of Disease, Insanity, and Deformity* (1860), that the propensity of curved spines in America proved that a terminal wasting was eating away at the nation's strength, a wasting he blamed on immoral life choices which had come to light through the growing number of individuals whose bodies displayed "crookedness and deformit[ies] of the spine" (121).

Lippard's choice in representing his inhumanly depraved characters makes great sense within the context of developing evolutionary theories concerning the upright human spine as the corporeal site which differentiates the human form from the nonhuman or animal. Scientific and philosophical thought, even in the early nineteenth-century, solidified the understanding of the developmental rise of the human from a curved over ape-like animal walking on all fours to a straight and erect being walking on two legs. This theory promoted the constituent belief that the straightening up of the human spine through the "upward progress" (Williamson 56) of evolution marked man's intellectual and moral development from bestial to human. The tall, straight, and erect human spine, opposed to the hunched, curved, and crouching spine of other animals, was the corporeal indication of advanced civilization and higher intelligence, evidence of man's enlightened trajectory upward from the earth. Those medical experts who denied evolutionary theories, made essentially the same argument while invoking biblical language to credit the "sublime privilege of standing erect" as irrefutable proof of human supremacy among God's earthly creatures (Bampfield 2). Medical practitioners further invoked theology in noting that the erect spine offered "peculiar advantages." The vertical human body is a physiological condition "exclusively granted" to human beings, providing a sense of "dignity" that directly indicated God's preference for the creature made in God's "Divine Image" (2).

Devil Bug: The Twisted Poor

Lippard's deployment of Devil Bug's misshapen spine to symbolize his stunted human development thus reflects the scientific, philosophical, and religious thinking of the time. Devil Bug's "strange" and "thickset" body is a disjointed "specimen of flesh and blood" characterized by inordinately "long arms," "thin distorted legs," and one "shriveled and orbless" eye socket sunken into a "ludicrously large head" (51). Describing Devil Bug as being overwhelmed by "broad" deformed shoulders, "protruding" from his back in "unsightly knobs," hunching him in a primordial lurch, Lippard relies on the visual abjection of Devil Bug's grotesquely "distorted" torso to indicate inherent evil and unrepentant sin. His "soul" like his "body" is an inchoate "mass of hideous and distorted energy" (105). Devil Bug's evil nature is substantiated when we learn that his "hideous" body (74) was formed by the devil himself as creative proof of Satan's own "inventive powers" (51). Devil Bug's disjointed body and his deformed frame thus reflect Satan's evil whim and link his bodily defects to inhuman depravity and demonic intent. Lippard's readers would have readily accepted the idea that corporeal deformities were evidence of corruption, sickness or sin, given the influence of mid-century health reformers like Dr. John Ellis who proclaimed moral corruption as the essential cause of physical disease.

Drawing on the principals of social Darwinism, Lippard adds eugenic overtones to the mix and suggests that Bug's "hideous soul" (106) and monstrous form is the product of the polluted lust of his biological parents, and his life in the low-class brothel where he was wretchedly born and inappropriately raised. Lippard implies that Devil Bug's "deplorable moral monstrosity" (107) is due to his situation as the offspring of "foulest sin" (105), "from his very birth." Nature is compounded by nurture: growing up in "continual sight" of "wretchedness" and "vice," surrounded by an "atmosphere of infamy" that separated him from the "human race," Devil Bug becomes a "wild beast, a snake," or even a "devil incarnate," "any thing" — Lippard writes — "but a man" (106).

The Twisted Jew

The social difference of poverty is not the only "vice" that Lippard figures through the image of the twisted body. He also embodies fears of ethnic and religious difference, through this trope. The other character in *Quaker City* who bears the mark of spinal deformity is Gabriel Von Gelt, disparagingly known as "The Jew" (198).[3] Incorporating long-held stereotypes about the Jewish population, Lippard describes Von Gelt as a plagiarizing thief and a social pariah who symbolizes the moral and economic threat posed to nineteenth-century America by Europe's Jewish masses, poised to infiltrate and thus eventually corrupt America's upstanding Christian landscape. Reflecting his ability to falsify handwriting, Von Gelt falsely presents himself to the world as a "respectable old gentleman in a white cravat," an elderly figure with "perfectly regular" features — an "aquiline" nose, a "well-proportioned" mouth and a "high forehead" — the apparent model of a fine-looking man from a morally-founded Christian race (175). Reflecting racial and religious bias that Sander Gilman notes long-pervaded Western thought, the novel shows that Von Gelt's genteel countenance is only a "mask" to obscure his inherently "corrupt" Jewish nature: Gabriel Von Gelt lines other men's purses with money procured through his talent for forgery.

Von Gelt's true nature is reflected in his twisted body: between the Jew's shoulders, rising "on either side as high as his ears" emerges a "shapeless" protruding "hump" clearly "visible above the outline of his head," a hump which deforms his "diminutive" frame and so inordinately hunches over his shoulders that his head seems to "lay upon his breast" (Lippard 175). The Jew's humped back curves him downward toward the ground and angles him into the grit and grime of the city, echoing the arch of a "horse's" longish "head" (175).[4] With hunched shoulders angling his face downward, Von Gelt's deforming hump also keeps him from looking people straight in the eye.

The hump of the Jew taps into popular and medical notions of Jews, advancing Lippard's condemnation of urban corruption. The nineteenth-century medical profession criticized the Jewish populations for living unhealthy lives, crowded together within the inner cities of Europe. The Jew thus represented the "ultimate example" of the negative "effect" which "civilization (i.e. the city and 'modern life') could have on the individual" (Gilman 49). Because of this, Gilman explains that the medical profession particularized Jews by assigning them pathological weaknesses of both the body and the mind.[5] Navigating urban life for long stretches of time was thought to have heightened the Jew's sinister nature, his propensity to swindle, and his cunning and unscrupulous character.

The Infectious Hunchback; Moral Contagion

The presence of the Jew is also a helpful way to understand the connection that Lippard makes between the deformity of the hunchback and the idea of moral contagion. As part of dehumanizing the Jew, there was a tendency to present his sexual drive in uncontrollable animalistic terms, thus leading to an association between the Jew and sexually transmitted diseases, as well as sexually criminal pursuits. Since spinal problems, specifically the hunching of the back, were also believed to be associated with syphilis,[6] Von Gelt's protruding hump, erupting from his upper back and growing out and above the outline of his head can be read as an atavistic phallic protrusion overtaking the civil rationality of his brain. This also suggests that in the case of Von Gelt, the required sexual restraints of civilization have been overrun by a prurient sexual drive, a bodily sign in the form of a metastasized spinal protrusion that indicates the Jew's inability to quell his inherently "deviant sexual nature" (Gilman 76). This medical context would certainly allow for an understanding of the Jew's hump as a symptom of syphilis and sexual perversion.

Bug and Von Gelt thus infect the rich with their own immorality as they make it possible for the rich to lead secretly twisted lives while holding on to the veneer of respectability. The two social outcasts both earn their ill-gotten gains by serving the immoral whims and criminal drives of the upper classes. Bug and the Jew purvey immorality to the rich, allowing them to maintain their facades: Fitz-Cowles who conspires with the Jew to pilfer and deceive is hailed as a "very fine man" (37). Although the upstanding resolves and spines of the pious and respectful men bend when they "stoop" to pass through the "narrow door" that leads them to Monk Hall's revelry and sin (54), their bodies bear no permanent marks of error. Devil Bug's "loathsome" body (105) with its disjointed parts, is a perverse and crooked receptacle for collecting and reflecting the libidinous indecency and hypocritical deceit amassed at Monk Hall. Wearing the sins of the rich on his own lawlessly vile form, Devil Bug's deformed body simultaneously stands as a visual threat, indicating the infectious nature of immorality and ruin, and as a containment device for consolidating the physical reflections of society's widespread decay. Devil Bug's physical ugliness, reflecting the sins of the rich as well as those of his own, allows the rich to maintain the superficial beauty that others incorrectly interpret as reflecting inner beauty. This service, even more than his various procurements, encourages the rich to succumb to Devil Bug's temptations.

Lippard thus uses Devil Bug's body and his relationship with the rich to literalize the emerging middle class fear of a contagious moral threat lurking within the disordered seediness of the lower-classes and spreading to the decadent, aristocratic rich. As the proprietor of Monk Hall's underground den of sin, Devil Bug's substantiates this belief. He spreads society's moral blight from the bottom up. With sinister joy and what David Reynolds's calls "gleeful evil" (xxiii), Devil Bug purveys debauchery, incest, rape and murder to Philadelphia's lawyers, doctors and even its "judges from the bench" (Lippard 55). Those partaking of Devil Bug's fiendish hospitality include "demure parson[s]" (55), enlightened "poets," upstanding "clerks," young "hopeful sons," refined and "distinguished millionaire[s]," and even "reputable married men" with "trustful wives," (56), all drinking to various degrees of "unconscious intoxication" (55). Converging in the "club room" (53) at the center of Monk Hall's "wickedness" (56), the "eloquent" and "learned," the "pious of the Quaker City" fall into drunken debauchery.

To further convey the communicable nature of sin as disease, Lippard details the response of the novel's fledging hero, Brynewood Anderson, to the hellish scene of Monk Hall. Confusedly standing in the midst of the city's most well-respected men, all inebriated and "scattered" about "the floor" of Monk Hall (71), Anderson is shaken by an "involuntary horror," a "strange feeling" like when "cold or heat" slowly "steal over you by slow degrees" (71). Equating the feeling to an invasion, Anderson asks himself whether this strange physical sensation is the "first attack of some terrible disease" (71), a disease that he senses is an evil infection that spreads into men's hearts like a "shadow" that slowly moves "over" them and overtakes their "souls" (71).

Anderson, a member of the hardworking middle class is the only person in Monk Hall who has not been infected by the sin and disease endemic to the place. His reason for being there is upright and moral: he is there to rescue his sister Mary from Devil Bug's infectious depravity. Mary's soul has been polluted by a "new world" of "desolation," because of Gus Lorrimer, the libertine habitué of Monk Hall, who tricks her into a fake marriage and then defiles her. Not surprisingly, the taint to Mary's purity, her moral degradation, and social ruin are depicted in the curve of her spine as she "crouch[es]" over in a "half-kneeling position" (146). No longer able to stand up straight in the righteous purity of undefiled maidenhood, she cowers in her shame.

The seduction by which Mary has been corrupted further highlights the contagion of evil in Lippard's novel. Bess, another victim of Bug's who has been reduced to a life of ill-repute within the Hall, had assisted Gus Lorrimer in his deception of Mary by gaining her trust and bringing her to Monk Hall for defilement and ruin. When questioned, Bess defiantly asks whether "this innocent [girl]" is "a whit better than [she] *was* when the devil in human shape first dragged [her] from [her] home?" Harboring her own sorrow at losing the "comforts [of] home ... the smile of a father ... the love of a mother," Bess bitterly states that she now feels "happy when she can drag another woman [down] into the same foul pit" where she is "doomed to lie and rot" (80).

The Upright Middle Class

While the upper classes are all too susceptible to the moral diseases of the poor, Lippard presents his middle-class hero as healthy enough to fight off the infection. Continuing to play off the visual economy of his plot's physical conceit, Lippard presents Anderson, his middle-class hero, as upright in both mind and body. Lippard uses the developing strength of Anderson's backbone to indicate his moral growth and hard-won self-possession. Anderson's initial resolve weakens when faced with the incarnation of sin, and his spine's "firmness" (74) crumbles at the sight of Devil Bug's "unsightly shoulders" (51) hunched over as if "an omen of death" (74). However, as soon as Anderson learns of his sister's ruin and defilement within the hellish halls of Devil Bug's lair, he transforms from a "quivering" (567) youth into a righteously strong American man whose "stern and erect" (149) backbone transforms him into a "towering ... Avenger" (149). Presenting a visual contrast between the "proudly erect" and "firm" (74) spine of young Anderson opposed to the "grotesque" and terribly "distorted form" of the evil Devil Bug, Lippard amplifies the moral and physical difference between the self-possessed middle-class hero and the cowering, bent villain. Anderson's conquest of Devil Bug represents the victory of the strong, upright middle-class man over the pernicious iniquity of the lower class and their secret allies in crime, the rich. Seemingly Lippard's novel ends with the normalizing and restorative eradication of the infection of immorality.

Confusions of the Cure

Yet no respectable Gothic novel ends with the certain restoration of normative order. The closure of the Gothic form usually erupts into a conflicted state of ideological confusion, pushing against the boundaries of social norms while at the same time solidifying them. Lippard's novel attempts to contain the social and moral threat presented by Devil Bug and the Jew while it simultaneously plants the seeds of what Elizabeth Napier describes as "fragmentation, instability, and moral ambivalence" (5). The novel's conservative "tendency towards moral and structural stabilizing" (5) is undercut by a lingering future potential for subversive social discord. In *The Quaker City*, moral containment takes place as the plot symbolically exorcizes the deviant and evil bodies of Devil Bug and Gabriel Von Gelt. They are both crushed to death, one on top of the other, in the deepest pit of Monk Hall's subterranean chambers. After pushing the Jew over a precipice into the "Dead-Vault" pit (534), Devil Bug sees Von Gelt's body at its most grotesque: smashed into an "undistinguishable mass of corruption and blood" (555). Thus Lippard takes the repressive tack in eradicating the foreign-born and native-born deviant and crooked bodies from his plot, in order to instigate national rebirth.

Yet, Lippard also points to wonderfully subversive and progressive possibilities in his conclusion, which elevates the death of Devil Bug as a selflessly sacrificial act. With a newly found spark of humanity and a "settled resolve" (556), Devil Bug stands uncharacteristically "erect" and thinks about the adult daughter whom he has recently discovered. As he offers the reader a "frightful" smile (556), he orders his servants to release the boulder that comes hurling down on his body, smashing it "beneath a big rock" in the Dead-Vault amongst the "pillars," the "ceilings," and the "walls" in this Gothic realm of darkness and death (554). By sacrificing himself for his daughter's stable and secure future, Devil Bug seems to have re-established the harmony of social life and quelled the horror that was ignited by the menace of the grotesque. However, in a final move toward Gothic transgression, Lippard undercuts his novel's seemingly conservative closure, with its restoration of social norms. For, we learn that Devil Bug has managed, with the help of the Jew, to pass off his daughter as the long-lost offspring of the novel's socially prominent millionaire, Albert Livingstone. Thus the novel ends scandalously with the insertion of the daughter of the outcast Devil Bug into the center of the privileged upper class. Lippard ends his novel by unleashing the seeds of Devil Bug's under-class contagion into the gene pool of the city's blue-blood elites, creating the ultimate horror of the upper classes: the specter of the lower-class person invisibly passing as the upper-class elite.

Thus in a novel hyperbolically obsessed with the danger of visible deformities, Lippard ironically gestures toward the invisible dangers of tainted blood, unseen defects, and invisible infections as being the most threatening and corrosive threats to America's moral base and its class designations. About to become a lingering threat to society even after his death, Devil Bug stands erect, awaiting the force from the falling boulder. He chuckles to himself, thinking that his offspring will "dress in silks," be a "lady" and "roll in wealth" as a "grandee o' th' Quaker City," a member of the respectable upper crust. All this despite the visible sign of his genetic corruption that she bears upon her flesh, the matching birthmark on her right upper temple, an image mimicking his own deformed curve and his sinister soul, that of a crooked and potentially corrupt "red snake" (556).

NOTES

1. Both Lennard J. Davis and Rosemarie Garland Thomson suggest that the association between disability and immorality was and still is the most common literary interpretation for disability. For an overview of the various interpretative shifts that took place in the modern era concerning what Thomson calls the extraordinary body, see her essay "From Wonder to Error — A Genealogy of Freak Discourse in Modernity." For a historical analysis of the scientific language used to identify grotesque and disabled bodily forms as abnormal or deficient see Lennard J. Davis's "Constructing Normalcy: The Bell Curve, the Novel, and the Invention of the Disabled Body in the Nineteenth Century."

2. Lippard also bestows the bent back upon the debased servants of Devil Bug, "Glow-worm" and "Musquito," "negro[es]," or what Devil Bug calls "black devils" (52), who are characterized with a variety of debasing and dehumanizing descriptions: they are "scarcely human" (52) with "receding foreheads ... immense lip[s]" and "bulging eyelids" (52). Yet, it is their "crouching in the darkness" (124) with bent-over backs that ultimately indicates their state of total submission and their acquiescence to another's will; like animals, they cower, "silent and motionless" (124), awaiting their master's command.

3. Gelt's name reflects the stereotypical notion of Jews as usurer ; the word "gelt," means "money" in Yiddish, deriving from the word "geld," in Dutch, German and Old English.

4. This image literalizes the long-held fear that Jews were primitive, "bestial," and "non-human" (Gilman 21).

5. Gilman notes that in the nineteenth century the Jewish foot — crooked, flat, or abnormally deformed — was hidden inside shoes. Evidence of the demonic nature of the Jew was the Jew's impaired gait, caused by structural defects in the legs, also signs of Jewish atavism and physical weakness or regression.

6. According to Gilman, as early as 1489, the physician Francisco Lopez de Villalobos marked the hunching of the spine as a symptom and an external sign of syphilis, writing in a poem titled "Syphilis" that its sufferers are "Hunchback'd and indisposed" as well as "pained and crippled" (100).

WORKS CITED

Anthony, David. "Banking on Emotion: Financial Panic and the Logic of Male Submission in the Jacksonian Gothic." *American Literature* 76.4 (2004): 719–747.
Bampfield, R. W. ESQ. *An Essay on the Curvatures and Diseases of the Spine, Including All the Forms of Spinal Distortion.* Ed. J. K. Mitchell, M.D. Philadelphia: Ed Barrington & Geo D. Haswell, 1845.
Botting, Fred. *Gothic.* New York: Routledge, 1996.
Davis, Lennard J. "Constructing Normalcy: The Bell Curve, the Novel, and the Inven-

tion of the Disabled Body in the Nineteenth Century." *The Disability Studies Reader*. Ed. Lennard J. Davis. New York: Routledge, 1997.

Ellis, John, M. D. *The Avoidable Causes of Disease, Insanity, and Deformity*. New York: Cooper Institute, 1860.

Gilman, Sander. *The Jew's Body*. New York: Routledge, 1991.

Lippard, George. *The Quaker City; or, The Monks of Monk Hall: A Romance of Philadelphia Life, Mystery, and Crime*. 1845. Ed. David Reynolds. Amherst: University of Massachusetts Press, 1995.

Mitchell, J. K. Editor's Preface. *An Essay on Curvatures and Diseases of the Spine, Including All the Forms of Spinal Distortion*. By R. W. Bampfield, Esq. Ed. J. K. Mitchell. Philadelphia: Ed. Barrington and Geo. D. Haswell, 1845.

Napier, Elizabeth. *The Failure of Gothic: Problems of Disjunction in an Eighteenth-century Literary Form*. Oxford: Clarendon-Oxford Press, 1987.

Reynolds, David S. Introduction. *The Quaker City; or, The Monks of Monk Hall: A Romance of Philadelphia Life, Mystery, and Crime*. By George Lippard. Ed. David S. Reynolds. Amherst: University of Massachusetts Press, 1995.

Tamplin, R. W. *Lectures on the Nature and Treatment of Deformities*. London: Longman, Brown, Green, and Longmans, 1846.

Thomson, Rosemarie Garland. "From Wonder to Error: A Genealogy of Freak Discourse in Modernity." *Freakery: Cultural Spectacles of the Extraordinary Body*. Ed. Rosemarie Garland Thomson. New York: New York University Press, 1996.

Williamson, Geo. M.D. *The Laws of Heredity*. San Francisco: Suzanne Bunker Williamson, 1898.

Ominous Signs or False Clues?
Difference and Deformity in
Wilkie Collins's Sensation Novels

Tamara S. Wagner

Victorian Sensation fiction derives its most startling effects from the Gothic intrusion into the domestic. As frightening bodies, dead or alive, are encountered within seemingly secure domestic confines, they create horror at home, often through corporeal deviations from the conventional norms. Useful for its intrinsically startling impact, physical deformity features centrally in the Sensation novels of Wilkie Collins who creates increasingly unusual forms of disability in the course of his novels. Collins's deformed figures respond to a growing cultural fascination with changing conceptualizations of disability, or affliction, and to the emergent paradigms of a specifically physical Gothic.[1] Collins's retention and revision of the Gothic trope of the Other who engenders horror work through an ambiguous doubling that shuttles between sympathetic accounts of deformity and warnings of the dangers of disability at home, in one's own body and in the bodies of eerie doubles.[2] What has, however, been largely sidestepped in critical discussion of the deformed villains of Victorian literature is the shifting significance of deformity as a false lead in detective plots. In playing out both sensational and Gothic clichés as misleading clues, Collins's reworking does more than simply dismantle or reinforce prevailing prejudices that were feeding reader expectations at the time. In fact, his increasingly intricate plots of detection trade on prevailing stereotyping at the time in order to turn them into false clues, that both startle the reader, and warn of the dangers of relying on conventional cultural categories.

The Gothic Villain of The Woman in White

Although the Victorian Sensation novel had important precursors, including traditional Gothic narratives, the Newgate novel, and Collins's early experiments with sensational themes and devices, the publication of *The Woman in White* (1860) exemplified the beginning of something different and innovative. In her regularly anthologized article, "Sensational Novels," published in *Blackwood's Magazine* in 1862, Margaret Oliphant refers to "a new fashion ... a most striking and original effort, sufficiently individual to be capable of originating a new school in fiction" (10). While Oliphant concedes that "Mr. Wilkie Collins is not the first man who has produced a sensation novel" (10) — mentioning Hawthorne, Bulwer Lytton, and the genre of the ghost story — Oliphant astutely notes Collins's shift from the international and supernatural to the mundane and domestic that later scholars of Sensation fiction describe as "domestic Gothic." There is however, a clear exception to Oliphant's statement that one of the domestic qualities of *Woman* is that it presents "neither startling eccentrics nor fantastic monsters" (11). Indeed, Count Fosco, "the arch-villain of the story" (11) is remarkably eccentric, fantastic and monstrous, although framed as human and realistic.[3]

Fosco is an embodiment of a number of paradoxical Victorian fears and fascinations. His status as a foreign, aristocratic spy leads a great number of critics to focus on his infiltration of the domestic, the way in which he serves as both foreign agent for the Austrian Empire and as Sir Percival's household spy.[4] His Italian otherness is amplified at the end of the novel when he is executed as a traitor by the secret society he has betrayed. This scene, in which Fosco ends up on display — his bloated body fished out of the river and exhibited at the Morgue in Paris — also reinforces another quality that identifies Fosco as inhumanly different: his grotesque obesity. The "great crowd clamour[ing] and heav[ing]" that views him, indulging in the sensational horror of the spectacle, respond to this frightening difference: "There was evidently something inside which excited the popular curiosity, and fed the popular appetite for horror ... and the account they were giving of the dead body to their neighbors, described it as the corpse of a man — a man of immense size, with a strange mark on his left arm" (639).[5] The shocking intrusion of Fosco's dead body solidifies the Gothic aura of Collins's novel. Set free from the domestic setting, and from the refinements that made him seem interestingly exotic, Fosco is exposed as a spectacular and inhuman monster.

That Fosco's monstrosity derives from his corpulence, rather than from his provenance, is evidenced by the other Italian in the novel, the benevolent Pesca who undercuts any easy alignments between Italian foreignness and villainy. This character gestures toward the Gothic in his role of Fosco's mirrored double, thus illustrating a central Gothic trope of ambiguous identity.[6] Pesca is indeed Fosco's counterpart on many levels. Both eccentrics display strategies of emulation and infiltration, and non-normative bodily proportions. Sutherland has termed them "dwarf and fat man, monsters of benign and malign deformity" (Introduction xix). This pairing, however, depends upon difference. Pesca's role as the non-threatening Italian derives from his diminutive size, the quality that directly opposes the defining quality of Fosco's body. He is thus "the eccentric little foreigner" (10) who befriends and ultimately assists Walter Hartright, the hero of the novel. Fondly introduced in the opening chapters, Pesca opposes Fosco's inhumanly gigantic proportions: "Without being actually a dwarf— for he was perfectly well-proportioned from head to foot — Pesca was, I think, the smallest human being I ever saw, out of a show-room" (7).[7] Pesca's non-threatening body neuters the danger of his foreignness. Thus, it is "harmless eccentricity" that compels Pesca to aspire "to become an Englishman in his habits and amusements, as well as in his personal appearance" (8), while Fosco's "unusual command of the English language" (221) threatens the English characters and is immediately linked to his international correspondence (and hence his activities as a spy).[8]

The Dangerous Gothic Husband

Although the prime source of Fosco's deviltry may not be his foreignness, his Italian identity does ally him with one of the recurring types of villainy in the traditional Gothic text: the dangerous Italian husband or suitor.[9] Fosco is married to Laura Fairlie's aunt,[10] Eleanor Fairlie who exemplifies the typically defeated and imprisoned Gothic wife. Formerly full of "pretentious nonsense" (218), an advocate of women's rights, "this once wayward Englishwoman" (219) is now completely submissive to the Count (236). Her "transformation" into Madame Fosco invests "the foreign husband who has tamed [her]" (219) with an ominous (and doubled) interest, anticipating Sir Percival's attempt to subdue Laura.[11] Even Fosco's seemingly innocent eccentricity — his characterization as an eccentric "Italian with white mice" (460, 467) — masks his role as the dangerous Gothic husband. His well-trained menagerie of pets, including "a cocatoo, two canary-birds, and a whole family of white mice," presents a grotesque parody of exotic domesticity. In fact, he confines his pets "in a little pagoda of gaily-painted wirework" (222), much as the dangerous Gothic husband confines his "pet," the wife that he possesses. As the captive white mice scamper across Fosco's body, Collins imbues the image with a distinctly Gothic flavor, presaging the mob's final feasting on the sight of Fosco's dead body: the image of the mice "suggests hideous ideas of men dying in prison, with the crawling creatures of the dungeon preying on them undisturbed" (233). Yet the Gothic possibilities of Fosco are invisible to most of the characters of the book; his seemingly soft and civilized demeanor allows him to present an even greater threat because it masks his danger.[12]

Monstrous Obesity

Only Marian, the unfeminine half-sister of the hyper-feminine and vulnerable Laura, is able to penetrate Fosco's mask. Marian's often remarked "masculine" intellectual qualities and her marginalized status as an intelligent, unfeminine spinster, allow her to interrogate the cultural stereotypes in which Fosco veils his identity. Marian is able to see Fosco for what he is because she rejects the contemporary association between obesity and benevolence:

> He is immensely fat.... I have always maintained that the popular notion of connecting excessive grossness of size and excessive good-humour as inseparable allies, was equivalent to declaring, either that no people but amiable people ever get fat, or that the accidental addition of so many pounds of flesh has a direct favourable influence over the disposition of the person on whose body they accumulate. I have invariably combated both these absurd assertions by quoting examples of fat people who were as mean, vicious, and cruel, as the leanest and the worst of their neighbours [220].

Marian's remarks thus reveal and reject the stereotypes of her time.[13]

In the narrative, Collins, like Marian, discards the Victorian stereotype, replacing it with the more archaic association between physical difference and dangerous monstrosity. Fosco's "monstrous corpulence" (581) warns the careful reader that this villain exemplifies two distinct forms of Gothic danger: he is at once the monstrous husband of the conventional Gothic, and the supernatural and inhuman Gothic monster, repackaged and modernized into one grotesque yet realistic human form. His disproportionate body shape renders "the horrible freshness and cheerfulness and vitality of the man" (581), combined with "his voracious vanity" (583), as ominous as sheer size itself. Much is made of his careful maintenance of his corpulence, as he "devours pastry" (226) and boasts of his "taste for sweets" as "the innocent taste of women and children" (294). His voracious production of his most recognizable characteristic hence externalizes an omnivorous desire that includes a gobbling up of identities, personal information, and Marian's purloined diary.

Yet only a particularly alert Victorian, like Marian, could be expected to anticipate Fosco's menace. To Victorians, fat men were jolly, if somewhat stupid,[14] anticipating the stereotypes of our times as articulated by Sander Gilman who describes the current "assumption that body size reflects mental acuity and emotional life" (514). Fosco's impressive intellect, charismatic wit, and internationally acknowledged achievements clearly go against this typecasting. The average Victorian would have been surprised indeed by the notion of an oversized villain who is notably un-jolly and un-genial. Thus Collins successfully plays into the cultural biases of his readers to confound their expectations and to provide his novel with a truly sensational villain.

The Monstrous Body in Collins's The Law and the Lady

While the monstrosity of Fosco's obesity is visible to the discerning reader, the horror of his body pales in comparison to that of the villain of *The Law and the Lady* (1875), Miserrimus Dexter, one of the most memorable freaks of Victorian Sensation fiction. A sad surprise to his healthy parents, he simultaneously evokes a peculiarly technological as well as biological Gothic. Linked to decay and discourses of degeneration, to the atavistic invocations of primordial birds, half-formed apes, and missing links, he sees himself as something radically new. He sets himself up as a newly evolved form of creation; when he propels his wheelchair, "man and machinery blended in one — the new Centaur, half man, half chair" (193). Teresa Mangum remarks that one might today well "substitute cyborg" for "new Centaur" (294).

Yet the notion that Dexter represents new development and transcendent genius really only exists in his own imagination, revealing that his mind is "as deformed as his body" (179). He believes he excels as a "poet-painter-composer-and-cook" (230), yet his works are mere "daubs" (213), random admixtures of "occult substances, of uninviting appearance" (228). Dexter's association with the old and the occult is furthered by his placement among the various "curiosities" the Victorians loved to exhibit in private and public spaces. In his own home, he deliberately stages a show for the benefit of the amateur detective Valeria, in which the display of his physical deformities is part and parcel of an exhibition that includes a number of startling items: the overrated truffles he (ineffectually) cooks to impress Valeria; a shirt seemingly of chamois leather that turns out to be the skin of a French Marquis tanned during the Revolution (230). In including his own body within this ghoulish exhibition, Dexter encourages the sense of his own monstrosity; to him, his deformity is a compelling demonstration of his exceptional status.

By definition, the monster interrogates the boundaries that conventionally and comfortably define the norm. Collins carefully shows that Dexter interrogates and transgresses the categories of the norm in a number of ways. Ambulating in his wheelchair, he is half-human, half-machine. The diagnosis of "latent insanity" (264) indicates that Dexter moves easily between the categories of the sane and the insane.[15] Moreover, Dexter demonstrates the permeability of the boundary that distinguishes the genders. Much critical ink has been spilled on the affinities between the androgynous Dexter and the female detective, Valeria. Kathleen O'Fallon has termed him "the androgynous figure of the earlier novels taken to its maddest extreme," suggesting at the same time that "Valeria senses a kinship with Dexter" (237). Mangum goes further in remarking that Dexter is born without legs "and, the novel coyly suggests, without genitals," and as he "is variously Valeria's associate, her antagonist, and her sensational counterpart, [he] raises questions about the relationship between the broader categories, normal and formal" (285).

The Monstrous Text

Examining Dexter's "biographical, spectatorial, and generic conditions" (293), Mangum draws vital connections between the novel's re-formation of the deformed, monstrous Gothic body (and mind) and its re-formulation of literary genre. Collins's case of the technological Gothic monster mixed with an elusive murder case work to render the novel as an intricate engagement with the shifting paradigms of sensational detective fiction. Of course, we need to remember that the detective novel, an emergent subgenre of popular culture at the time, grew out of Sensation fiction and was rooted in its precursor's domestication of the Gothic. Mangum points to Collins's re-formulation of detective plots in the novel: "formal paradoxes that characterise detective fiction" (287) can be seen to "re-form" themselves "around the socially anomalous body of the female detective" as they become at once literalized and partly upstaged by "the physically anomalous masculine figure" (Mangum 286). Since amateur detectives, both male and female, have long held the upper hand in such novels, the structures of detection are not necessarily "a masculinist plot" that is disrupted by the introduction of a female (amateur) detective, as suggested by Mangum (286). On the contrary, the novel is centered on the juxtaposition between the successful efforts of "the lady" and the failures of "the law." Valeria refuses to accede to the power of a legal verdict and is ultimately proved right in her firm belief that she can more successfully solve the mystery of her husband's alleged crime: "What the Law has failed to do for you, your Wife must do for you" (108).[16]

Doubled Disability

The narrative unfolds as recently-married Valeria Woodville discovers that her husband has married her under an assumed name. This is because he does not wish her to know that he has been accused of murdering his first wife, a crime for which he has never been entirely acquitted because of the intricacies of the Scottish legal system. Tried in Scotland, Eustace Macallan (alias Woodville) suffers under the peculiarities of the "Scotch Verdict," which allows a verdict of "Not Proven." Collins thus provides a critique of legal injustice in Victorian Britain through the eyes of a woman, and empowers his female character to rewrite and correct the printed narrative of the trial, *A Complete Report of the Trial of Eustace Macallan For the Alleged Poisoning of his Wife.*[17]

False Clues of Disability

As in *The Woman in White*, Collins resists the easy answers provided by conventional stereotypes. In the official account of the trial, the dead woman is described as having been "a very plain woman" with "a cast in one of her eyes" and "one of the most muddy, blotchy complexions" (124). This depiction leads participants at the trial to believe mistakenly that she must therefore have been saintly, a stereotype that undermines attempts to establish the usual motives of love and jealousy for her "murder." Testimony of Eunice's weakness as the result of the pain from her rheumatic knee work to heighten the sense of her pathos and of the villainy of Eustace who has supposedly poisoned his prostrated wife. And yet, Eunice is not the suffering saint that she appears. Her death is the direct consequence of Dexter's passion for her. Moreover, the testimony of her nurse identifies her as one of the manipulative, sometimes hypochondriac invalids of Collins's earlier fiction. As "the inflammatory look" disappears, her symptoms are confined to "weakness from lying in bed, and irritability of temper," while otherwise "there was really nothing the matter with her" (126).

Just as the figure of Fosco confounds Victorian notions of obesity, so does the figure of Dexter confound sentimental cultural ideas of the sexually neutered, pathetic victim of disability. Dexter's lack of lower body parts suggests that he is an unlikely candidate for amorous passion, let alone sexual misconduct. Yet in scene with Valeria the "lustful cripple put his arm round her waist and tried to kiss her." This passage was considered "unfit to appear in the pages of a family newspaper" (Peters 371). Certainly the offense to morality derived as much power from the notion of a sexualized "cripple" as from the presence of lust. In fact, everything we know about Dexter confounds our expectation that eventually we will come to a sense of sympathy for this tragically deformed man. His deformity surprises the reader because it accurately reflects his deformity. He is a monster not because of his appearance, but because he cruelly mistreats a mentally disabled servant, attempts to seduce his friend's wife, contributes to her suicide, and remains silent when the truth could liberate his friend.

Collins also confounds our expectations in his representation of Eustace, the hero of this novel. A mysterious, scarred, older husband, he could be read by a reader familiar with the Gothic trope of the dangerous husband as yet another representative of that murderous crew. But Eustace's limp complicates our reading of this man as dangerously powerful patriarch. The image pushes the novel from the Gothic and taps into associations with physical impairment in nineteenth-century culture. As Peter Hays points out in *The Limping Hero: Grotesques in Literature*, the special emotional significance of the limp in literature spans maimed figures of sterility as well as images of the Devil, "another lame prototype" (8). Dickens, notorious for his sentimentalizing of disability, also "makes obvious use of lameness as a sign of evil with Quilp and Rigaud, the *diaboli ex machina* of *The Old Curiosity Shop* (1840–1841) and *Little Dorrit* (1855–1857) respectively" (Hays 107).[18] A rejection of Tiny-Tim types, as much as of tragic Byronic hero-villains bearing the sign of the devil's cloven foot, Collins's limping hero capitalizes on this mixed metaphorical potential.[19]

By the end of the novel, the reader is left with the doubled image of a hero, Eustace, and a villain, Dexter, both physically disabled. Collins pairs the mentally unstable legless cad–who sports a perfectly shaped muscular upper torso — with the fragile, limping husband. The doubles also mirror each other's emasculation. Eustace is a delicate, emotionally unsettled, even weepy middle-aged man and Dexter is a disconcertingly effeminate "halfman" (168), lacking the lower half of his body, and presumably his genitals, hopping like a bird, clad in frilly pink. The competing stereotypes of disability — "cripple" as demon or as victim — appear to cancel each other out. In *Woman* Collins deploys the figure of Fosco to reverse stereotypes without abandoning them — at the end of the novel, the reader has learned that fat men may be dangerously unjolly, and that physical difference denotes menace. Yet *The Law and the Lady* concludes with the suggestion that resorting to the lazy strategy of stereotyping to determine the inner worth of a character can be misleading. Although this detective tale trades on the sensational effects of deformed bodies, it self-consciously reacts against clichés, both sensational and sentimental, in the process dismantling prejudices evoked to mislead and to surprise unsuspecting readers.

False Clues in The Legacy of Cain

In his later writing, Collins's fiction increasingly derives its structure by playing deliberately with the generally false physical signs mapped out by a corporal Gothic. *The Legacy of Cain* (1888), the last novel Collins completed, raises questions about the "hereditary transmission of qualities" (19), which may be mapped on the body. The narrative tension of the novel focuses on the identification of a murderess's daughter. The novel opens up with a prison governor's account of a strikingly beautiful woman's conviction for the murder of her husband, and her final request that a minister adopt the child she leaves behind. The mother's startling resemblance to pictures of the Madonna in Italian art reintroduces the question about the inscription of criminality, or innocence, on the body. The governor is skeptical about the linkage: his extensive experience "has considerably diminished [his] faith in physiognomy as a safe guide to the discovery of character" (7). He recognizes that "there would be two forces in a state of conflict in the child's nature as she grew up — inherited evil against inculcated good" (29). The optimistic governor believes that upbringing can temper temperament, and thus opposes the belief articulated by a physician regarding "the growth of that poisonous hereditary taint" (18). The doctor argues: "I have been studying the question of hereditary transmission of qualities; and I have found vices and diseases descending more frequently to children than virtue and health" (19). The prevailing question whether "the tempers of children are formed by the accidental influences which happen to be about them" or whether they "are inherited from their parents" (14) — nature versus nurture — structures the plot.[20]

Set seventeen years after the trial, the novel's next section consists of the diaries kept by the minister's two daughters, Helena and Eunice Gracedieu: one, the adopted daughter of the murderess; the other, the daughter of the minister and his late wife. Neither knows that one of them is adopted. Investing the diary format with an intriguing ambiguity, their alternating doubled accounts tell a conventional story of romance, jealousy, and attempted murder.

But there is tension in this dyad. In a rather contrived plot-twist, Eunice falls in love with Philip Dunboyne, the cousin of the adopted girl. While this coincidence slowly drives Mr. Gracedieu to distraction, which ultimately results in complete imbecility, Helena deliberately steals the deplorably weak young man from Eunice. Helena confides to her diary that she feels she has a "wicked heart" and wonders "[w]hat has become of [her] excellent education" (115). Eunice's simplicity and intensely passionate nature — tantrums included — thus contrast favorably with the ploys of her cleverer, but also more conniving sister.

Throughout the novel, Collins plants many clues, some mutually exclusive, as to the identity of the girls, another example of one of Collins's affinity for the strategy of the red herring. The phrenological feature of the slanting forehead and her innate nastiness seem to mark Helena as a potential murderess. Yet, just when the governor (and with him, the reader) has become convinced of Eunice's well-directed passionate energies and Helena's transference of her mother's murderousness into destructive ploys, Eunice takes her father's sleeping draft and is promptly visited by "an Evil Spirit" that announces itself as her mother come "to harden [her] heart" (146). Eunice terms the vision her "mock-mother" and "hateful second self" (205–6). Guided by this psychological double, she almost kills her sister. Helena's cruelty reasserts itself when the morally weak Philip remorsefully creeps back to Eunice. Helena forges a prescription and begins to poison Philip. In a heavily sensational crescendo of chases and last-minute rescues, Helena is arrested; the minister, broken down in health, loses his memory entirely; Eunice marries Philip. The governor decides not to disclose what only he knows — that the latter thereby marries his murderous aunt's daughter, and the novel ends with a postscript that partially, ambiguously, acknowledges the influence of the much disputed "accidental obligation to our fathers and mothers" (202). Yet Collins's statement regarding the inheritance of evil is far more ambiguous.

As in *The Law and the Lady*, Collins sets up the doubled image of two opposing characters, one inherently good, one inherently evil, both marked by difference. In *The Law*, the mark is the clearly visible mark of disability; in *The Legacy of Cain*, the mark is the more metaphorical mark of the murderer borne by the first murderer, Cain. Since in *Cain* both halves of the double are capable of misdeeds, we could conclude that Collins suggests that the daughter of a minister and the daughter of a murderess are equally influenced, or uninfluenced, by heredity. Yet, if we remember that the minister's wife was a heart-hearted woman, reluctant to take in the homeless child of the murderess, we might consider that both flawed girls show the inherited taint of their flawed mothers. Collins thus engages in a deeply ambiguous interrogation of the concepts of the signs mapped on the body and on the mind. In doing so, he defies readers' expectations of easy solutions to the mysteries he poses.

NOTES

1. Meegan Kennedy speaks of "Gothic medicine," pinpointing the narrative use of "the 'clinical' case history of the nineteenth century" as singularly Gothic in "its interest in the supernatural and the unexplainable and its narrative aim of arousing suspense, horror, and astonishment in the reader" (327). On sentimental discourses of affliction see Holmes.

2. Gothic body forms in Victorian fiction should be situated within the larger cul-

tural engagement with the "abnormal," with fear not only of aberration itself, but also of a policing of harmless eccentricity. This multilayered concern with typecasting ensured that the most strikingly unusual body forms were always more than a rehearsal of "freakish idiosyncrasies" (Julia Miele Rodas 53). As Rodas points out, such "freakish idiosyncrasies" (53) predominated in the early sketches of Dickens, yet his mid-century fiction increasingly illustrated "that illness and disability are a part of the ordinary course of life" (80), suggesting that this depiction of disability as an integrated part of daily life was part of a general development in mid-Victorian society. Of course, Rodas adds, "that earlier query persists: 'who or what am I in relation to this other creature?'" (61).

3. Fosco's "combination of gifts" (12), and his versatility, distinguish him as one of the first clever criminals of popular fiction. Winifred Hughes has called him a "swashbuckling foreign agent" (157) as well as "one of the most delightful villains in literature" (143), and John Sutherland suggests that Fosco founded a line of arch-villains that was to include "Professor" Moriarty and "Doctor" Nikola.

4. As Lisa Surridge asserts, "one of the text's jokes rests on the confusion between private and political spying" (146). Alison Milbank has linked Fosco to the aristocratic villains of traditional, eighteenth-century Gothic to suggest that he "imposes his aristocratic will on society, and his narrative of omnivorous desire upon the text of the novel itself, in a series of first-person interpolations" (12).

5. This is a fitting end for a larger-than-life villain who delights in displaying not only his multifaceted talents, but also his sheer size and remarkable presence, including his seemingly harmless eccentricities: "There he lay, unowned, unknown; exposed to the flippant curiosity of a French mob!" (640). In suggesting a connection to the Crystal Palace, Steve Dillon reads this display as a critique of transparency: "the final picture of the dead Fosco is one seen *through glass*— yet it is a vault of layers" (252). It remains unclear, Dillon admits, whether this is really a critique of display or of concealment.

6. Thus, there are two Italians in Collins's novel; there are several Italians in Ann Radcliffe's iconic Gothic novel, *The Italian*. Similarly, there are a number of women in white in Collins's novel. In fact, an encounter between Pesca and Fosco serves to reinforce the loss of identify of the latter. The novel's conclusion reveals that Pesca and Fosco are both members of the brotherhood that Fosco betrays. Yet Pesca fails to recognize Fosco because of the deterioration in the Count's appearance: he is "so altered, or so disguised" (592), "so changed that [Pesca] could not recognise him" (638). This lack of recognition on the part of his own double reveals the severity of Fosco's loss of identity.

7. In considering Collins's emphasis on bodies that deviate from the norms of scale, Catherine Peters points to Collins's "sensitivity about his physical disproportion" (20). Describing his own physiognomy, Collins regularly remarked that "Nature in his case had been a 'bad artist' who had depicted his forehead 'all out of drawing'" (Peters 20).

8. The paired foreign imports, united by nationality, divided by body type and moral nature, provide an important touchtone for the eponymous *Woman in White*, the set of half-sisters Laura Fairlie and Anne Catherick. The plotline of the novel hinges on the swapping of Laura's identity with that of her half-sister, Anne. Here too, doubleness depends on qualities other than physical similarity. The substitution of the titular Woman in White is facilitated not so much by the startling physical resemblance of the half-sisters as by their shared nervous susceptibility, a doubled characteristic in that what translates as impracticable oversensitivity in the lower class Anne, is perceived as sensibility in the upper-class Laura. *Woman* is thus a novel that focuses on the significance of fixed identity, and the impossibility of achieving this ideal. Collins also illustrates this motif in destabilizing the gendered identity of a number of important characters. Mr. Fairlie's "wretched nerves" are not merely a "selfish affectation," they are an illustration of his troubling and — as far as the effect on other characters — dangerously passive femininity. There is "something singularly and unpleasantly delicate in its association with a man, and, at

the same time, something which could by no possibility have looked natural and appropriate if it had been transferred to the personal appearance of a woman" (39–40). This
confusion of gender markers poses Mr. Fairlie against Laura's resolute, masculine other
half-sister, Marian, who has been termed "almost the only moustached heroine in English
fiction" (Symons 59). While Fairlie's "effeminately small" (39) feet put him on the list of
unusually sized weak or villainous men, Marian stands out in her unconstrained, un-
policed natural proportions. Still, there is no easy division between the supposedly natural, the socially approved, and the unpleasantly incongruous. Indeed, what Hartright
endorses as Marian's perfect waist because it is "visibly and delightfully undeformed by
stays" (31) imbues the appearance of her masculine head — sporting a "dark down on her
upper lip [that] was almost a moustache" (32) — with an additionally startling effect: "Never
was the old conventional maxim, that Nature cannot err, more flatly contradicted — never
was the fair promise of a lovely figure more strangely and startlingly belied by the face and
head that crowned it" (32). This early reference to erring nature simultaneously introduces
the complicated issue of deformity (and the fluidity of what constitutes natural body
forms), while nevertheless trading on its sensational effects.

    9. This trope begins with Manfred in Horace Walpole's *Castle of Otranto* and is
consolidated by the many Italian villains of Ann Radcliffe, most notably Montoni in *The
Mysteries of Udolpho*.

    10. A relationship that echoes the relationship of Montoni to the heroine of *Udolpho*.

    11. In the same vein Percival's assumed urbanity is soon exposed as "the artifices of
a mean, cunning, and brutal man, who had dropped his disguise when his practised duplicity had gained its end" (255). It is hardly surprising, therefore, that his hacking cough and
shiny scar become more pronounced as he reveals his violent temper.

    12. Conversely, Pesca and Hartright display their authenticity in rejecting the kind
of disguise that Fosco adopts. Pesca follows the orders of his brotherhood "to emigrate to
England" without attempting a physical disguise (589). Stalked by Sir Percival's men,
Hartright might be justified in claiming the protection of a physical disguise, yet such
concealment is emphatically rejected: "But there was something so repellent to me in the
idea — something so meanly like the common herd of spies and informers in the mere act
of adopting a disguise — that I dismissed the question" (492).

    13. Her disputation of the image of the genial fat man is backed by similar remarks
regarding Sir Patrick's solicitor, the misnamed Mr. Merriman, who seems "all in a glow
with the warmth of his own amiability" while striking a mercenary bargain. Merriman,
"a fat, well-fed, smiling, friendly man of business is of all parties to a bargain the most
hopeless to deal with" (154).

    14. In a recent discussion of obesity as a form of disability that underscores the slip-
periness of the concept itself, Sander Gilman remarks that mid-nineteenth-century American medical discourse began explicitly to connect "gross obesity" to "mental stupidity"
and "coarseness of feeling," so that in "this world of physiognomic equivalents, obesity is
a sign of mental vacuity and emotional insensitivity" (514).

    15. Rylance has shown that at first mental pathology was "an all-or-nothing game....
Theorists liked to think that insanity was either all there, and the lunatic is therefore a
pariah to the human community (as in literary representations like that of Bertha Mason
in *Jane Eyre*), or not there at all" (114). It was only in the century's second half that conceptions of the self became more complicated.

    16. It moreover turns out that Valeria is not just a female, but a pregnant detective,
yet despite some early hints, this revelation is too sudden and its connection to any physical change too tentative to introduce any additional dimension into the prevailing dismantling of paradigms. Instead, it primarily underscores Valeria's self-identification as a
wife (and mother) who seeks to succeed where the law has failed. Awareness of her pregnancy, a "strange medley of joy and fear, and wonder and relief, and pride and humility,"

makes "a new woman of [her]," investing her with "a new resolution and a new courage" (293). This strength helps her to breaks through the deformities of the law.

17. The first Mrs. Macallan, Eunice, a hard-featured, overbearing, emphatically plain woman with a violent temper, is linked to the villainous wheelchair-bound Dexter by a temporary impairment when she is bedridden due to a rheumatic knee. Moreover, she articulates a sense of connection to Dexter: "I have indeed almost a fellow-feeling for [deformed persons]; being that next worst thing myself to a deformity — a plain woman" (360). This difficulty with her leg, moreover, links her (and Dexter) to her limping husband, Eustace, who suffers from a "slight limp" (15). Eunice thus suggests an important link between the two men. In fact it is Dexter's sense of connection to Eunice that leads to her death and the accusation of murder lodged against her husband. After Dexter purloins Eustace's diary as "proof" of the latter's indifference to her, she commits suicide. Dexter steals and attempts to destroy her last letter. It is the retrieval and reconstruction of this torn-up paper that ultimately prove Eustace's innocence.

18. Reminding us that Goethe's Mephistopheles "has no obvious hooves, but does limp" (106–7), and that Captain Ahab in Melville's *Moby-Dick* (1851) is both maimed and a victimizer himself, Peter L. Hays traces the traditions that "such characters should be deformed — that they should, in particular, limp" to two essential sources: "deformity, from the Platonic concept that a man's character is reflected in his appearance; limping, from the tradition that Satan has cloven hooves which he can disguise but not entirely conceal should he take human shape" (106–7).

19. Eustace is but one of Collin's limping characters: Limping Lucy, the messenger of a deformed suicidal servant girl in *The Moonstone* (1868) and the kind-hearted, club-footed baronet, "a gentleman of the byegone time" in knee-breeches who "carried his lameness, as he carried his years, gaily" (57–58) to triumph over a murderous man of "muscular education" in *Man and Wife* (1870) prepare the reader for the reworking of clichés in *The Law and the Lady*.

20. The identification of the daughter of the murderess is complicated by the birth of the minister's own daughter, which induces his wife to consult the governor about getting rid of the adoptive child. Although the governor refuses to assist her, and she dies before she can carry out her otherwise undisclosed plan, her introduction is a crucial lead. As her "long slanting forehead and the restless look in her eyes" (142) play right into phrenology, they complicate the novel's ambiguous redeployment of the theories of the time.

Works Cited

Collins, Wilkie. *The Law and the Lady*. 1875. London: Penguin, 1998.

———. *The Legacy of Cain*. 1888. Stroud: Sutton, 1993.

———. *Man and Wife*. 1870. Oxford: Oxford University Press, 1998.

———. *The Woman in White*. 1860. Oxford: Oxford World's Classics, 1996.

Dillon, Steve. "The Archaeology of Victorian Literature." *MLQ* 54.2 (1993): 237–261.

Gilman, Sander. "Defining Disability: The Case of Obesity." *PMLA* 120.2 (March 2005): 495–641.

Hays, Peter L. *The Limping Hero: Grotesques in Literature*. New York: New York University Press, 1971.

Hughes, Winifred. *The Maniac in the Cellar*. Princeton: Princeton University Press, 1980.

Kennedy, Meegan. "The Ghost in the Clinic: Gothic Medicine and Curious Fiction in Samuel Warren's *Diary of a Late Physician*." *Victorian Literature and Culture* 32.2 (2004): 327–51.

Mangum, Teresa, "Wilkie Collins, Detection, and Deformity." *Dickens Studies Annual* 26 (1998): 285–310.

Milbank, Alison. *Daughters of the House: Modes of the Gothic in Victorian Fiction*. New York: St Martin's, 1992.

O'Fallon, Kathleen. "Breaking the Laws about Ladies: Wilkie Collins' Questioning of Gender Roles." *Wilkie Collins to the Forefront: Some Reassessments*. Eds. Nelson Smith and R. C. Terry. New York: AMS Press, 1995.

[Oliphant, Margaret]. "Sensational Novels." *Blackwood's Edinburgh Magazine* 91 (May 1862): 564–580. *Varieties of Women's Sensation Fiction: 1855–1890*. Ed. Andrew Maunder. London: Pickering & Chatto, 2004.

Peters, Catherine. *The King of Inventors: A Life of Wilkie Collins*. London: Secker & Warburg, 1991.

Rodas, Julia Miele. "Tiny Tim, Blind Bertha, and the Resistance of Miss Mowcher: Charles Dickens and the Uses of Disability." *Dickens Studies Annual* 34 (2004): 51–97.

Rylance, Rick. *Victorian Psychology and British Culture*. Oxford: Oxford University Press, 2000.

Surridge, Lisa. *Bleak Houses: Marital Violence in Victorian Fiction*. Athens: Ohio University Press, 2005.

Sutherland, John. "Introduction." *The Woman in White*. By Wilkie Collins. Ed. John Sutherland. Oxford: Oxford World's Classics, 1996.

_____."Wilkie Collins and the Origins of the Sensation Novel." *Wilkie Collins to the Forefront: Some Reassessments*. Eds. Nelson Smith and R. C. Terry. New York: AMS, 1995.

Symons, Julian. *Bloody Murder: From the Detective Story to the Crime Novel: A History*. London: Pan Books, 1994.

The Dangerous Mr. Casaubon: Gothic Husband and Gothic Monster in *Middlemarch*

Elizabeth Hale

Readers who know of the stereotypical image of the scholar — physically feeble and unattractive, short-sighted, absent-minded and pedantic — will readily recognize the Reverend Edward Casaubon in George Eliot's *Middlemarch* (1874). Early chapters of the novel show him assiduously conforming to type in his appearance, his approach to human interaction, and his obsession with his "great work," the "Key to All Mythologies." He acknowledges that his preference for ancient narratives is determined by his sense that the modern world is a place of "ruin and confusing change" (40). Yet shortly after making this statement, Mr. Casaubon decides to become part of modern society in the most conventional way possible: by marrying Dorothea Brooke, an eager young heiress with a brain. The result is a disastrous marriage, played out over the course of the novel, in which Casaubon proves not merely to be an ordinarily unpleasant pedant, but a husband so monstrous and selfish that he poses a serious threat to Dorothea's happiness and selfhood, even after his death. In fact, during the course of the novel, the image of Casaubon changes from an unworldly Victorian pedant to a character more at home in the Gothic as Eliot's descriptions move from benign social stereotype to Gothic convention.

Dorothea's Gothic Husband

Eliot carefully aligns Casaubon with the typical Gothic husband,[1] selfish and uncaring, consigning his wife to a life of unhappiness at best. The honeymoon in Rome quickly devolves to a Gothic scene of misery and decay. Abandoned by her new husband while he researches in the Vatican Library, Dorothea is reduced to weeping at his neglect and emotional coldness. Dorothea's own view of Rome, its Gothic ruined excess clashing horribly with her idealistic purity, is filtered through her distress at her disastrous honeymoon; all she sees are "ruins and basilicas, palaces and colossi, set in the midst of a sordid present, where all that was living and warm-blooded seemed sunk in the deep degeneracy of a superstition divorced from reverence (225). A major disappointment for Dorothea is her realization that Casaubon's scholarship is not, as he states, a great work; it is outmoded and lacking in penetration or insight.[2]

From the start it is evident that Casaubon, like the conventional Gothic patriarch, sees marriage as a fulfillment of his needs; he seems to have no thought about Dorothea's wishes and desires — including her sexual desires.[3] Casaubon's neighbor, Mrs. Cadwallader, knowingly asserts that for Dorothea entering the marriage would be as "good as going to a nunnery" (82). Nor ultimately does he satisfy her intellectual desires. His grudging teaching leads to her difficulties in learning Greek and Latin, although she blames the stupidity of her own gender. He denies her the sense of self-worth she hopes to attain by contributing to his work; he reduces her assistance to making marks in directed places and rejects her offers of insight and critique. The cruelest consequence of this rejection is that he withholds a true sense of communion between their intellects and souls, which had been Dorothea's vision of the marriage. Casaubon is, of course, oblivious to the insensitivity of his behavior. After all he deliberately chooses a young wife who will make no demands — in the "most horrible of virgin sacrifices" says Will Ladislaw (397). Casaubon values Dorothea for her "submissive" (312) nature and for her ability to "lighten my solitariness" (67). The narrator comments that he requires her to "irradiate the gloom which fatigue was apt to hang over the intervals of studious labor with the play of female fancy" (87).[4]

In behaving like the typically cruel and selfish Gothic husband, Casaubon maneuvers Dorothea into the confined situation of the typical Gothic wife. She finds herself limited and controlled by the husband whom she thought would be her intellectual, spiritual and romantic partner. The absolute control is evident when Casaubon denies Dorothea the pleasure of speaking to Will at church. Eliot invokes the language and the imagery of the Gothic to contextualize Dorothea's enforced passivity:

> She longed for objects who could be dear to her, and to whom she could be dear. She longed for work which would be directly beneficent like the sunshine and the rain, and now it appeared that she was to live more and more in a virtual tomb, where there was the apparatus of a ghastly labour

producing what would never see the light. To-day she had stood at the door of the tomb and seen Will Ladislaw receding into the distant world of warm activity and fellowship — turning his face towards her as he went [516].

Confined to the tomb of "Lowick," Casaubon's aptly named residence, Dorothea feels as trapped as any woman married to a typical Gothic tyrant.

Casaubon as Gothic Monster

Yet, Eliot also suggests that ultimately Casaubon is more horrifying than the worst Gothic husband. Will Ladislaw is on to this when he describes the marriage as "beautiful lips kissing holy skulls" (399). Casaubon's neighbors think of him as a ghoulish vampire of sorts. When Sir James expresses his opinion that Casaubon is well on the way to death — "he has one foot in the grave" (82), Mrs. Cadwallader responds: "he means to draw it out again" (82). Later Sir James adds that Casaubon is a desiccated ghoul who "has got no good red blood in his body" (96).[5]

A strong clue to Casaubon's monstrosity is the repulsive state of his body. In proposing to Dorothea, Casaubon regales her with a catalog of decay taken from Sir Thomas Burton's description of unpleasant scholarly afflictions in the *Anatomy of Melancholy* (1621):

> Hard students are commonly troubled with gowts, catarrhs, rheums, cachexia, bradypepsia, bad eyes, stone, and collick, crudities, oppilations, vertigo, winds, consumptions, and all such diseases as come by over-much sitting; they are most part lean, dry, ill-coloured ... and all through immoderate pains and extraordinary studies [67].

This list, emphasizing atrophy (cachexia), blockage and poor digestion (bradypepsia, oppilations), and difficulties with sight, reinforce the association between the scholar and physical decay. Yet this catalogue omits an alternate cause of these symptoms — much of Casaubon's bodily decay, including the weak heart that eventually kills him, is a consequence of his advanced age. His age too links him with the old dead past that fascinates him. His age also could be seen as a link to the Gothic tradition with its fascination for antique moments.

Casaubon's "spare form and ... pale complexion" (38) sound like the features of a skeleton and at the end of his life, Casaubon does attempt to function as a living skeleton — a dead desiccated body that still retains the power of animation — or as a haunting ghost. Deathly in life, he attempts to live on after his death, and intends to use Dorothea as the tool of his immortality: "he willingly imagined her toiling under the fetters of a promise to erect a tomb with his name upon it. (Not that Mr. Casaubon called the future volumes a tomb; he called them the Key to all Mythologies)" (535). Eliot shows us the metamorphosis of this man from Gothic husband, controlling his wife in life, to ghost, controlling her from the grave: "he sought to keep his cold grasp on Dorothea's life" (535). Casaubon's will further demonstrates his ghostly intent; when he dies, Dorothea discovers that he has made a codicil to his will, directing his property away from Dorothea if she should marry Will Ladislaw (532). Ironically, his final attempt at controlling her after his death backfires — it makes Dorothea "conscious of another change which also made her tremulous; it was a sudden strange yearning of heart toward Will Ladislaw" (532). At the end of the novel the ghost is exorcised and defeated — in coming to a full realization that her husband's motives "had been lower than she had believed" (535), Dorothea frees herself entirely from his control. She renounces her claim to Casaubon's money, decides to marry Will, and leaves the shadow of the grave behind.

The Monstrous (Un)Self

Eliot scrupulously avoids drawing upon popular and Gothic stereotypes that link exterior bodily decay with monstrosity by emphasizing that it is Casaubon's interior that renders him a monster. Eliot invokes imagery of death, desiccation, burial, contagion, petrifaction, and decay to describe Casaubon's mind and soul, as well as his body. Indeed he is painted, as Henry James observed in his review of *Middlemarch*, with an "admirably sustained greyness of tone" (66). His character is uniform; his inner self in consonance with his outer self. Eliot's ability to sustain the unremitting "greyness" of tone — rather than displaying a lack of imaginative power — thus shows Eliot at her finest, defining a character whose inhuman consistency makes him monstrous. The absolute correlation between the stereotyped exterior and the inner world of Casaubon suggests that he is monstrous in that he is not subject to human irrationality and inconsistency. In this, as in most things, Dorothea provides the human counter to Casaubon's inhumanity. When he is close to death, Dorothea sits "as if she had been turned to marble, though the life within her was so intense that her mind had never before swept in brief time over an equal range of scenes and motives" (323). This description provides a powerful illustration of human inconsistency. The stark contrast between Dorothea's body, pale and still as marble, and her mind, racing through many different thoughts and ideas, highlights the inhuman congruity between Casaubon's mind and body.

The work that is the obsession of the passionless Casaubon is also gray, dead and monotonous. When he informs Dorothea that as his wife, she will assist him with "graver labours" (66), he seems to mean serious work. However, his characterization does allow for the Gothic image of the two of them at work disinterring a corpse, an image that anticipates Dorothea's later notions of Casaubon's "ghastly labours" (316) and her future imaginings of her participation in his work: "And now she pictured to herself the days, and months, and years which she must spend in sorting what might be called shattered mummies, and fragments" (520).

In fact Casaubon's narcissistic obsessive focus on his work, his scholarship, his perception, keeps him from fulfilling himself as a scholar as well as a human being. He aims for scholarship that is "unimpeachable" (314), in its perfection avoiding the need for engagement with other scholars. He locks criticism of his work away "in a small drawer of [his] desk, and also in a dark closet of his verbal memory" (314), not caring or wanting to know what others think of his work. As the narrator notes, this attitude results in the sad isolation of the scholar who is shielded from the world behind the narrow lens of his scholarship:

> For my part I feel very sorry for him. It is an uneasy lot at best, to be what we call highly taught and yet not to enjoy: to be present at this great spectacle of life and never to be liberated from a small hungry shivering self— never to be fully possessed by the glory we behold ... but always to be scholarly and uninspired, ambitious and timid, scrupulous and dim-sighted [314].

Because his desiccated obsession fills his mind and heart, Casaubon's inner life has no space for anything connected to the world of the living — perhaps the most serious accusation that Eliot levels against her villain. When Eliot takes the narrative inside Casaubon's mind, it is ostensibly to show that he has as rich, complex and real an inner persona as other characters in the novel, and to defend him against his critics: "In spite of ... the want of muscular curve which was morally painful to Sir James, Mr. Casaubon had an intense consciousness within him ... spiritually a-hungered like the rest of us" (312), the narrator insists. Yet somehow the narrator fails to illustrate this point with any actual examples. What we discover on this trip inside Casaubon's mind is the profound narrowness of his outlook and character. His view of marriage is chillingly practical — "he reflected that in taking a wife, a man of good position should expect and carefully choose a blooming young lady — the younger the better, because more educable and submissive" (312). Little mention is made of love; indeed, the narrow propriety of Casaubon's ideas defeats the narrator's stated plan to defend Casaubon by entering his mind and understanding his position. Sadly, his soul is virtually an un-being, a thing "too languid to thrill out of self-consciousness into passionate delight; it went on fluttering in the swampy ground where it was hatched, thinking of its wings and never flying" (313). It is this essential emptiness that solidifies Casaubon's role as the monster of the novel. By definition a monster is an object to be observed from the outside. By convention a monster is the quintessential Other with no subjectivity, no visible inner self. Casaubon is thus the full-fledged monster of *Middlemarch*, a repulsively decaying body with a vacuum at its core.

Although Casaubon is a Gothic figure, *Middlemarch* is certainly not a Gothic novel. This is largely due to Dorothea's actions after his death. Upon exorcising Casaubon's ghost, and putting a stake through his vampiric heart, she departs from the world of the Gothic: moving from the role of subdued wife and passive heroine to fully developed woman. And in doing so, she takes the novel with her to the world of the *Bildungsroman* where she can act as the main character in the narrative of her life, exploring her own rich, complex and dynamic identity and self.

NOTES

1. Starting with Horace Walpole's Manfred in *The Castle of Otranto* (1764).
2. In this view, Dorothea is influenced by Will Ladislaw, whose studies in Germany reflect a radical shift in philological work that had not yet reached England. Casaubon's cold response to her tentative inquiries about learning German to gain access to the powerful scholarship taking place in Germany, reflects his intellectual rigidity as well as an incipient jealousy of Will and Dorothea's youthful friendship.
3. Although Casaubon is unaware, the narrator gives the reader a strong sense of what attracts Dorothea to him and what she expects from the marriage. Casaubon's outward appearance suggests to her that he is a model of humanist endeavor, a "man of profound learning" (7); he is a well-off clergyman whose independent wealth allows him to pursue a career as a scholar. When we first meet him, he is working on his impressively named "Key to All Mythologies." His name suggests further gravitas as it honors the eminent Swiss Renaissance theologian, Isaac Casaubon. These scholarly associations lend him a certain physical charm. To Dorothea he resembles a portrait of the father of the English Enlightenment, John Locke, in the "set of his iron-grey hair and his deep eye sockets" (38). But Dorothea is mainly disposed to admire Casaubon because of her intellectual rather than physical yearnings; she is seeking spiritual enlightenment and a wider role than those normally available to women of her class. She is attracted to Casaubon's professed allegiance to the life of the mind because it coincides with her own intellectual yearnings. To Dorothea, Casaubon's narrow pedantry compares favorably with the scattershot approach to learning of her uncle, Mr. Brooke. In the first bloom of love, Dorothea even finds Casaubon's bony and gray figure to be a refreshing contrast to the "blooming Englishman of the red-whiskered type" (38).
4. Casaubon's desires also recall the obsession of the Gothic patriarch, starting with Walpole's Manfred, to replicate himself in order to sustain his dynasty. Casaubon too wants to leave a "copy of himself" (313). As Joseph Wiesenfarth observes, "having failed to produce a copy of himself from [Dorothea's] body, he asks her to produce a copy of himself from her mind" (115).
5. Carol Senf identifies Rosamond Vincey, as another vampiric character who preys

on the living because she stifles the heroic potential of her husband, the young doctor, Tertius Lydgate. The narrator relates: "He once called her his basil plant; and when she asked for an explanation, said that basil was a plant which had flourished wonderfully on a murdered man's brains" (897). Rosamond is a more successful monster than Casaubon because she is a more modern monster than he, a monster for a new age. Tertius is unable to destroy Rosamond, while Dorothea is able to put a stake through the damaged heart of Casaubon, a figure of the past, a monster weakened by the corruption of his body.

WORKS CITED

Eliot, George: *Middlemarch*. Harmondsworth: Penguin, 1985

James, Henry. Rev. of *Middlemarch*, by George Eliot. *Galaxy* (March 1873). In *George Eliot: Middlemarch A Casebook*. Ed. Patrick Swindon. London, Macmillan, 1972.

Maxwell, Catherine: "The Brooking of Desire: Dorothea and Deferment in *Middlemarch*." *Strategies of Reading: Dickens and After*. Spec. issue of *Yearbook of English Studies* 26. (1996).

Senf, Carol A. "The Vampire in *Middlemarch* and George Eliot's Quest for Historical Reality." *New Orleans Review* 14.1 (Spring 1987): 87–97.

Wiesenfarth, Joseph. *Gothic Manners and the Classic English Novel*. Madison, Wisconsin: University of Wisconsin Press, 1988.

Folk Medicine, Cunning-Men and Superstition in Thomas Hardy's "The Withered Arm"

Simon J. White

Reason or Witchcraft?

Thomas Hardy's "The Withered Arm" (from the *Wessex Tales* 1888) is an account of a love triangle in a remote part of Hardy's Wessex, set in the 1820s and 30s. It is also a meditation on the opposition between the older supernatural way of understanding the world and the rational scientific modern approach. These opposing explanations for the title disability vividly illustrate the divergent approaches. All of the principal characters in the story profess a modern and rational world-view. Yet the story traces the re-emergence of the latent superstitions, and the tragic consequences of this return, as Hardy suggests that it is the residual belief in witchcraft that leads to the horrific dénouement.

The withered arm of the title comes about in a mysterious way. About thirteen years before the narrative thread is taken up, Farmer Lodge, who owns land in the village of Holmstoke and in the adjoining parish, had seduced and then abandoned Rhoda Brook, a dairy maid whose son is twelve years of age at the start of the story. The narrative begins with the arrival in Holmstoke of Farmer Lodge and his new wife Gertrude. Despite her jealousy, Rhoda befriends Gertrude, but later the two rivals have parallel dreams. Rhoda dreams that Gertrude is sitting on her chest, like a succubus. She grasps the arm of the "confronting spectre" (335) and pushes it away. At roughly the same time Gertrude, dreams that she is in a distant strange place. Shortly afterwards she discovers marks upon her arm. The marks seem to resemble the imprint of a human hand and the limb begins to waste away.

Some recent critical studies have suggested that Rhoda has somehow caused harm to Gertrude through the intensity of her obsession with the wife of her lost love. For Tony Fincham, "The Withered Arm" is "a story of the triumph of the psyche over the soma" and he goes on to argue that "Lodge's cruelty ... has crippled her [Rhoda] inside" so that the "accumulated hurt and anger has built up within her to the point where it can no longer be suppressed [and] has to spread outwards to touch those around her [Gertrude in particular, but Farmer Lodge too] with a psychological intensity over which Rhoda has no control" (142). Hardy's narrative superficially points to this explanation, because before she goes to bed on the night that she has the dream, Rhoda meditates upon Lodge's new wife so intently that she loses track of time. But Fincham's argument does not work in the context of the state of the sciences of mind in the late Victorian period or, for that matter, the detail of the narrative. It could be argued (although Fincham does not do so) that Rhoda has employed some form of mesmerism to cause harm to her rival.[1] But practices like mesmerism required the practitioner and patient to be in the same place at the same time, and necessitated a conscious effort on the part of the practitioner to affect the patient. Notwithstanding the fact Rhoda is unsettled by the arrival of Gertrude, it is not clear that she wishes to cause her rival harm (she feels considerable affection for her and sees her as a friend), even if she had possessed the knowledge and ability to do so with mind power alone.

The Survival of Witchcraft

Gertrude Lodge's immediate response to her disfiguring injury is that it is a biologically explicable mishap that can be cured by a physician. When the people around Holmstoke first suggest that she should visit "some clever man over in Egdon Heath" she "thought they meant some medical man" (340–41). It does not occur to Gertrude that her neighbors would think her in need of the assistance offered by Conjuror Trendle, who, as Rhoda explains "had [magical] powers other folks have not" (341).[2] As a proponent of the modern scientific attitude toward healing that was developing during the nineteenth century, Gertrude expresses surprise that "[her] people" could be as superstitious as to recommend a cunning-man (341).

Yet Gertrude's new neighbors in the remote and sparsely populated country are less attuned to the process of medical enlightenment than she is.[3] Hardy was well aware of the powerful belief in magical cures still held by people within rural villages in Dorset, even at the end of the nineteenth century. The anthropologist John Lubbock wrote in the 1870s: "a belief in witchcraft still flourishes among our agricultural labourers and the lowest classes in our cities" (136). In fact, Hardy's story shows the power that this belief can have over a scientifically modern person. As Romey T. Keys notes, Gertrude "has moved from the advanced world of the educated urban class to which she belongs toward the primitive world of the fieldworkers and Egdon Heath" (118).

Although Hardy explains in the preface to *Wessex Tales* (1888) that "The Withered Arm" is based upon an account of an actual tragedy told to him by "an aged friend who knew 'Rhoda Brook'" (xiii), he was certainly not a believer in magic as a cause for disability, nor in the curative powers of cunning-folk, despite the persistence of these beliefs in parts of Dorset in the 1880s. In a review of *The Folklore Record* for the *Saturday Review* written in 1882 he recounts the story of a man who applied for relief because he could not work, despite a surgeon finding no cause for his disability. The man provided his own explanation: "he had been 'over-looked' by his sister in law." Hardy's condemnation of this attitude is clear: "It is not a little disgusting to learn that an annual gathering is, or was until lately, held in the same neighborhood, called the Toad Fair, because a cunning man of great fame there sold to crowds of admirers legs torn from the bodies of living toads. These placed in a bag, and worn round the neck, were declared to be a sovereign remedy for scrofula, for the 'over-looked,' and for sufferers generally.... [Such superstition] is of the most groveling and mischievous kind" (Hardy "*Facts*" 303).

Because of the prevalent superstitious attitude, Gertrude's withered arm arouses fear and gossip in her community. Rather than considering the possibility of a physical cause and possible physical cures, the people around Holmstoke immediately link the disfigurement to darker and more intangible phenomena, finding cause to attribute a malignant and jealous motive to Rhoda, the mother of the illegitimate son of Farmer Lodge. In part III of the story, when Rhoda herself first entertains the idea that she might be in some way responsible for Gertrude's ailment, the reader is reminded that "she knew ... she had slily been called a witch [by the Holmstoke folk] since her fall" (338).[4] Earlier in the story the narrator provides another possible cause for the people's distrust: Rhoda holds herself aloof from the other inhabitants of Holmstoke. She does not participate in the dairy gossip, and seems to withhold herself from the social life of the community, thus presenting sufficient cause for the community to attribute Gertrude's unexplained disfigurement to Rhoda's malevolent witchcraft.

The circumstances represented in "The Withered Arm" mirror actual accusations in early-modern England where any bodily deformity, especially if grotesque or unexplained, could be attributed to witchcraft. As Keith Thomas points out, any private misfortune could be ascribed to witchcraft "but a supernatural explanation was particularly seductive in the field of medicine, where human impotence in the face of a variety of hazards was only too obvious" (639). Until recently most historians either assumed that a belief in witchcraft had ceased to be a significant influence upon the world view of the English people by the nineteenth century, or simply did not interest themselves in the history of witchcraft after the Witchcraft Act of 1736. But more recent work on the subject, particularly in a number of important studies by Owen Davies, has transformed our understanding of witchcraft in modern England. In fact Davies asserts that the traditional world view, which was inextricably bound up with witchcraft, and which, at the same time, helped to sustain a belief in the supernatural, did not disappear in the eighteenth and nineteenth centuries.

Gertrude's Disability: Natural or Supernatural?

If Hardy's story depicts the kind of traditionally oriented world that clearly survived into the second half of the nineteenth century, it also represents the painful collision between the old and the new within the individual mind. The advent of Gertrude's disability and its aftermath gradually reveals the instability of a personal commitment to a modern rational explanation of disability. Rhoda Brook initially has too much "common sense" (341) to pay much attention to superstitious gossip. But her gradual movement toward implicit acceptance of the possibility of witchcraft suggests that her "common sense" does not have a very solid foundation. The apparent congruence between her dream and Gertrude's, added to her feeling of guilt, leads her to suspect that she is somehow responsible for the injury: "'can it be ... that I exercise a malignant power over people against my own will?'" (338). Eventually Rhoda's doubts lead to her self-exile. As time passes her face grows "sadder and thinner" and she disappears from the "neighborhood of Holmstoke" (344). Tony Fincham responds to Rhoda's fear by noting "psychologically this is certainly possible" (143), citing Flanders Dunbar who says "a pain is a pain, and it hurts as much whether it is caused by an emotion or a club, a fear or a poison" (61). But Dunbar is reflecting upon the link between the mind and the body of the sufferer rather than the psychological ability of one individual to cause harm to another. What is, however, possible, is that Rhoda's guilt is powerful enough to destroy her.

Suzanne Johnson forcefully argues that "The Withered Arm" tends to undermine the possibility of a scientific medical explanation. The story "resists all realistic explanations for the strange events it chronicles" largely because the "temporal correspondence between the vision, the loud noise which the

son hears, and the shooting pain in Gertrude's arm push coincidence to breaking point" (131, 133). Yet Johnson also concurs with Leslie Stephen's critique
that it is not entirely clear whether Hardy's reader is supposed to believe that
the events depicted have a supernatural explanation (393–94).

For the reader to make a judgment, it is necessary to properly understand the events as they occur in Hardy's story. The dreams of the two women
in particular warrant further consideration. Rhoda dreams that "the young
wife, in the pale silk dress and white bonnet, but with features shockingly
distorted, and wrinkled by age, was sitting upon her chest as she lay ... and
then it [the specter] thrust forward its left hand mockingly, so as to make the
wedding-ring it wore glitter in Rhoda's eyes" (335). Rhoda seizes the specter's
left arm and flings it away from her, starting up as she does so with a cry.
Gertrude dreams that "[when she] was away in some strange place, a pain
suddenly shot into [her] left arm there, and was so keen as to awaken [her]"
(338).[5] As Johnson suggests, there is a temporal link between the two dreams,
which lends credence to the supernatural interpretation. Rhoda's son hears
the noise at two in the morning, and "the clock striking two" (338) reminds
the confused Gertrude where she is when she awakes. Rhoda dreams about
grasping Gertrude's arm at the very time the latter wakes with a pain in her
arm, suggesting a supernatural causality for the injury.

Yet apart from the temporal link there is no real evidence that Rhoda's
and Gertrude's dreams are supernaturally connected; the temporal link, the
sound Rhoda's son hears at two, is simply her own cry upon awakening. Since
Rhoda is completely preoccupied by Gertrude during her waking hours it is
unsurprising (and not particularly supernatural) to note that her dreams are
dominated by her rival. It is also unsurprising that it is the left hand, to which
the wedding ring — the ultimate symbol of her loss — is attached, that is the
focus of her dream, and that she grasps the left arm to push the "specter" away.
Indeed as Romey T. Keys points out "Rhoda's 'vision' is the culmination of a
prolonged effort of imaginative creation" (112). After all Gertrude does not
dream that she is in Rhoda's room (at the time of the dream she is unaware
of her husband's connection with Rhoda), simply that she is "away in some
strange place." The spasm that awakens her might have nothing to do with
the dream, except in so far as a painful injury to her arm would cause her to
sleep fitfully. The most likely scientific, medical, cause of the pain is peripheral neuropathy, in which a nerve is damaged by trauma or pressure. The
symptoms of this disorder range from numbness and pain to lack of coordi-
nation, muscle weakness, and even paralysis. In most instances patients recover
following appropriate treatment (not available to Gertrude), but in serious
cases peripheral neuropathy can cause muscle wasting and permanent damage to the affected area (Latov 7–9).

Rather than trying to impose either a supernatural or natural diagnosis on the reader, Hardy's text ultimately seems to allow both possibilities. The characters, however, are left with less of a sense of ambiguity. Like Rhoda, Gertrude and Farmer Lodge eventually move toward a supernatural explanation for Gertrude's injury. Neither Gertrude nor Farmer Lodge is aware of the temporal link between the dreams because Rhoda cannot bring herself to tell them, even though "it seemed treachery in the presence of her friendliness" to keep silent (340). Even so, the fallout from Gertrude's disability gradually wears down the Lodges' ability to adhere to a scientific explanation, and cure. Gertrude's struggle to heal the disfigured arm that she feels is somehow responsible for her husband's shrinking from her leads her to Conjuror Trendle, where she dabbles in the "mystic herbs, charms, and books of necromancy, which in her schoolgirl time she would have ridiculed as folly" (345). Farmer Lodge is overtly contemptuous of his wife's superstitious attempts: "'Damned if you won't poison yourself with these apothecary messes and witch mixtures some time or other'" (345). Lodge is angered by his wife's apparent superstition, "partly because he half entertained ... [superstitious ideas] himself" (348). As the narrator suggests and as his wife senses, there is a grain of belief in Lodge's apparent jokes about the marks on Gertrude's arm: "it is as if some witch, or the devil himself, had taken hold ... and blasted the flesh" (339). So it seems that Gertrude's wounded arm becomes a source of horror on two planes. To the local people the arm represents a revisiting and reviving of the traditional fears that link disability to supernatural agency. But even more frightening to the modern reader, Gertrude's mysterious injury represents a failure of modern thought and a return to the ancient dark ways.

The Traditions of Horror

The tendency of the Holmstoke community to link Gertrude's disfigurement to the practice of witchcraft, thus constructs her disabled arm as a source of supernatural horror, rather than as a simple example of a physical mishap. Indeed, Gertrude's arm cannot be cured by scientific modern medicine. When Farmer Lodge insists on a visit to a doctor, the result is a failed scientific attempt. Conjurer Trendle is dismissive of the powers of science: "'Medicine can't cure it.... Tis the work of an enemy" (343, 346). Because Gertrude is represented as an ideal of womanhood — Rhoda's own son describes her as "'a lady complete ... her face [is] as comely as a live doll'" (333) — her deforming disability is even more noticeable, spectacular. The withered arm draws attention away from her doll-like ideal beauty, towards her status as a breathing, eating and ultimately corruptible material being.[6] The shocking spectacle of the contrast between the grotesque withered arm and the beautiful woman it defaces also contributes to a horror whose source must be unworldly. The imagined origin in the curse of a malevolent supernatural enemy is compounded by the fact that by its very nature it is meant to degrade, to spoil and to destroy, the arm, and by extension its owner. Hardy's text thus partakes in the kind of grotesque abjection that Julie Kristeva imagines in *The Power of Horror*: "the theme of suffering-horror is the ultimate evidence of such states of abjection within a narrative representation" (141). For Kristeva the grotesque-abject body is a body of fear, but it is fear tempered with fascination: "like an inescapable boomerang, a vortex of summons and repulsion places the one haunted by it literally beside himself" (1). In the eyes of the community, Gertrude's body, tainted by Rhoda's curse, is marked by the witchcraft that still cast a dark shadow in the nineteenth century.

Modern Horror

Most horrifying is the effect of the arm upon Rhoda and the Lodges, the three characters who are initially committed to the scientific world-view. Their context of modernity actually amplifies the horror of the witchcraft that they presumably encounter. In *The Female Thermometer,* Terry Castle argues that an awareness of, or sensitivity to the grotesque or uncanny is heightened by the context of the "function of [rationality or] *enlightenment*" (7). That is, the rational perspective amplifies the fear engendered by phenomena unavailable to rational explanations and categories of understanding. Castle defines this set of threatening phenomena: that which "disturbs identity, system, order," that which "does not respect borders, positions, [and] rules. The phenomena appear as the "in-between, the ambiguous, the composite" (4). Thus Gertrude's mysterious and undiagnosible (uncategorizable) condition causes more acute horror and revulsion to its modern observers (characters and readers) because it reveals the fragility of the boundaries that the modern world constructs to maintain cognitive order, including the boundaries between magic and science, health and illness. Thus while the curse of the twisted arm comfortably confirms the received notions of the laborers, it shocks and destabilizes the Enlightenment world-views of Rhoda and the Lodges, disturbing their belief that they inhabit a modern world, that is available to understanding through science and reason.

Farmer Lodge responds to the impossibility of supernatural disability by distancing himself from Gertrude and her Gothic mark. With the passing of "half a dozen years" their "married experience sank into prosiness and worse" (344). He is "gloomy and silent" (344) and despite himself he is repelled by his wife. His latent superstition emerges and he ascribes their lack of children to a "judgement from heaven" (345), arising out of his treatment of Rhoda Brook and her son. The withered arm thus destroys their marriage as both come to believe that the very purpose of her affliction is to punish her and spoil her beauty. In their minds the arm becomes a monstrosity, the result of a devilish curse. Thus it is their belief in the supernatural, rather than the physical affect of the ailment that destroys their marriage.

As the object of the "curse," Gertrude, who comes from the outside rational modern world, is most visibly affected by her encounter with supernatural agency. After the failure of modern medicine to help her,[7] Gertrude overcomes her skepticism, convincing herself that she is visiting Conjuror Trendle "from curiosity" (341).[8] Yet Gertrude comes to believe that she has seen Rhoda's face in Trendle's water and egg solution. She tells herself that Conjuror Trendle is "entitled to certain credence, for the indistinct form he had raised in the glass had undoubtedly resembled the only woman in the world who — as she now knew, though not then — could have a reason for bearing her ill-will" (346). Gertrude discounts the (rational) possibility that Trendle might be engaging in a typical strategy of the cunning folk[9] — using his knowledge of local gossip in order to identify Rhoda as the witch responsible for the injury. Similarly, Gertrude does not entertain the possibility that her own fears have led her to identify Rhoda Brook in Trendle's mixture of water and egg.

That Gertrude Lodge should come to rely upon Conjuror Trendle's diagnoses of her arm after modern medicine fails her is understandable, socially and psychologically, if not rationally. In the new world that she inhabits, her decision to seek out a cunning-man of renown would be the *normal* thing to do. Thus although Gertrude is breaching the norms of the progressive modern world she comes from, her use of Trendle's services makes perfect sense to the superstitious community to which she now belongs. Moreover, the scientific medical establishment did not vociferously condemn the healing practices of cunning-folk during the early-nineteenth-century (Davies "Cunning-Folk in the Medical Market Place during the Nineteenth-Century" 57).[10] So in turning to Trendle, Gertrude is not even explicitly violating the norms of her previous, modern society. Since Trendle seems to give her an answer that is unavailable to modern medicine — what Davies characterizes as "a firm diagnosis, witchcraft, and a cause, a witch" (Davies *Popular Magic* 105), his methodology seems even more comforting and reliable to Gertrude. From the moment she forms the idea that the problem is witchcraft, orthodox medicine is put aside for the "mystic herbs, charms, and books of necromancy" that anger her husband so much. Over the next six years Gertrude's natural personality is also transformed as the result of her sense that she has been cursed: "The once blithe-hearted and enlightened Gertrude was changing into an irritable, superstitious woman" (345).

The End of Reason; The Beginning of Monstrosity

Thus Hardy shows that the supernatural continues to wield power, not because it is an accurate accounting of the world, but because even seemingly rational people continue to succumb to its mysteries. His story reveals an anxiety of the modern age: the fear of sliding back into dark superstition. Once Gertrude loses her anchor of rationality, her previously dormant superstition leads her into an increasingly horrific and primeval world. Ultimately Gertrude returns to Conjuror Trendle, and as a result of her second visit her disfigurement takes on further horrific associations. At this point (six years after her first visit) Trendle informs Gertrude that the one possible remaining cure will be "hard to carry out especially for a woman'" (346). Because Gertrude has been cursed by an enemy, the means of countering the curse must necessarily be extreme and horrifying. Trendle tells the anxious Gertrude that she "'must touch with the limb the neck of a man who's been hanged ... Before he's cold — just after he's cut down'" (346–47).[11]

Although her mind has been infected with the superstition that structures the lives of the people around her, Gertrude continues to feel the need to find a rational justification for this appalling procedure. She repeatedly returns to the words "'It will turn your blood'" (348), attempting to find a reasonable explanation. Yet Gertrude clearly knows that she has left the world of modern science, and that the "corpse cure" is inexplicable in rational terms. In face she sinks into greater irrationality, her obsession for cure now replaced by the obsessive need for a hanged body, irrespective of whether the hanged person is guilty or innocent. As Romney T. Keys remarks, Gertrude's "decision to make the trip [to Casterbridge Assizes in search of a body] marks the final stage in Gertrude's abandonment of her views 'as a woman of common sense'" (118). But the truth of the matter is that her descent goes much further than Keys suggests. This beautiful and sophisticated modern woman has become a ghoulish monster, a vampire of sorts whose only wish in life is to embrace the still-warm body of a hanged man.

The depth of Gertrude's macabre descent becomes clear when we discover that the hanged man is the son of Rhoda and Lodge. Gertrude's arm has been laid across the neck of the hanged man by the executioner when a shriek is heard in the enclosure. Gertrude looks round to find Rhoda and her husband before her. Lodge curses her for her presence and Rhoda cries out, "'This is the meaning of what Satan showed me in the vision! You are like her at last!'" Rhoda then pushes Gertrude "unresistingly" against the wall, where she collapses into an unconscious stupor (356). The shock of the discovery also turns Gertrude's blood "too far" and she dies in Casterbridge "three days after" (357). In fact it is the loss of her anchor of rationality, and the gradual emergence of her suppressed superstition, that has transformed Gertrude into the horrible specter of Rhoda's vision. With this image of reason transformed to monstrosity, Hardy leaves his modern readers to deal with their own fears of the return of the repressed monster of superstition.

NOTES

1. During the nineteenth century numerous theories of the relationship between mind and body emerged. The pioneering psychiatrist Henry Maudsley argued that "we do not, as Physicians, consider sufficiently the influence of the mental states on the production of disease, and their importance as symptoms" (38). But many went further than Maudsley and claimed that individuals could affect others simply by the power of mind. Mesmerism which, according to Alison Winter, "was practised widely and continuously from the 1830s through the 1860s and beyond" incorporated a range of techniques all of which were characterised by the claim that one person with the right training and skill could "affect another's mind or body" (2–5). Winter demonstrates that in Victorian Britain "almost any member of society — from the factory worker to [the] aristocrat or priest — might succumb to the powerful attractions of the mesmeric séance" (1). Some orthodox practitioners condemned mesmerism; in 1851 an anonymous writer in *Blackwood's Edinburgh Magazine* described it as "the magnetic superstition" (85). But it is also important to note that boundaries between the orthodox and the heterodox were not as great as some historians have argued, and, as Henri Ellenberger notes, from the 1870s onwards aspects of mesmerism, such as hypnotism and magnetism, were incorporated into the emerging discipline of dynamic psychiatry (110–81).

2. As Owen points out in *Popular Magic,* an important recent study, cunning-folk (also known as wise-men or women, wizards or conjurors in some regions) "have often been air-brushed out of representations of the past" (xiv). This is partly because historians of witchcraft have focused on the period before the Witchcraft Act of 1736, and medical historians have concentrated on developments in medical knowledge and the growth of the medical profession during the nineteenth century. But because "cunning-folk generally left no record of the cunning-profession" it is difficult for historians to place them (xiii-xiv). The lack of interest within academia does not alter the fact that they "were as much a part of eighteenth- and nineteenth-century society" as they were of the seventeenth-century world (xiii). They were generally individuals who stood out because they possessed more knowledge than their neighbors. This special knowledge would often be attributed to "a supernatural source, or ... innate, hereditary ability, or [simply] from being able to understand writing" (vii). Cunning-folk offered a range of services to their clients. They could locate hidden treasure, heal the sick, exorcise the bewitched, identify thieves and induce love (vii-viii). Particularly in rural areas, where there was limited redress for loss following theft and little access to expensive medical professionals, cunning-folk provided a much-valued service. Indeed people would often travel a considerable distance to visit a wise-man or a wise-woman with a potent reputation.

3. Kristin Brady suggests that the setting of the story illustrates the moment on the cusp between superstition and science. Holmstoke dairy is "an emblem of its transitional time exemplifying the beginnings of modern agricultural organization and management

in its status as a rented farm, but continuing to appear 'old-style' in its appurtenances and in the garb of its workers — as well as in their superstitious beliefs" (24).

4. Witchcraft was often associated with female sexual liberty.

5. Tony Fincham relates that in the story as told to Hardy "the visitation occurred on a hot summer afternoon as Rhoda relaxed on her bed 'before falling asleep'" (142). In fact Hardy explicitly describes Rhoda's vision as a "dream" and does not say that it occurred before she fell asleep in his account of the story as told to him (*Wessex Tales*: xiii). In the story itself the dream takes place at night and the narrator remarks: "Rhoda Brook dreamed — since her assertion that she really saw [the spectre], before falling asleep, was not to be believed" (335). The earlier *Blackwood's* version of the story has "if" instead of "since" so Hardy clearly wanted to insist more clearly that Rhoda's assertion is not to be believed. Fincham's argument that Rhoda experiences a "hypnagogic phenomenon [inducing or leading to sleep]" (142) is based on his particular reading of Hardy's preface to *Wessex Tales*.

6. The response to Gertrude is also driven by an instinctive "loathing" towards the material detritus of life that Julia Kristeva identifies in *Powers of Horror: An Essay on Abjection* (1980): "filth, waste, or dung ... defilement, sewage, and muck ... a wound with blood and pus [and the] sickly, acrid smell of sweat, of decay" (2–3).

7. Before "the advent of pharmaceutical analgesics, anaesthetics and antibiotics, general practitioners could provide little relief, let alone successful treatment for many of those who consulted them" (Davies *Popular Magic* 104).

8. Writing during the first decade of the nineteenth century, the Reverend Thomas Hawkins suggests that several of his parishioners had gone to cunning-folk only after orthodox practitioners had failed to cure what they initially thought were natural ailments. He writes that one particular individual "applied first to the faculty [probably a general practitioner], but obtained little or no relief" and as a consequence "his wife suspected that he might have had 'hurt done' him" by a malevolent neighbour (ix). In this instance a "wizard" or cunning-man was able to cure the ailment that had proved too much for science-based modern medicine. He helped identify "the culprit," whom his client was instructed to shun and as a result became "well and [was] thankful to God for his recovery" (Hawkins: x–xi).

9. Cunning-folk would often rely upon their client's pre-existing suspicions to aid their attempts to identify the enemy who had caused them harm. Their divinatory practices would thereby be transformed into a process of "confirmation rather than detection" as "the client saw what they wanted to see; in other words, the person they already suspected" (Davies 107).

10. This is partly because healing was only one of the numerous services that cunning-folk provided. But it is also because, unlike many other kinds of unorthodox medical practitioners, cunning-folk did not generally dispense medicine. They were not therefore "so visible to the medical profession" (Davies "Cunning-Folk in the Medical Market Place during the Nineteenth-Century" 57). They did not escape opprobrium altogether; for example *The Lancet* occasionally published articles about the prosecution of cunning-folk in order to highlight the risks that people took when they sought help from unlicensed healers (1849: 572 and 1864: 444). But in the main, cunning-folk were left alone to do their work for anyone who was prepared to pay for it.

11. According to Ruth Firor, the purpose of this "corpse-cure" is to turn the blood, to transfer the parting life of the hanged victim to the dead limb of the living person (111). Trendle and later the narrator suggest that the practice had fallen out of use: "'The last I [Trendle] saw was in [18]' 13 — near twenty years ago'" (347). Yet even up to the turn of the nineteenth century "hangmen made a business, for fees, of admitting several persons at a time to the scaffold at the time of executions" (Firor 111). Tony Fincham implies that Trendle's cure might actually have some value: "It is perfectly reasonable that laying a psy-

chologically wounded arm across the neck of a recently hung man should 'turn the blood and change the constitution.' Drastic diseases require drastic remedies. Hysterical symptoms characteristically disappear instantly once the correct psychological button is pressed" (144).

WORKS CITED

Brady, Kristin. *The Short Stories of Thomas Hardy.* London: Macmillan Press, 1982.

Castle, Terry. *The Female Thermometer: Eighteenth-Century Culture and the Invention of the Uncanny.* Oxford: Oxford University Press, 1995.

Davies, Owen. "Cunning-Folk in the Medical Market Place during the Nineteenth-Century." *Medical History* 43 (1999): 55–73.

_____. *Popular Magic: Cunning-Folk in English History.* London: Hambledon Continuum, 2003.

_____. *Witchcraft, Magic and Culture 1736–1951.* Manchester: Manchester University Press, 1999.

Dunbar, Flanders. *Mind and Body: Psychosomatic Medicine.* New York: Random House, 1947.

Fincham, Tony. *Hardy the Physician: Medical Aspects of the Wessex Tradition.* Basingstoke: Palgrave Macmillan, 2008.

Firor, Ruth A. *Folkways in Thomas Hardy.* New York: A. S. Barnes, 1962.

Hardy, Thomas. *The Life and Works of Thomas Hardy.* Ed. Michael Millgate. Athens: University of Georgia Press, 1985.

_____.Preface. *Wessex Tales.* Ed. F. B. Pinion. London: Macmillan, 1986.

_____.*The Return of the Native.* Ed. George Woodcock. London: Penguin, 1978.

_____. *Thomas Hardy's "Facts" Notebook.* Ed. William Greenslade. Aldershot: Ashgate, 2004.

_____. *The Withered Arm and Other Stories 1874–1878,* ed. Kristin Brady. London: Penguin Books, 1999.

Hawkins, Thomas. *The Iniquity of Witchcraft, Censured and Exposed: Being the Substance of Two Sermons, Delivered at Warley, Near Halifax, Yorkshire.* Halifax: Holden and Dowson, 1808.

Johnson, Suzanne R. "Metamorphosis, Desire, and the Fantastic in Thomas Hardy's 'The Withered Arm.'" *Modern Language Studies* 23.4 (1993), 131–41.

Keys, Romey T. "Hardy's Uncanny Narrative: A Reading of 'The Withered Arm.'" *Texas Studies in Language and Literature* 27.1 (1985): 106–23.

Kristeva, Julia. *Powers of Horror: An Essay on Abjection.* Trans. L. Roudiez. New York: Columbia University Press, 1982.

Latov, Norman. *Peripheral Neuropathy: When the Numbness, Weakness and Pain Won't Stop.* New York: Demos Medical Publishing, 2006.

Lubbock, John. *The Origin of Civilization and the Primitive Condition of Man. Mental and Social Condition of Savages.* 2nd ed., with additions. London: Longmans, Green, 1870.

Maudsley, Henry. *Body and Mind: An Inquiry into Their Connection and Mutual Influence.* London: Macmillan, 1873.

Stephen, Leslie. *The Life and Letters of Leslie Stephen.* Ed. Frederic William Maitland. London: Duckworth, 1906.

Thomas, Keith. *Religion and the Decline of Magic: Studies in Popular Beliefs in Sixteenth- and Seventeenth-Century England.* London: Penguin, 1973.

"What Is Mesmerism?" *Blackwood's Edinburgh Magazine* 70 (1851): 84–85.

Winter, Alison. *Mesmerized: Powers of Mind in Victorian Britain.* Chicago: University of Chicago Press, 1998.

Lucas Malet's Subversive Late-Gothic: Humanizing the Monster in *The History of Sir Richard Calmady*

Catherine Delyfer

The daughter of novelist Charles Kingsley, niece of Henry Kingsley, George Kingsley, and J. A. Froude, and cousin of African explorer Mary Kingsley, Mary St. Leger Kingsley Harrison (1852–1931) started her literary career in 1878–1879. Her first novel *Mrs. Lorimer: A Sketch in Black and White* was published in 1882 and was quickly followed by *Colonel Enderby's Wife* (1885), *A Counsel of Perfection* (1888), *Little Peter: A Christmas Morality for Children of Any Age* (1888), *The Wages of Sin* (1890), *The Carissima* (1896), and *The Gateless Barrier* (1900). *The History of Sir Richard Calmady: A Romance*, her most acclaimed novel, was published in 1901.[1] Widely admired by critics, these ambitious and often controversial novels elicited comparisons with those of George Eliot,[2] Charlotte Brontë, and Elizabeth Gaskell. Rapidly moving into the highest literary circles in London and abroad under the pseudonym "Lucas Malet,"[3] the woman whose father had forbidden her to read novels until she was twenty wrote, in the course of her life, seventeen novels and numerous short stories, novellas and essays, while her works inspired several leading novelists of the day, including Henry James and Thomas Hardy.[4] In her online entry on "Lucas Malet," Talia Schaffer asserts that Lucas Malet is an author whose "current neglect is remarkable considering her radical expansion of the capacities of the English novel and her world-wide fame at the peak of her career. Her ground-breaking works are central to understanding the development of the novel from the nineteenth to the twentieth century."

The History of Sir Richard Calmady: A Romance was Malet's eighth published novel. In *An Inward Necessity*, Patricia Lorimer Lundberg suggests that she started writing this novel in 1887 (114–117).[5] Yet it was only finished and published in 1901, when it became an immediate best seller. No doubt Malet knew that her book would stir up controversy and contemporary reactions were strong. Some critics gave this powerful book unqualified praise; others wished to burn it.[6] Her beautifully rich prose could not make people completely forget that she had chosen a disabled man as the hero of her novel and savior of his noble lineage — a feminized man, who is moreover surrounded by three dangerously powerful women: a passionate mother who has incestuous feelings for him; his cousin, a perversely manipulative adulteress who seduces him; and a wife who is a bisexual socialist. In short, the book fuelled contemporary fears about norms and abnormality, changing gender roles, sexuality, class conflicts and the so-called "decadence" or "degeneracy" of the age. Several reviewers even wondered if her father, Charles Kingsley, the champion of Muscular Christianity, was not turning in his grave (Lundberg 239) since, in conscious contradistinction to her father, Malet selected a type of manhood that was neither athletic nor physically "healthy," and made deformity the crux of her reflection on manliness. Not every reader could be as discerning as G. K. Chesterton, who praised the book as a compelling call for critical reflection on the discourse on disability. Drawing upon Ann Radcliffe's famous literary distinction between the awful and the sickening, terror and horror, in her 1826 essay "On the Supernatural in Poetry," Chesterton described Malet's achievement in a 1901 review as a "wholesome horror which shakes the nerves, not the unwholesome terror which betrays the keys of the spirit."[7]

The History of Sir Richard Calmady *as Gothic Text*

The History of Sir Richard Calmady: A Romance is a deliberately hybrid book resisting classification. In 1901 it was often considered a "monstrous" book to have been written by a woman, but it is also a "monstrous" book today, in the sense that it brings together styles not typically found together. It displays affinities with the Sensation novel of the 1860s, with the Aesthetic and Decadent novels, with the French Naturalist novel, with the New Woman novel, and with the horror novels of the late nineteenth century. Furthermore, it constantly and deliberately weaves a plethora of intertextual and intermedial references which function either parasitically to conceal the real (political) nature of the text or prosthetically, to convey a layer of meaning that would otherwise be lacking in the text, just like a prosthesis supplements a missing or defective part of the body. Malet's aestheticism as a strategy of concealment in *The History of Sir Richard Calmady* has already been the subject of critical attention.[8] In fact, the text of this novel is very much like the body of baby Richard Calmady wrapped in multiple layers of clothes before his mother undresses him to reveal the hidden horror. After unwrapping the baby and examining the perfection of the upper half of his infant body:

> she turned her eyes, with almost dreadful courage, upon the mutilated, malformed limbs, upon the feet — set right up where the knee should have been, thus dwarfing the child by a fourth of his height [48–49].

The monstrously hybrid body of Malet's text is equally concealed and protected under multiple networks of references, images and styles. The novel's full title clearly states its ambition of being both a history and a romance.[9] The archaic language and the references to historic people and events lend credence to the book's claim that it is based on archival research, reports, diaries and chronicles. On the other hand, like a romance, it blends historical facts with mysterious or miraculous events. Dense with a profusion of palimpsestic resurgences, it constantly quotes or refers to former stories, artwork, texts and allegories. It appeals to readers' fascination with the past, legends and prophecies, horrible transgressions, the irrational, and monstrosity.

In fact, the two sets of tropes — those which evoke history and those which evoke the romance — are typical of the Gothic novel, that hybrid which also questions the constructions of categories, generic and otherwise. Just before publishing *The History of Sir Richard Calmady*, the novelist had been exploring the ghost story tradition while she was writing *The Carissima: A Modern Grotesque* (1896) and *The Gateless Barrier* (1900). With *The History of Sir Richard Calmady*, she draws on the Gothic tradition again, using its potential to interrogate and subvert the categories of literature and culture.

Throughout the novel, the imagery is unmistakably Gothic. Richard grows up in an isolated manor, "Gothic in its main lines, but with much of Renaissance work in its details" (3), under the attentive gaze of his 225-year-old ancestor's statue:

> From the niche in the ... gable, arrayed in sugarloaf hat, full doublet and trunk hose, his head a trifle bent so that the tip of his pointed beard rests on the pleatings of his marble ruff, a carpenter's rule in his right hand, Sir Denzil Calmady gazes meditatively down [4].

The interior of Brockhurst manor is graced with recognizably Gothic and Queen Anne furniture, such as Richard's mother's bed, on which is embroidered a parable with direct bearing on the understanding of Richard's fate. The supernatural of the Gothic intrudes via the terrible nightmares that Richard experiences as a boy; these dreams actually reveal the truth of Richard's life. In the nightmare, as in the imagery of Thomas De Quincey's opium eater's Oriental dream, the feeling of incarceration prevails; innumerable hordes of fanatic Chinamen come after him and the elements of decoration leap out from the lacquered furniture to assault him. Later in the same nightmare, Richard becomes a "winged seagull, with wild, pale eyes, hiding, abject yet fierce," lying "among the vegetable beds in the Brockhurst kitchen-gardens, and picking up loathsome provender of snails and slugs,"[10] crawling away "ignominiously, covered with the shame of its incompleteness and its fallen estate" (70). Shouting aloud in angry terror Richard wakes up trembling, wet with perspiration, bewildered by the "wild phantasmagoria of his dream" (71), a phrase directly borrowed from De Quincey's *Confessions*.[11]

Malet pointedly evokes *The Castle of Otranto* (1764) by Horace Walpole, the progenitor of the English Gothic. As in *Otranto,* an ancestor's statue looms over all; the plot of Malet's novel, like Walpole's hinges on a story discovered in an ancient text, telling of the fulfillment of a cryptic ancient prophecy.[12] That a curse hangs over the destinies of the Calmadys is hinted from the opening of the book, and the actual prophecy is disclosed to the reader when the archivist of the Gothic manor of Brockhurst discovers in the library "four tiny volumes tied together with a rusty, black ribbon" (17). Even before reading the volumes, Julius March the archivist feels instinctive "disgust" (17), like all the characters who hear about the prophecy. Piecing together the information contained in all four volumes, Julius is able to come to a full understanding of the whole matter. He realizes that the legend of Brockhurst belongs to "a gross and vulgar order of history": it is a tale written in broken verse by an illiterate poet which recounts the story of a beautiful forester's daughter once seduced under the promise of marriage by the ancestor of Richard, Sir Thomas Calmady. Abandoned by Sir Thomas, the forester's daughter, who was "inconveniently defiant of custom and common sense" and refused to be "cast into the social wilderness," tried to arrest the carriage taking away her lover and his newly-wed wife, which resulted in her infant son, Calmady's son, being thrust under the carriage, his legs severed from his body above the knee (18–19). So she cursed the man who had brought ruin upon her, along with his descendents. The "terrifying stor[y]" (39) which serves as the core text, the matrix of Malet's rich and elegant narrative, is thus a coarse legend written in broken verse.[13] In *The History of Sir Richard Calmady*, this archetypal story of exploitation and abandonment of a women by a man is repeatedly alluded to in Book I of the novel as if to announce the inevitable confrontation that will ensue in the rest of the book between history/story, high culture/low culture, upper class/working class, past and present, the rational and the irrational, the natural and the supernatural. "History repeats itself" as the narrator tells us (90) and repetition, with slight variations, is the only mode of discourse that seems possible in the cyclical, mythic time created in this Gothic novel. Since the casting of the curse, all Calmadys have died young by violent deaths, including Richard's father whose riding accident, surgical amputation and subsequent agony are described in the most graphic details. It is only at the end of the story that Richard Calmady discovers what most other characters and the reader have suspected all along, that his life is enacting the prophecy and that his martyrdom has meaning: it means that the curse will die with him, that he is putting an end to the degenerate Calmady patriarchy (as the fulfillment of the prophetic curse puts an end to the evil dynasty in *Otranto*).

Richard as Gothic Monster and Gothic Hero

Lucas Malet's novel is, however, no conventional Gothic ghost story. Typically, the Gothic is characterized by a troubled encounter with otherness, usually represented in supernatural terms. But here Gothic fear and horror are relocated onto the maimed body of Richard, the male hero of the book. He is the Gothic monster of this tale, born shortly after the death of his father. Like his Shakespearian namesake, he is a cripple.[14] His invalid, possibly diabolic, un-whole/unholy body[15] is the locus of the abject, the non-human.[16]

Born with feet growing in place of the knees, the eponymous hero struggles to cope with his condition throughout his life. Like Mary Shelley's monstrous creature in *Frankenstein*, Richard is both "an abortion" (106) and "a Modern Prometheus" (330), consumed with self-hatred as soon as he becomes aware of his difference and the awe and repulsion it causes in others. This realization comes slowly though, as he is protected by his mother from contacts with the exterior world and assisted in his daily needs and movements by loving and devoted friends and servants who treat him deferentially as the master of the house. Significantly Richard's self-recognition comes mainly as the result of discourse. As an infant, at the pre-linguistic stage, Richard seems unaffected by his condition. Because of his initial seclusion, his self-awareness and his sense of identity are mostly constructed in and by literary and pictorial discourses. For example, Richard feels inexplicably touched by the character of Witherington, the crippled fighting-man from the "Ballad of Chevy Chase," who haunts his dreams; and he also identifies with the grotesque dwarf represented in a painting by Velasquez that hangs in the Brockhurst library. Richard's fear of the non-human and the horror of his own body which surfaces during his nightmares are eventually acknowledged and Richard is provided with a label when his cousin, the lovely Helen, mockingly calls Richard "un avorton, un monstre" (89)[17] to his face. The status of Richard as a Victorian aberration is made crystal clear when Malet describes

him riding by a freak show at the end of Book II. Despite the class difference, Richard immediately senses a kinship with the "freaks" in the freak
show. As an adult Richard comes to fully realize his situation as a horrifying
monster, especially after the failure of his marriage prospects with Lady Constance Quayle. The mutilated Richard travels across the earth like Frankenstein's creature in an attempt to find someone able to love him. His progress
as a "rake" deeply affects his mother and causes Honoria to loathe him. Sir
Richard Calmady thus *seems* bound to become a monster because of his abnormally monstrous body like Frankenstein's monster.

Yet, unlike Walter Scott's dwarf, Elshender the Recluse (*The Black Dwarf*
1816), or Wilkie Collins's crippled Misserrimus Dexter, of *The Lady and the
Law* (1875), Richard Calmady is not actually a misanthropic outcast. An avid
reader of Scott, Malet was no doubt familiar with *The Black Dwarf,* which
owes much to Scott's attitude to his own deformity as well as to the immediate inspiration for the novel, a dwarf by the name of David Ritchie of
Tweeddale (Garbin 78). Sunie Fletcher has argued, however, that a more likely,
more positive, real-life model for Malet's Richard is Arthur MacMurrough
Kavanagh (1831–1889), an educated member of the Irish gentry who traveled
the world, married, and achieved public recognition as a Member of Parlia-
ment despite a deformity even greater than Richard's (174). While Richard
experiences a moral lapse after he is made to renounce his promised bride Constance, it is only temporary. Generally, he impresses those who know him,
like Mrs. Chifney, who sees him as the "noblest looking young gentleman ...
[u]nearthly beautiful.... [H]is face ... like a very angel's from heaven" (145).

Realistic Science or Gothic Supernatural?

Just as Richard is divided by his monstrous appearance, and angelic interior, so is the novel torn between two explanations for his condition: the scientific or the supernatural. Is Richard's condition the result of a medical
anomaly or a magical curse? This tension is illustrated in a conversation
between the priest/librarian Julius March and the agnostic Dr. Knott, two
people who are said to stand "at opposing poles of thought — the one spiritual and ideal, the other material and realistic" (39). This confrontation leads
to the defeat of the "half sneering rationalism" of Dr. Knott, who loses his
composure when he realizes how precisely the facts match the terms of the
prophecy (39–40).[18] Dr. Knott's repeated attempts to find a scientific solution to compensate for Richard's missing limbs merely delay the supernatural resolution: it is only after the doctor's help has been unsuccessful that at
long last Julius March deigns to reveal to Richard the prophecy and the mythic

origins of his mutilation, thus performing a talking cure of sorts for Richard and bringing the narrative to a point of catharsis.

If the doctor's scientific attempts to explain Richard's body or to fix it by providing a prosthetic solution[19] come short of the mark, Dr. Knott's assessment is, however, crucial to confirm that Richard's deformity is in no way the sign of a thwarted mind or a devious personality. Unlike Robert Louis Stevenson's Mr. Hyde (1886), whose body is similarly described as "dwarfish" and "deformed," Richard's body is emphatically not "the mere radiance of a foul soul" (Stevenson 23). Indeed, Richard is an "angelic" monster, a Christological figure of goodness whose suffering for the sins of his forefathers averts future suffering,

Malet's Subversive Gothic: Resisting Conventions

Richard's inner purity leads one to wonder why the novel stirred so much controversy, especially considering that, despite the practical, physical, and emotional difficulties imposed on him by his disability, Richard is perfectly successful at the conventional career of a fine Victorian gentleman: ultimately, he goes to Oxford where he excels; he marries, raises a child and works to contribute productively to the betterment of society. Yet, in setting up an angelic monster as the hero of her novel, Malet powerfully subverts the social norm as well as the conventions of the Gothic novel. The novel's Gothic tendency intersects with her reflection on normality from the beginning of the novel: it is significant that Sir Denzil's statue holds a carpenter's rule. Indeed, Lennard J. Davis reminds us that the carpenter's rule, also called a "norm," provides the etymological meaning of words such as "normal" and "abnormal," which appeared in the modern sense only in the middle of the nineteenth century.[20] Davis's observation reveals the meaning of the narrator's speculations about the poor statue's hypothetical bewilderment:

> among the varying scenes ... upon which Sir Denzil had looked down during the two and a quarter centuries of his sojourn ... there was one his eyes had never yet rested upon — one matter, and that a very vital one, to which, had he applied his carpenter's rule, the measure of it must have proved persistently and grievously short [4].

The shortness here alluded to refers not only to the unnatural brevity of Sir Denzil's male descendents' lives but also, more literally, to the short lower limbs of Richard Calmady. Such facts, Malet suggests, cannot be accounted for by Sir Denzil's carpenter's rule, or norm; in other words, different tools are needed to appraise and understand data that do not square with the average, with socially constructed standards.

The History of Sir Richard Calmady is not the first text in which Malet had shown an interest in reflecting on corporeal otherness, nor was it to be the last. In her children's tale *Little Peter* (1888),[21] for example, Malet describes the friendship between a boy and a monstrous-looking man, who later saves the child. In her Naturalist novel *The Wages of Sin* (1890), the crippling past of James Colthurst combined with his foreign "Tartar" looks, his disproportionate body, his compulsive stammer, his interest in physical deformity and his revolutionary artistic views all make him appear monstrous and loathsome to most; in the end, the otherness he embodies is silenced definitively when "his body turn[s] ... traitor to his brain" (470), and he is unable to speak and justify himself. In *The Gateless Barrier* (1900), Mr. Rivers is a "disabled" old man (91). Much later in Malet's career, in her post-war novel *The Survivors* (1923), the trope of the dysfunctional body crops up again: crippled and mutilated veterans abound in Lady Aylwin's hospital. But the horror comes from an unexpected source: the wonderful Lady's devotion, which feeds off soldiers' broken bodies and pains. The true source of horror becomes even more clear when she orders additional maiming to be performed surgically on the body of the young warrior she has fallen in love with, in the hopes of securing his life-long dependence on her. Thus, awareness of the situation of the invalid traverses Malet's works for reasons both aesthetic[22] and biographical.[23]

Disability and Interdependency: The New Woman and the New Man

Ultimately, the contemporary opposition to *Richard Calmady*, stemmed from the recognition by Malet's audience that Richard, the Gothic monster provides a distracting cover ploy to allow for the discreet entrance of the real late-Victorian bugbear, the monstrous New Woman — as well as her equally threatening masculine correlate, the New Man. In the narrative itself the necessary recourse to such a stratagem is indirectly suggested when Dr. Knott decides that he, and not a servant, must be the one to tell Lady Calmady of her son's infirmity. The announcement of monstrous deviance from the norm must be:

> well told — the *whole thing kept at a high level* ... this announcement must come to Lady Calmady *from an educated person, from an equal*, from somebody who can see all round it [43, italics mine].

While the New Woman novel was dismissed as poor literature, Malet's Aesthetico–Gothic treatment of such bold themes as adultery, incest, same-sex love, the woman's question, manliness and disability kept her novel "at a high level," the level of an author who aspired to be the equal of the best English novelists of her time. Malet's novel thus remains beautifully elegant, deploying Gothic and Aesthetic styles to produce a form of political discourse otherwise unacceptable. From this perspective the character of Richard essentially acts as diversion from and foil to that of Honoria, the New Woman of the novel. Or rather, Richard and Honoria may be envisaged in their *interdependence*, as representing new models for both genders. As Martha Stoddard Holmes has remarked, Victorian disability narratives often remind us that "almost all lives are based on interdependence and mutuality" (187). In her novel, Malet shows the value of mutual dependency as well as the interaction of gender and disability.

Richard is associated with three compelling female characters, who were identified even by some contemporary critics as the real focus of the novel. They may also be the real monsters of the novel. As one outraged critic wrote:

> That book is false to everything we have been trained to hold most sacred. The deformity of Richard is monstrous — nothing but the most diseased and morbid imagination could conceive and develop such a plot. Katherine ... is shown from the first to be ... weak mystic, irrational and vindictive.... Sin brings no punishment — Helen to the last is radiant, charming, happy and triumphant ... Honoria St. Quentin, too, is false ... to all standards of womanly purity and delicacy.... [I]t is coarse, impure, and degrading [qtd. in Lundberg 241].

In fact, Richard and the three heroines of the novel need to be read *together*, as a nexus of signification, as the four poles of the same argument, just like the four bound volumes which together tell of the old prophecy. These books "all proved to be ragged and imperfect copies of the *same* work" (17, italics mine) and it was only by "supplying the deficiencies of torn or defaced pages by reference to another of the copies" (18) that Julius was able to understand the full story. The same is true of each of Malet's four characters, who paint an incomplete picture unless analyzed comparatively as incarnations of the same plight.

Richard's monstrously incomplete body is clearly the product of powerful female passion. Either his body is the result of the old curse cast on the Calmady family by the rejected female servant, or it is the consequence of his mother's fancies during pregnancy. Katherine Calmady, herself, suggests that it was the trauma caused by the sight of her husband's amputation that made her give birth to a child suffering from what Dr. Knott calls "spontaneous amputation" (42). Katherine's archaic supernatural interpretation aligns itself with the long tradition of folk belief in "monstrous progeny [resulting] from the disorder of the maternal imagination.... The monster thus erased paternity and proclaimed the dangerous power of the female imagination" (1), as

Marie-Hélène Huet argues in *Monstrous Imagination*. Conceived as he was under the auspices of female curses, fears, desires and imaginations, very much like the limping, parthenogenetic Greek god of fire Hephaestus, Richard can only build his identity and regain a degree of wholeness through the agency of female characters: his mother, Honoria and Helen, who reveals him as a sexual being in an extremely daring scene.[24] Richard's incomplete body, forged by female power, thus places him in a situation of dependence on the women around him.

The obstacles Richard has to overcome to release himself from his dependence on women and to become the masculine public Victorian success that he wants to be are linked to the fact that he is a new kind of man. Like Victorian women, he is trapped in a body deemed inferior by Victorian society. Much like the unconventional New Woman, he is deemed "monstrous" because he refuses to lead a domestic life in the privacy of his beautiful Gothic home, despite his supposed inferiority. Instead, he achieves public recognition and does what any normative man of his class would do: he learns to ride horses; he graduates from Oxford; he sows his wild oats, travels, sails, breaks women's hearts.

Richard's initial plight of dependence is similar to that of many Victorian middle-class and upper middle-class wives.[25] After all, women — especially married women — *were* all among "the disabled," to quote Victorian feminist Mona Caird.[26] Calling upon the metaphor of the caged bird, often used to convey Victorian women's constricted lives, Malet describes Richard feeling "like a caged wild beast — blinded, its claws cut, the bars of its cage soldered and riveted, no hope of escape, and yet the vigour, the immense longing for freedom, activity" (203). The narrator stresses Richard's dual nature describing his perception of events both "as a woman" *and* "as a man" (114). Richard's ambiguous gender identification and socialization are particularly striking when he explains to his mother his intense desire to marry and have a son. The terms he uses might have been those uttered by an aspiring Victorian wife hoping to realize her ambitions indirectly, through her offspring: "Mother, I — I want to marry.... I want to marry because — because I want a child — I want a son ... to give me an object and keep up my pluck, and keep me steady. I, giving him life, shall find my life in him, be paid for my wretched circumscribed existence by his goodly and complete one" (202–203).

Additionally, Richard's dependence on Katherine, Honoria and Helen thrusts into relief these women's own non-normative independence from men. Katherine is a widow; Honoria has no interest in conventional marriage; Helen is an adulteress who has abandoned her husband. Each of them clearly represents one of the three categories of useless women defined by the famous Victorian anti-feminist, Eliza Lynn Linton, in her article "Nearing the Rapids"

(1894): widows, spinsters and prostitutes (Linton 379). Yet in Malet's telling, Katherine, Honoria, and Helen are women whose displacement from society actually provides them with power and independence. Each also gains power from Richard's disability: Katherine manages Richard's estate and his horses; Honoria beats him at racing as a child and later guides him emotionally, intellectually, morally and professionally as an adult; Helen derives a perverse erotic pleasure and sense of power from the contrast of her own beauty and Richard's deformity. The three thus reject traditional feminine subservience and take on the non-normative role of women who are assertive and vigorous in action and in thought. In doing so, they threaten social boundaries as much as Richard does.

Honoria, the most advanced and challenging character in the novel, is the most daringly new of Malet's female characters. She demonstrates "loyalty to the oppressed" (194), socialist views and suffrage activism, dedication to the cause of women and wounded industrial workers, together with a lesbian sensibility. Helen describes this New Woman in the following manner:

> Honoria is quite a woman's woman. Men do not care very much about her as a rule ... and men are usually conscious that Honoria does not care so very much about them.... Her wealth left her free to espouse the cause of womanhood at large.... She says women must be encouraged to combine and to agitate [166].[27]

As opposed to New Woman novelists such as George Egerton or Sarah Grand, Lucas Malet allows her heroine to be rewarded for her political and sexual boldness. Malet's Honoria experiences political, emotional and erotic awakening and development without being denied personal fulfillment, a family, and a good marriage. As her husband, Richard complements her in being a man who is similarly non-normative, an unconventionally New Man for the future, a man unheard of and never yet seen who would be (as Richard describes himself): "not as other men are [but instead] abnormal, extraordinary" (170). In valuing these usual qualities in himself, Richard recognizes the "privileges of his disabilities" (170), the difference that frees him (and Honoria) from the obligations of society and gender roles, allowing exploration and self-fulfillment.

The New Monster: Re-Creation of a Category

Malet thus contrives a highly subversive happy ending, as the non-normative (monstrous) man and the non-normative (monstrous) woman each finds a partner in the other. Even though Richard can never recover from his dismemberment, he finds peace in wedlock and parenthood, with Honoria;

he discovers the possibility of entering and integrating the realm of normative Victorian manhood. Yet this happy ending has nothing normative about it. On the level of literary convention, it disrupts the Gothic tendency toward a closure in which the deviant monster is inevitably dead or doomed. The means to the marriage with which the book ends is equally unorthodox. Possibly inspired by the subversive notion of the active female lover, especially as espoused by Bram Stoker's Mina in *Dracula*,[28] Malet has Honoria propose to Richard at the end of the book:

> "Richard," she cried fiercely, "if you don't care for me, if you don't want me, be honorable, tell me so straight out and let us have done with it! I am strong enough, I am man enough for that ... but, if you do care, here I am. I have never failed anyone yet. I will never fail you. I am yours body and soul. Marry me," she said [414].

It takes a monster to recognize a monster, or to recognize that the monster is human. Here clearly the transgressive nature of Honoria is comparable to Richard's. Each of them is both man *and* woman, both non-normative monster, and fully sentient and sexual human being: as Honoria puts her hand on the "peak" of Richard's saddle she offers herself "body and soul." Yet this blending of "monsters," far from leading to the degeneracy of the race so violently feared by the eugenically-conscious Victorian, *enables* the perpetuation of a healthier race. In fact Richard stops the cycle just by being his own self: "half-angel, half-demon" as the prophecy foretold. He achieves this ultimately human state of tension — between perfection and imperfection — by virtue of a set or competing dualities: his beautiful upper body and maimed lower body; his external monstrosity and internal humanity; his typically human shifting of behavior between the poles of angelic nobility and bitter cruelty. Similarly the imperfect and unorthodox (and thereby human) union between Honoria and Richard restores balance and brings an end to the curse. Lucas Malet's narrative thus unequivocally validates the new political ideas and values for which Honoria stands. Inspired by honor rather than by convention and fear, Honoria is bold enough to subvert the binary of non-normative monster and normative human that provides Victorian society with its Gothic underpinnings. This is Malet's final statement; as Patricia Lundberg notes (234), the name, Honoria is the very last word of the novel. Thus Malet's depiction of the New *Monsters* anticipates Jacques Derrida's definition of the term:

> A monster is a species for which we do not yet have a name.... Simply it shows itself — that is the etymological meaning of "monster" (from the Latin "monstrare"/to show). It shows itself as a thing that has never been shown before and which therefore looks like a hallucination whose sight

strikes us and scares us precisely because nothing could have helped us anticipate and identify this figure [400, translation mine].

Malet's thinking illustrates the influence of Charles Darwin, whose works she read extensively. Darwin saw the development of the non-normative — "the monstrous" deviation that was never before seen in a species — as a necessary step in evolution, the movement toward a more advanced stage. Malet suggests that perhaps her own monsters might effect a *speciation*, that the models in her text might contribute to the construction of a new species in which the notions of ability and disability might be redefined. In fact, Malet reminds us that difference is an integral part of being alive and human: Helen is a "psychological aberration"; Honoria in an unfeminine woman; Katherine has incestuous feelings for her son; Constance Quayle is notably unintelligent; Dr. Knott looks like a gargoyle; Shotover is "monstrously extravagant" (150); Lord Fallowfield has difficulties with communication. In Malet's valorization of the grotesque, all bodies are in some sense "disabled."

Like the ancient Antinous,[29] whose striking bronze statue adorns the Brockhurst library, Richard thus sets new standards of beauty and able-bodiedness, causing the reader to question the boundaries between the normal and the abnormal and to reassess the value that we attach to the ideal body. In *The History of Sir Richard Calmady*, Malet asks the reader to recognize the fecundity and the revolutionary potential of the extraordinary body of the "monster" as the vessel of the radically new, the vehicle of the future. Breaking the conventions of the Gothic, Malet proposes that we value "monstrous" difference, rather than fearing it.

The Privilege of Difference

In Malet's novel, Richard's body clearly concentrates repressed Victorian anxiety in response to what Lennard J. Davis calls the "enforcement" of normalcy, the shaping of human identity through the pervasive use of statistical norms in the late-nineteenth century. Sir Calmady's physical difference embodies Victorian anxiety about the dangers posed to the contours of British manhood and womanhood by changing gender roles. In this respect Malet's novel is a powerful contribution to fin-de-siècle constructions and destructions of limiting sexual binaries. *Richard Calmady* draws on Gothic stories of violent and frightening transgression to challenge the patriarchal norms and structures of society.

At the same time, more importantly perhaps, Richard's nonnormative body is exemplary of repressed difference *in all its forms*. As David T. Mitchell and Sharon L. Snyder explain in *Narrative Prosthesis: Disability and the Depen-*

dencies of Discourse, the disabled body is emblematic of the social category of "deviance" in general. Read from this perspective, the disabled body in *The History of Sir Richard Calmady* serves as a symbolic vehicle for the author's critique of oppressive social rhetoric which brands difference as inferior. Malet's novel thus challenges the reader to acknowledge the fecundity of the monster and the creative potential of difference in society and in literature.

NOTES

1. In her introduction to the 2003 edition of *The History of Sir Richard Calmady*, Talia Schaffer quotes Stephen Gwynn's 1901 assertion that "Sir Richard Calmady is the best novel since *Middlemarch* written by a woman.... It seems to me quite clear that no woman now living, and none recently dead, has written in English anything of equal importance." W. L. Courtney too was impressed by Malet's novel and wrote that "we have to go back a good many years, back to the best work of George Eliot, or even of Thackeray, to find its equal" (Schaffer ix).

2. The connection with George Eliot was especially deliberate on Malet's part throughout her career, as Patricia Lorimer Lundberg's biography shows.

3. In her biography, Lundberg explains that Malet chose her pseudonym by combining the last names of her grandmother and great-aunt, in order to win recognition on her own merit, and possibly to replace her famous father and uncles with a female lineage (82–83).

4. As Talia Schaffer shows in "Malet the Obscure," *The Wages of Sin* greatly influenced Thomas Hardy's *Jude the Obscure*. In "Some Chapter of Some Other Story," Schaffer asserts that Henry James appropriated Lucas Malet's 1900 novel *The Gateless Barrier* for his *The Sense of the Past*. Furthermore, in "Dialogic Fiction of the Supernatural," Lundberg argues that Malet's ghost story *The Carissima* (1896) anticipates Henry James's *The Turn of the Screw* (1898), *The Ambassadors* (1903) and *The Beast in the Jungle* (1903).

5. The writing and publishing of the novel may have been delayed by Malet's fear of scandalizing her husband, the Reverend William Harrison.

6. For contemporary reactions to *The History of Sir Richard Calmady*, see Lundberg (236–254).

7. Quoted by Lundberg (240) from the *Pall Mall Magazine*.

8. See Talia Schaffer, "Connoisseurship and Concealment in *Sir Richard Calmady*: Lucas Malet's Strategic Aestheticism" (44–62).

9. In her biography Lundberg quotes Malet defining romance as "life at its greatest fullness — at its highest emotional intensity" (268).

10. The parallel with De Quincey's *Confessions of an English Opium Eater* is striking: "I was ... laid, confounded with all unutterable slimy things, amongst reed and Nilotic mud" (73).

11. The opium eater also talks of the "wild phantasmagoria of his dreams" (De Quincey 5).

12. In her biography Lundberg claims that the novel's curse was inspired from an actual curse cast on the Craven family in Berkshire Downs (230).

13. As in Vernon Lee's contemporaneous Gothic short story "Prince Alberic and The Snake Lady" (1896), the embedded legend is a poem written in very poor style about the unfaithfulness of men. Vernon Lee's short story similarly involves socially unacceptable love between a man and a good woman whose upper body is fair while her lower body is monstrous, like Richard's.

14. His nickname, Dick, also suggests parallels with *Moby Dick*.

15. "The unwhole body is the unholy body" writes Lennard J. Davis in "Nude Venuses, Medusa's Body and Phantom Limbs: Disability and Visuality" (57).

16. *The History of Sir Richard Calmady* is quite representative of fin-de-siècle Gothic as Kelly Hurley defines it. In *The Gothic Body*, she explains that the British Gothic fiction of the end of the nineteenth century and the beginning of the twentieth century focuses primarily on what she calls the "ruination of the human subject ... the destruction of 'the human.'" Instead of being considered "stable and integral" the human body, in its late Victorian Gothic representation, becomes repulsive, "metamorphic and undifferentiated ... continually in danger of becoming not-itself, becoming other ... abhuman." (Hurley 3–4). Critics have persuasively argued that the Gothic mode is instrumental in negotiating the cultural anxieties that accompany socio-epistemological changes and crises in a society. In fact, *The History of Sir Richard Calmady* should be read in the context of this Gothic re-making of the human subject, within the context of a general anxiety about norms, the nature of human identity, gender categories and the social meanings assigned to bodies male, female, crippled or otherwise marked.

17. French for: "a dwarf and a monster." The French "avorton" is etymologically close to "abortion"; it suggests the arrested development of the fetus and conjures up Aubrey Beardsley's disturbing images of old fetuses and dwarfs at the end of the 1890s.

18. Dr. Knott recalls Dr. Simson, from Margaret Oliphant's 1881 fantastic short story "The Open Door," whose skepticism is opposed to the minister Moncrieff's insight into things spiritual and irrational. While Simson refuses to see that his scientific knowledge is incapacitated and that he is "disabled" by the supernatural, Moncrieff immediately identifies the wandering soul whose wailing has been terrifying villagers for years and succeeds in placating it and liberating it from purgatory

19. For a detailed analysis of the failure of Richard's prosthesis, see Sunie Fletcher's dissertation.

20. Lennard J. Davis has astutely demonstrated that the "invention" of the disabled body dates from the late eighteenth and nineteenth centuries, resulting in a new use of words such as "normal," "normalcy," "normality," "norm," "average," "abnormal" around the middle of the nineteenth century: "

> The word "normal" as "constituting, conforming to, not deviating or different from, the common type or standard, regular, usual" only enters the English language around 1840. (Previously, the word had meant 'perpendicular'; the carpenter's square, called a "norm," provided the root meaning.) Likewise the word "norm," in the modern sense, has only been in use since around 1855, and "normality" and "normalcy" appeared in 1849 and 1857, respectively. Thus it is possible to date the coming into consciousness in English of an idea of "the norm" over the period 1840–1860 ["Constructing Normalcy" 24].

21. According to Lundberg, Malet wrote *Little Peter* while also at work on *The History of Sir Richard Calmady*.

22. For an analysis of disability as a deep interest of literary narratives, see David T. Mitchell and Sharon L. Snyder's *Narrative Prosthesis: Disability and the Dependencies of Discourse*.

23. In her biography of Malet, Lundberg describes Malet's "own gendered crippling within her familial and social spheres" (1), and her being afflicted with depression, which sometimes made her lose the power of speech (138). She was also a thwarted painter, who gave up her artistic ambitions for marriage (Lundberg 65, 142).

24. Schaffer interprets this episode as a depiction of Helen giving oral sex to Richard, when they are suddenly interrupted by his mother.

25. Like Daniel's mother in George Eliot's *Daniel Deronda*, Richard's fight is against society's misconstruction of his stunted body as inherently too "small" to house such aspirations. In the words of Eliot's character:

Every woman is supposed to have the same set of motives, or else to be a *monster*. I am not a monster, but I have not felt exactly what other women feel — or say they feel, for fear of being thought unlike others.... You are not a woman. You may try — but you can never imagine what it is to have a man's force of genius in you, and yet to suffer the slavery of being a girl. To have a pattern cut out — this is what you must be; this is what you are wanted for; a woman's heart must be of such a size and no larger, else it must be pressed small, like Chinese feet; her happiness is to be made as cakes are, by a fixed receipt [573–576].

26. In "The Morality of Marriage"(1890), Caird wrote:

Between husband and wife it is absolutely degrading, not only to the disabled, but to him who disables. It is the fatal sense of power and possession in marriage which ruins so many unions" [640].

27. Honoria is certainly bolder and wiser than Mary Crookenden, Malet's heroine from *The Wages of Sin*. In the latter novel, Mary compares her own choice with Honoria's extraordinary marriage but is ultimately unable to love and marry her own monstrous Colthurst.

28. I am referring to the seemingly out-of-the-blue mention of the New Woman in one of Mina Murray's journal entries: "Some of the 'New Woman' writers will some day start an idea that men and women should be allowed to see each other asleep before proposing or accepting. But I suppose the New Woman won't condescend in future to accept; she will do the proposing herself. And a nice job she will make of it, too!" (Stoker 111).

29. Antinous, the Roman Emperor Hadrian's favorite, is reported to have had a heavier torso than that defined by the conventional ideal of male beauty. In *The Nude: A Study in Ideal Form*, Kenneth Clark explains that after Antinous's death, Hadrian was so distraught that he ordered that his lover's body serve as model for statues of the gods, thus subverting the traditional notions of proportion, introducing a type of beauty taken from a distinctive human form rather than from theoretical and ideal standards.

WORKS CITED

Caird, Mona. "The Morality of Marriage." *Prose by Victorian Women*. Eds. Andrea Broomfield and Sally Mitchell. New York: Garland Publishing, 1996.

Clark, Kenneth. *The Nude: A Study in Ideal Form*. London: Penguin, 1956.

Davis, Lennard J. "Constructing Normalcy: The Bell Curve, the Novel, and the Invention of the Disabled Body in the Nineteenth Century." *Enforcing Normalcy: Disability, Deafness and the Body*. London, New York: Verso, 1995.

_____."Nude Venuses, Medusa's Body and Phantom Limbs: Disability and Visuality." *The Body and Physical Difference: Discourses of Disability*. Eds. D. T. Mitchell and S. L. Snyder. Ann Arbor: University of Michigan Press, 1997.

De Quincey, Thomas. *Confessions of an English Opium Eater and Other Writings*. Oxford: Oxford University Press, 1985.

Derrida, Jacques. *Points de Suspension*. Paris: Galilée, 1992.

Egerton, George. "The Cross Line." *Daughters of Decadence: Women Writers of the Fin de Siècle*. Ed. Elaine Showalter. New Brunswick, New Jersey: Rutgers University Press, 1993.

Eliot, George. *Daniel Deronda*. New York: New American Library, 1979.

Fletcher, Sunie. "Beauty, Flowers and Flesh: Fin-de-Siècle Female Aestheticism in the Novels of Elizabeth von Arnim, Netta Syrett, Victoria Cross, Jane Findlater and Lucas Malet." Diss. University of Exeter, 2006.

Garbin, Lidia. "Literary Giants and Black Dwarfs." *Scottish Studies Review* 1 (2000): 78–93.

Grand, Sarah. *The Heavenly Twins.* New York: Cassell, 1893.

Heiland, Donna. *Gothic and Gender.* Oxford: Blackwell, 2004.

Holmes, Martha Stoddard. *Fictions of Affliction: Physical Disability in Victorian Culture.* Ann Arbor: University of Michigan Press, 2004.

Huet, Marie-Hélène. *Monstrous Imagination.* Cambridge: Harvard University Press, 1993.

Hurley, Kelly. *The Gothic Body: Sexuality, Materialism, and Degeneration at the Fin de Siècle.* Cambridge: Cambridge University Press, 1996.

Lee, Vernon. "Prince Alberic and the Snake Lady." 20 March 2008. <http://gaslight.mt royal.ca/princalb.htm>

Linton, Elizabeth Lynn. "Nearing the Rapids." *Prose by Victorian Women.* Eds. Andrea Broomfield and Sally Mitchell. New York: Garland Publishing, 1996.

Lundberg, Patricia Lorimer. "Dialogic fiction of the supernatural: 'Lucas Malet.'" *English Literature in Transition (1880–1920)* 41.4 (1998): 388–407.

_____. *An Inward Necessity: The Writer's Life of Lucas Malet.* New York: Peter Lang, 2003.

Malet, Lucas. *The Gateless Barrier.* New York: Dodd, Mead, 1900.

_____. *The History of Sir Richard Calmady.* Ed. Talia Schaffer. Birmingham: Birmingham University Press, 2003.

_____. *Little Peter: A Christmas Morality for Children of Any Age.* London: Hodder and Stoughton, 1909.

_____. *The Survivors.* London: Cassell and Company, 1923.

_____. *The Wages of Sin.* London: Thomas Nelson and Sons, 1907.

Mitchell, David T., and Sharon L. Snyder. *Narrative Prosthesis: Disability and the Dependencies of Discourse.* Ann Arbor: University of Michigan Press, 2000.

Oliphant, Margaret. "The Open Door." 29 January 2008. http://www.gutenberg.org/ files/10052/10052-8.txt

Schaffer, Talia. "Connoisseurship and Concealment in *Sir Richard Calmady*: Lucas Malet's Strategic Aestheticism." *Women and British Aestheticism.* Eds. Talia Schaffer and Kathy Alexis Psomiades. Charlottesville: University of Virginia Press, 1999.

_____. "Lucas Malet." *The Literary Encyclopedia.* 2 December 2007. <http://www.litEncyc. com>.

_____. "Malet the Obscure: Thomas Hardy, 'Lucas Malet,' and the Literary Politics of Early Modernism." *Women's Writing* 3 (1996): 261–86.

_____. "Some Chapter of Some Other Story." *Henry James Review* 17 (1996): 109–128.

Stevenson, Robert Louis. The *Strange Case of Dr. Jeckyll and Mr. Hyde.* London: Penguin, 1994.

Stoker, Bram. *Dracula.* London: Penguin, 1994.

Walpole, Horace. *The Castle of Otranto.* Mineola, New York: Dover Publications, 1966.

Encounters with the Monster: Self-Haunting in Virginia Woolf's "Street Haunting"

Tara Surry

Virginia Woolf's essay "Street Haunting: A London Adventure" (1927) presents itself as a celebration and an "adventure," but it is tinged throughout with disquiet. Woolf anxiously observes the juxtaposition between the rich consumers who are located within the system and the poor outcasts who inhabit the margins, the social "crevices and crannies" (484).[1] In part, "Street Haunting" is a Gothic ghost story set in the modern city. Woolf's narrator encounters both monsters and ghosts. And although the essay is set in modern London, it actually inhabits the undefined border territory of the Gothic, both in terms of temporality and spatiality; Woolf sets her essay "between tea and dinner" (480), in the space "between Holborn and the Strand" (484).

Woolf's use of Gothic elements may seem surprising given her alignment with Modernism. However, "Street Haunting" is a knowingly uncanny modern(ist) Gothic text that draws attention to its own hauntedness. The essay presents a modernist haunting without the traditional Gothic trappings, revising the conventional Gothic tropes and narrative strategies. Ultimately, Woolf's modernism gives the old conventions an afterlife, as the Gothic return in new and strange ways.[2]

"We are no longer quite ourselves": London as Gothic Space

In setting sets her essay outside in the city streets, Woolf radically alters the conventionally enclosed Gothic space of the haunted house. Yet modern

London is an appropriate site for the narrator's encounters with the unknown. Woolf suggests that urban space provokes a sense of ghostliness, both the subject and the people she encounters are spectralized because all are alienated by the anonymity of the streets. Thus the narrator herself "haunts" the city, while apprehensively co-existing with other ghostly presences.

The very modernity of the city might account for its susceptibility to haunting. In her introduction to *The Second Ghost Book*, Elizabeth Bowen comments on the power of ghosts to adapt themselves to the modern world: "they ... shift their hold on our nerves and, dispossessed of one habitat, set up house in another ... telephones, motors, planes and radio wave-lengths offer them self-expression" (101). Similarly, Jacques Derrida observes that "the experience of ghosts is not tied to a bygone historical period ... but on the contrary is accentuated, accelerated by modern technologies" (61). In diminishing the significance of the materially present human body, allowing people to be present, even when the body is elsewhere, modern technology creates a new species of everyday ghosts.

Within the setting of a gothicized London, there is another liminal space: the shop that is both private space and public place, both inside and outside because of the large windows that subvert the division. This setting taps into Walter Benjamin's use of the term "phantasmagoria" in a more modern sense, in relation to the seductive culture of the commercialized commodity (165). The narrator is attracted to the shops, averting her gaze from the homeless people and looking into the shop windows. She admires the beauty of the objects on display and incorporates them into a fantasy home, building up and demolishing an "imaginary house" (485). The narrator knowingly contrasts the "derelicts" with the world of consumption that surrounds them: "They lie close to those shop windows where commerce offers to a world of old women laid on door steps, of blind men, of hobbling dwarfs, sofas which are supported by the gilt necks of proud swans; tables inlaid with baskets of many-coloured fruit; sideboards paved with green marble the better to support the weight of boars' heads." (485). The juxtaposition of the grotesque and valueless street people with the equally grotesque and valuable items of luxury is Woolf's critique of a world with devalues and excludes the human while valuing and welcoming the luxury commodity.

The narrator's need for a less luxurious and more inherently valuable commodity necessary to the writer, a pencil, is her "pretext" (480), her excuse to voyage out from the private space of her room and to cross over into the public space of the city streets. She rejoices in "the irresponsibility which darkness and lamplight bestow. We are no longer quite ourselves ... we shed the self our friends know us by" (480). This Jekyll-like impulse is a deliberate relinquishment of the social self and an escape from the boundaries of the room and the body: "[t]he shell-like covering which our souls have excreted to house themselves, to make for themselves a shape distinct from others, is broken" (481). To shed, in imagination, this specific body is to reject the social conventions and expectations which are mapped on to it, a liberating, emancipating move.

The narrator also moves from the conventional situation of the female as passive object in the male Gothic text. She emphasizes her role as imaginatively disembodied, observing self: "a central oyster of perceptiveness, an enormous eye" (481). She also emphasizes her role as the writing self, one who writes, rather than one who is written by others; hence her need for a pencil so that she can insert her own "instincts and desires" (486) into the narrative, while sketching out new possibilities. Yet she fluctuates between the two roles: she is simultaneously object —"part of that vast republican army of anonymous trampers" (481) and subject — disengaged from "the army of human beings" (482) that she observes. She also moves uneasily between interior and exterior spaces: inside she "find[s] anchorage in these thwarting currents of being" (486), but she also wants to go outside, to branch out into other paths. In addition to shifting subject positions, she plays with different narratives of identity. The city offers a variety of costumes, allowing the narrator to temporarily explore various identities: "Let us choose those pearls, for example, and then imagine how, if we put them on, life would be changed.... Wearing pearls, wearing silk, one steps out on to a balcony which overlooks the gardens of sleeping Mayfair" (485). This passage also indicates another aspect of the narrator's modern agency: she is the consuming subject, the female shopper rather than the female object to be consumed.

Woolf also aligns her narrator with the conventional male model of recording subject, the *flâneur*, the idle male wanderer in the city. By acknowledging that the search for a pencil is merely "an excuse for walking half across London" (480), the narrator positions herself as taking up the detached, observing position of the traditional rambler of the city streets. Yet abandoning the protective carapace of her "shell-like covering" (481) leaves her vulnerable, emphasizing that the position of the woman in public space is not the same as that of the male *flâneur*. Although the narrator moves through the streets, "passing, glimpsing" (485), her position is very different from that of the traditional *flâneur*. She is not, as Walter Benjamin describes Baudelaire, at home on the streets (37). In Gothic terms this woman is as anxious on the streets as the conventional Gothic heroine is at home. To adopt Freud's terms: just as the conventional heroine's home is uncannily *unheimlich*, so is the narrator's street; both spaces are, in fact, haunted and teeming with monsters.

"A maimed company of the halt and the blind": Monsters and Ghosts on the Streets

The narrator's journey thus becomes a kind of gothicized *flânerie* as she encounters profoundly disturbing figures. As *flâneur* the narrator revels in the "variegated" (486) nature of internal subjectivity, praising carnivalesque disorder when she ventures into a second-hand bookshop (487). But when faced with homeless and "wild" (484) individuals, she recoils in horror. In her walk, the narrator encounters the disquieting figures of a "dwarf" woman, two blind men, a "feeble-minded" boy and a whole "hobbling grotesque dance" of "the humped, the twisted, the deformed" (484). These outcast on the streets, lack a place in society: "a bearded Jew, wild, hunger-bitten ... the humped body of an old woman flung abandoned on the step of a public building with a cloak flung over her like the hasty covering thrown over a dead horse or a donkey" (484).[3] In representing these outcast grotesques as monsters, sources of fear and mystery, Woolf adopts the Gothic strategy of displacing Gothic fear of the unknown onto fear of the human Other. The gaze of the narrator renders the Other visible and thereby monstrous by virtue of the spectacular non-normative status. Yet as the title of the essay suggests, until the figures fall under the gaze of the narrator, they are invisible ghosts haunting the teeming city.

The dwarf that the narrator encounters in a shoe shop illustrates the way that the representation of human difference can shift from monster, to ghost, to human. When the narrator sees the dwarf, she abruptly asks "'What, then, is it like to be a dwarf?'" (483). The focus of the scene switches to the (imagined, human) perspective of the "deformed" woman, who is accompanied by two relative "giantesses."

Woolf gives a lengthy description of the woman's pleasure in selecting shoes for her "shapely, perfectly proportioned" feet (483). The dwarf is thus humanized, distanced from the grotesque figures outside the shop, by demonstrating her ability to consume, to belong to the inside space of the shop. Yet her identity is paradoxically normative and non-normative: she is an unattractive dwarf with beautiful feet. The perfection of her feet additionally suggests an attractive sexuality, as the feet are the body parts most likely to be fetishized due to their relative physical distance from the displaced genitalia. Yet this is only the dwarf's interior (psychologically and spatially) identity, invisible to the spectator. Within the shop, the dwarf can engage in a fantasy of cultural reversal in which she is Cinderella rather than one of the two "giantess" step-sisters who cannot fit into her shoes. She thus attempts to gain a foothold, so to speak, within a society organized around the gaze, which assigns value based on cultural norms of the body.

However, as the dwarf exits the store, she reluctantly discards the inner identity of a confident, "aristocratic," "well-grown woman" (483) and reverts to her exterior public identity in the city street, displaying her commonality with the "monsters" in the street. Crossing back into public space she becomes the object of the gaze, of pity or derision as the outside world re-fixes and reduces her identity: "the ecstasy faded, knowledge returned ... by the time she reached the street again she had become a dwarf" (483). The dwarf returns to a world in which her non-normative stature translates to monstrosity[4]; her humanity is invisible.

A Hobbling Grotesque Dance: The Monster within the Unstable Self

The narrator's representation of the dwarf reveals that although Woolf evokes the conventional representation of physical deformity as monstrosity, she ultimately stages a resistance to this trope. In his discussion of the dwarf Quilp in Dickens' *The Old Curiosity Shop*, David Punter suggests that disability is threatening to the normative gazing subject because it "replace[s] the quasi-permanence of the perfected body and of the transparent mind ... with a measure of opacity, an unassimilable difference" ("A Foot is What Fits the Shoe" 43). The observer of the disabled body assumes that the non-normative body reflects a mind that is inhuman and impossible to fathom. Yet Woolf's depiction of the dwarf vigorously disputes this assumption. The narrator radically dismantles the fiction of the dwarf's seeming opaque otherness by imaginatively entering into the dwarf's subjective self to reveal a woman who dreams of beauty, and perhaps, of love. Just as the dwarf's shoes hide the beauty of her feet, so does her misshapen body veil the beauty of her psyche.[5]

The narrator's recognition of the dwarf's humanity and subjective reality allows her to make the unsettling discovery that this "monster" is, in fact, her mirrored double. The narrator recognizes that, as Woolf articulates in "Gothic Romance," "[i]t is at the ghosts within us that we shudder" (306); the external monstrous spectralized figure is disturbing because it is mirrors that which lies hidden within the self. Just as the monstrosity of the dwarf hides the human within, so does the narrator's normative appearance of the narrator veil her inner monstrosity, the unique individual qualities that define all humans as idiosyncratic deviations from an ideal norm.[6] As Woolf argues in "Across the Border," the anomie of modern times is conducive to this sense of self-haunting: "our sense of our own ghostliness is much quickened" (218–9). Woolf accounts for this modern tendency in "Henry James's Ghost

Stories": the ghosts are "present whenever the significant overflows our powers of expressing it; whenever the ordinary appears ringed by the strange" (324). This is certainly an accurate way to describe the history and culture of the early twentieth century. The disturbing figures encountered in "Street Haunting" thus trouble the attempt to maintain a stable, rational normal self. They are "called into being" (484) by efforts to repress the narrator's unspoken fears or desires; indeed, they represent the return of the repressed. Woolf thus enacts a complex haunting, an inescapable spectralization of the self. The present self is no longer "calm, aloof"; it has become aware of the "element of uncertainty" (489), the sense that the Others without mirror the Other within. Woolf's essay thus promotes a sense of being other to one's own self. The disabled and different bodies are an outward manifestation of this, but they are also independently human, resisting subjects.

On returning from the shop to the outside world, the narrator finds that the introduction of the dwarf "had changed the mood"; suddenly the streets are full of "the humped, the twisted, the deformed," the blind, the "feeble-minded" (484). Woolf's own fears play a significant role in her representation of monstrous otherness. In an early diary entry she recorded: "we met & had to pass a long line of imbeciles.... Every one in that long line was a miserable ineffective shuffling idiotic creature, with no forehead, or no chin, & an imbecile grin, or a wild suspicious stare. It was perfectly horrible. They should certainly be killed" (*Diary* 1.13). Underlying this chilling remark, written shortly before she had a major breakdown, is the fact that Woolf herself felt vulnerable to being judged an "outcast" (*Diary* 2.270). She considered herself one of those "outside the envelope, foreign bodies" (*Diary* 2.12–13) and she confronted this in her writing. In "Street Haunting" such anxieties are projected onto the disabled, the homeless, or the otherwise outcast, so that the narrator can maintain her own secure position.

The street is also strangely populated by mirrored doubles. The two "giantesses" who flanked the dwarf are oddly mirrored by the two bearded blind men "resting a hand on the head of a small boy between them" (484). There is a continual effect of distortion and doubling. The "giantesses" perversely mirror the blind men; the frontispieces of two writers in a bookshop window give back a dim reflection of each other (487, 490); a mirror is glimpsed in one of the shop windows (485); a man who is quarrelling with his wife in the stationers' shop tells the story of discord between another man and his wife (490), which is itself presaged by the story of another quarrel between an innkeeper and his wife (481). The narrator even encounters her own double: a previous self standing by the river, a "person, who six months ago stood precisely where we stand now ... soon it becomes apparent that this person is ourselves" (489).[7]

These uncanny doublings are part of an ongoing and escalating breakdown of boundaries in the text: between inside and outside, subject and object, self and Other, conscious and unconscious self, disabled and non-disabled, different and normative. As Freud argues in "The Uncanny," a sense of "a doubling, dividing, and interchanging of the self" (234) is part of the experience of the uncanny, an awareness that the familiar self hides a self that is strange and unknown. Thus in recognizing her self mirrored in the distorted figures around her, the narrator experiences a breakdown of the identifying divisions, hierarchies and taxonomies which leads to a destabilizing of her own identity. The multiple reflections of her dark irrational self encroach upon and undermine the boundaries of the narrator's own stable identity and place in society. The monstrous ghosts the narrator encounters on the street are, in fact what Woolf calls in "Henry James's Ghost's Stories," the "baffling things that are left over, the frightening ones that persist" (324). The narrator is haunted by the recurring surplus of meaning and identies, the return of the repressed. She actively invites the dissolution of identity and the presence of the uncanny — "a ghost has been sought for" (490) — but simultaneously she fears an irrecoverable collapse of identity: being split, "cleave[d] asunder" (484). Having initiated this drift, the narrator fears that it will become unstoppable: an infinite fragmentation of identities with no stable referent. The perceived horror of the experience lies in the disintegration of the boundary between, in this case, the normative and non-normative body, the self of the narrator and the selves of the Other. However, this collapse is also potentially liberating.

In fact others on the street also participate in this public breakdown of a stable identity that is based on the binary of normal/abnormal. The various unsettling figures outside the shoe shop threaten the self-possession of the spectators by drawing them into "a hobbling grotesque dance to which everybody in the street now conformed" (484). The crowd recognizes the danger to their identity and sense of self that is posed by their mirroring the action of their non-normative doubles. The blind men convey "terror and inevitability" and "the little convoy seemed to cleave asunder the passers-by with the momentum of its silence, its directness, its disaster" (484). But all do participate in this dance of difference. Woolf discards the distinct category of monstrosity, as her narrator acknowledges that monstrous difference is a permeable category that embraces all, including herself.

In her discussion of the identification of the self with the Other in *Strangers to Ourselves*, Julia Kristeva argues that the visceral and sometimes vicious response to the outcast or figure of difference is an unconscious acknowledgement that "the foreigner lives within us: he is the hidden face of our identity, the space that wrecks our abode, the time in which understanding and identity founder" (1). To Kristeva, rejection of the foreigner is a self-protecting, self-consolidating and self-aggrandizing attempt to deny our own otherness. This is the ambivalent impulse underlying "Street Haunting." On one hand, opposition to the Other is crucial in the construction of individual identity, yet that encounter also results in the loss of the sense of a unique, identity, a identify that deviates from the homogenous ideal norm. As Kristeva puts it, encountering the Other forces us to see that "we are our own foreigners, we are divided" (*Strangers* 181). A consequence of our own foreignness, Kristeva suggests may be that we no longer "hunt" the "foreigner ... but rather ... welcome them to that uncanny strangeness" (*Strangers* 192), which we share with them. Judith Halberstam also urges that we "celebrate our own monstrosities" (27), which may involve learning to acknowledge our own difference without gothicizing the difference of the Other.

Woolf's narrator comes to understand that the continued maintenance of a single and stable identity, a given set of roles, a coherent normative body, is a socially produced limitation: "The good citizen ... must be banker, golfer, husband, father" (486). She criticizes the demand for homogeneity: "Circumstances compel unity; for convenience's sake a man must be a whole" (486). She argues instead that "the true self [is] neither this nor that, neither here nor there, but something so varied and wandering that it is only when we give the rein to its wishes and let it take its way unimpeded that we are ourselves" (486), unique individuals, defying the categorical social norms, that define and limit identify.

The recognition of our multiplicity is not easy; it involves an acknowledgment of kinship with "those wild beasts, our fellow men" (491). Yet despite the confusions, the narrator ultimately celebrates the several selves of each individual: "we are streaked, variegated, all of a mixture; the colours have run. Is the true self that which stands on the pavement in January, or that which bends over the balcony in June? Am I here, or am I there?" (486). Of course, this difficult recognition of a self that is "cleave[d] asunder" (484) results in questions, instead of any certain answers: "a question is asked which is never answered" (484–5).

Towards a Conclusion: A Gothic Modernism?

Thus, when the narrator arrives at her purported destination, she feels suddenly, strangely blocked: "the mind cringes to the accustomed tyrant.... Was it not for this reason that some time ago, we fabricated the excuse ... of buying something?... Ah, we remember, it was a pencil." (489). Yet the narrator has managed to invade the public space of the city, to acquire the phallic pencil, "the only spoil we have retrieved" (491) — and to adapt the defining and limiting male gaze. With the powerful instrument and the powerful perspective she inscribes a narrative that troubles the conventional certainties of generic categories. This is a different kind of travel narrative, focusing on shifting identities rather than spaces; it is instead an internal Gothic journey to the unknown. She has used Gothic tropes to investigate the Gothic questions regarding the stability of social categories, forcing the reader to ask: Who is the monster? Who is the human? Who is the self? Who am I? The narrator's return to her room is ostensibly presented as a return to the sanctuary of a private space and a unitary identity: "it is comforting to feel the old possessions, the old prejudices, fold us round" (491). However, the questions raised about identity and the relatively privileged, secure position of the normative body remain. Although the narrator insists that she is once again "shelter[ed] and enclose[ed]" (491) she has become part of a complex and ongoing process of haunting: "Walking home ... one could tell oneself the story of the dwarf, of the blind men ... of the quarrel in the stationer's shop. Into each of these lives one could penetrate a little way, far enough to give oneself the illusion that one is not tethered to a single mind, but can put on briefly for a few minutes the bodies and minds of others" (491).

The narrator's inconclusive conclusion thus points to yet another set of literary categories that Woolf destabilizes in her essay: the distinct categories of the Gothic, and the Modern. In fact, the interest of "Street Haunting" in otherness and transgression of boundaries results in a text that is simultaneously modernist and Gothic. Woolf amplifies the mirrored relation of these seemingly distinct genres, which both seek to disrupt convention and certainty, transgress boundaries, confront the hauntings of the past, accommodate the fragmentation of the self, and celebrate the new.

NOTES

1. Elizabeth Grosz has pointed out that representations of the body politic presume "an organized cohesive, integrated body, regulated by reason" as the ideal inhabitant of the well-ordered modern city. Grosz argues that when this rational order breaks down, what is produced instead is "a body depleted, abandoned, and derelict insofar as it is cast outside those nets" (*Space* 107).

2. Woolf's writings examine the shift in the twentieth century away from the traditional motifs of "monks and monsters" ("Gothic Romance" 306) towards more psychological ghost stories such as those of Henry James. Woolf argues that one cause for this change was the unavoidable awareness of terrible contemporary events, such as (she implies) the Great War: "Nowadays we breakfast upon a richer feast of horror than served ... for a twelvemonth" ("Henry James's Ghost Stories" 321).

3. The Jew here is a figure of difference, his appearance and behavior marked by starvation. As Kristeva argues in *Powers of Horror*, the Jew as Other is fantasized as a threatening figure (185); the Jew has also been gothicized as the subject of racialized stereotyping

(Anolik 164). The old woman with the "humped body," meanwhile, is excluded from a "public building" and public discourse and hidden from view, reduced to the status of a dead animal. As Woolf shows, such figures are cast out in order to maintain the myth of a coherent society and a non-vulnerable body; this ideal, she implies, is phantasmal and phantasmagoric.

4. Woolf's figure becomes less human and more like the sinister woman dwarf in Daphne du Maurier's "Don't Look Now"; she is "monstrous spectacle" (du Maurier 220), with an unstable identity. In their reading of the story, Horner and Zlosnik note du Maurier's turn to "the Gothic tropes of the monstrous body, veiling, freakishness and masquerade to interrogate the uncanny nature of identity itself" (231). Yet it is not the dwarf's identify that changes; the change is in the perspective from which she is viewed. As Rosemarie Garland Thomson argues, the so-called "freak" is a product of the outside spectator; the unstable image reassures the spectator of the security of his or her own status.

5. Indeed, Woolf's resistance to the demonization of difference is also rooted in Gothic convention, and in the strong Gothic tendency to destabilize the norm — including the ideal of the normative body — and to normalize the monstrous. The othering of the disabled or different body is a reaction to what has been called "the conviction that difference is always, in some sense, deficit ... we defend ourselves against the knowledge that difference surrounds us and *is* us" (Scully 61). Price and Shildrick have suggested that bodies which are disabled or ill "define and haunt" the bodies which are not, and that the attempted denial of such bodies leaves an "irreducible trace, the spectre of the other who is at the same time the self" (242). Woolf's Gothic may offer an escape from the gothicization of the disabled body, by continually destabilizing boundaries and by drawing attention to and acknowledging the non-normative otherness within.

6. Elizabeth Bowen notes that this recognition of kinship with the monster is the impulse that lies at the heart of the Gothic: "Our irrational, darker selves demand familiars" (102).

7. There is also an uncanny gender confusion in the scene: we assume that the narrator is female, but the self that she observes is referred to as male.

WORKS CITED

Anolik, Ruth Bienstock. "The Infamous Svengali: George Du Maurier's Satanic Jew." *The Gothic Other Racial and Social Constructions in the Literary Imagination.* Eds. Ruth Bienstock Anolik and Douglas L. Howard. Jefferson, NC: McFarland, 2004.

Benjamin, Walter. *Charles Baudelaire: A Lyric Poet in the Era of High Capitalism.* London: Verso, 1997.

Bowen, Elizabeth. Introduction. *The Second Ghost Book. Afterthought: Pieces about Writing.* London: Longmans, 1962.

Derrida, Jacques. *The Architecture of Deconstruction: Derrida's Haunt.* Ed. Mark Wigley. Cambridge: MIT Press, 1993.

_____. "The Ghost Dance: An Interview with Jacques Derrida." *Public.* 2 (1989).

Du Maurier, Daphne. "Don't Look Now" (1971). *Don't Look Now and Other Stories.* London: Penguin, 1996.

Freud, Sigmund. "The Uncanny" (1919). Trans. Alix Strachey. *The Standard Edition of the Complete Psychological Works of Sigmund Freud.* Vol. 17. London: Hogarth, 1955.

Grosz, Elizabeth. *Space, Time and Perversion: Essays on the Politics of Bodies.* St. Leonard's, NSW: Allen and Unwin, 1995.

Halberstam, Judith. *Skin Shows: Gothic Horror and the Technology of Monsters.* Durham: Duke University Press, 1995.

Horner, Avril, and Sue Zlosnik. "Deaths in Venice: Daphne du Maurier's 'Don't Look

Now.'" *Spectral Readings: Towards a Gothic Geography.* Ed. Glennis Byron and David Punter. New York: St. Martin's, 1999.

Kristeva, Julia. *Powers of Horror: An Essay on Abjection.* New York: Columbia University Press, 1982.

_____. *Strangers to Ourselves.* New York: Columbia University Press, 1991.

Price, Janet, and Margit Shildrick, "Uncertain Thoughts on the Dis/abled Body." *Vital Signs: Feminist Reconfigurations of the Bio/logical Body.* Eds. Margit Shildrick and Janet Price. Edinburgh: Edinburgh University Press, 1998.

Punter, David. "'A Foot Is What Fits the Shoe': Disability, the Gothic and Prosthesis." *Gothic Studies* 2.1 (Spring 2000): 39–49.

_____. *Gothic Pathologies: The Text, the Body and the Law.* New York: St Martin's, 1988.

Scully, Jackie Leach. "Admitting All Variations? Postmodernism and Genetic Normality." *Ethics of the Body: Postconventional Challenges.* Eds. Margit Shildrick and Roxane Mykitiuk. Cambridge: MIT Press, 2005.

Thomson, Rosemarie Garland. "The Beauty and the Freak." *Points of Contact: Disability, Art, and Culture.* Eds. Susan Crutchfield and Marcy Epstein. Ann Arbor: University of Michigan Press, 2000.

Woolf, Virginia. "Across the Border." *The Essays of Virginia Woolf.* Vol. 2. Ed. Andrew McNeillie. London: Hogarth, 1986–1994.

_____. *The Diary of Virginia Woolf.* Ed. Anne Olivier Bell. London: Hogarth, 1976–84.

_____. "Gothic Romance." *Essays.* Vol. 3. Ed. Andrew McNeillie. London: Hogarth, 1986–1994.

_____. "Henry James's Ghost Stories." Vol. 3. *The Essays of Virginia Woolf.* Ed. Andrew McNeillie. London: Hogarth Press, 1986–1994

_____. "Street Haunting: A London Adventure." *Essays.* Vol. 4. Ed. Andrew McNeillie. London: Hogarth, 1986–1994.

PART II

Visible Specters:
Horrifying Representations
of Invisible Pathology

Revising Ophelia: Representing Madwomen in Baillie's *Orra* and *Witchcraft*[1]

Melissa Wehler

"Oh flower too soon faded!": Ophelia's Gentle Madness

When the doomed heroine of *Hamlet* makes her entrance as a madwoman, she evokes great pity on the part of the other characters and of the audience. But it would be hard to imagine any reading of Ophelia that could inspire the horror evoked by her literary successors, the madwoman of the Gothic, a genre deeply influenced by Shakespeare. With her affecting madness and premature death, Ophelia illustrates the figure of the tender madwoman, isolated and confined by her gender even as her madness takes her beyond the social norms. Ophelia thus represents the literary tradition of the madwoman whose gender is the most obvious and most threatening mark of difference. In Shakespeare's text, Ophelia's ladylike madness is not *madness*: she is not angry or wild, indignant or ecstatic. She does not attempt to terrorize those who terrorize her. Rather, as the various stage directions indicate, her iconic entrance embodies a sort of tragic innocence. While the directions differ in various manuscripts, in each, the directions demonstrates a concern for the appearance of Ophelia's femininity, despite her distraction. In Q1, Ophelia enters "playing on a Lute, and her haire downe singing," while in 20F Ophelia enters "distracted." The emphasis placed on her courtly female attributes, her hair, her lute, and her singing, illustrates a concern for retaining her femininity.

For the other characters in the play also, the mad Ophelia is the object of the pitying and diminishing patriarchal gaze, rather the irrational subject.

Scorned as a lover, used as a daughter, she is Claudius' "poor Ophelia" who has "divided from herself and her fair judgment" (IV.v.84, 85). Of course, Shakespeare too plays a part in this: Ophelia's role in the play is little more than a thing to be pitied. This objectification thus reduces Ophelia to the status of the Other, the unknowable, inhuman object, lacking human (male) subjectivity, who is, through her difference, isolated and submerged. Her submersion is quite literal as she slips into death, off-stage, quietly and "mermaid-like" (IV.vii.174) — at last revealed as being fully non-human (though not at all threatening).

Perhaps because of the absence of her subjectivity, Ophelia has attracted great critical investigation over the centuries. Not surprisingly critics have greatly admired her tight grasp on femininity even as she is going mad. Indeed, they have read her as a model of subdued femininity. Samuel Johnson, for example, describes Ophelia filling "the heart with tenderness" and casts her as "the young, the beautiful, the harmless, and the pious" maiden (311). Samuel Taylor Coleridge refers to her as that "sweet girl" (151), and William Hazlitt portrays her as a "character almost too exquisitely touching to be dwelt upon. Oh rose of May, oh flower too soon faded!" (75). Instead of focusing on her passionate madness, almost all of the critics describe her death — the symbol of her subdued femininity — as her "touching" characteristic. Thus, Ophelia is re-packaged as a model for eighteenth- and nineteenth-century women: the example of retaining femininity at any cost. Only the seventeenth-century theater critic and theologian Jeremy Collier seemed to sense the dangerous and subversive qualities of madness, that would later be exploited by Joanna Baillie and others. In criticizing Shakespeare's representation of a madwoman, he asserts "such People ought to be kept in dark Rooms, and without company. To shew them, or let them loose, is somewhat unreasonable" (10). Certainly Collier's approach had many adherents: the mad have always been locked away in enclosed spaces, both in literature and in life.

If the literary or dramatic character is formed simultaneously by text and reception, then Ophelia certainly has many authors — Claudius, Collier, Johnson, Coleridge, Hazlitt, and, of course, Shakespeare — yet the one perspective still missing is that of Ophelia herself. Refused the voice and the agency to contribute to her own story, Ophelia is at the mercy of other authors who construct her, part by part, century by century, according to changing ideas and beliefs about the female and about madness. However, in the dawn of the Romantic era, with its attendant emphasis on self-awareness and self-expression, the Ophelia character-type was efficaciously and sweepingly reconsidered from the inside by Joanna Baillie. Baillie's dramas illustrate the development of the passively feminine Renaissance madwoman into the dangerous and wildly subversive madwoman of the Romantic Gothic era.

The Wise Fool

At the turn of the eighteenth century, Edward Ward produced *The London Spy* (1698–1700), a periodical meant, according to its subtitle, "to expose the vanities and vices of the town." Adopting a satirical perspective on contemporary institutions, the philosophical narrator attempts to reveal London through the eyes of lived experience. In the eighteen-month print run, the "spy" visits several of the town's "attractions," including Covent Garden, Fleet Street, Drury Lane, and the Tower, where the follies of London citizens are put on display for a general audience. Not least among such "attractions" are the "inmates" of Bethlehem Royal Hospital, otherwise known as Bedlam or "The College." For the cost of a donation, the leisurely spectator could spend the afternoon viewing and interviewing the mad.[2] In one notable instance, Ward recounts meeting a madman who tells him:

> "We madmen have as much privilege of speaking our minds, within these walls, as an ignorant dictator, when he spews out his nonsense to a whole parish. Prithee come and live here, and you may talk what you will, and nobody will call you in question for it. Truth is persecuted everywhere abroad, and flies hither for sanctuary" [56].

Removed from society's surveillance, madness offers Ward's "wise fool" the freedom to speak "the truth" from the sanctuary provided by the madhouse. Indeed, from the vantage point of his madness, the fool questions society's authority by asking who (and what) is mad? In so doing, he revises the general conviction that madness is a disability, an illness that inhibits one's freedom, physical and otherwise. Ward's liberated madman is one of many types identified in an ongoing socio-historical narrative of non-normative psychologies in the Western world.[3] These wise fools resist the label of madness that is deployed as a tool of social control. Whereas eighteenth-century psychology emphasized the need for Enlightenment ideals — reason, temperance, and prudence — in order to counteract the effects of dangerous deviations from the prescribed norm, the wise fools utilized their social invisibility to safely announce the irrationality of the "truths" of the normative world.

The madwomen of the eighteenth- and nineteenth-century Gothic are the heirs of the wise fools. Marginalized and imprisoned by virtue of their gender, these women turn to madness in order to state dangerous truths that interrogate and subvert the patriarchy. Only as madwoman do they have the freedom to refuse normative female behavior and normative female psychology that accepted the diminishing and dehumanizing limitations of patriarchy. Roy Porter points to an explanation of the feminization of the wise and subversive fool: "with the coming of the age of sensibility from the mid-eighteenth century ... disorder [was] effectively 'feminized'" (*A Social History* 104).

Certainly, the feminization of disorder plays upon the popular notion of women as emotional, unreasonable creatures, thereby positioning them in a dialectical relationship to the normative rational male, the emblem of the Enlightenment. By synthesizing the dual pathologies of irrationality and femininity, the madwoman became the emblem of the anti–Enlightenment. With the advent of the Gothic/Romantic valorization of the subjective and irrational self, the figure of the madwoman took on additional power. But, when played by a woman, the marginalized role of the harmless though subversive fool took on the lineaments of horror

Insane Agency: Joanna Baillie's Mad Women

Joanna Baillie was a prolific Scottish poet and dramatist and a prominent voice for Scottish nationalism, whose poetic and dramatic work spanned sixty-one years, from her first published work *Poems: Wherein It Is Attempted to Describe Certain Views of Nature and of Rustic Manners* (1790) until *The Dramatic and Poetical Works of Joanna Baillie: Complete in One Volume* (1851), a compendium volume and the final work published in her lifetime. Informed by an interest in non-normative psychology as well as by extensive reading, Baillie inhabited a confluence of literary and social perspectives.[4] According to Margaret Carhart, one of her earliest biographers, Baillie was especially inspired by Shakespeare: "The influence of Shakespeare is very evident even in her first volume, and many lines have been criticized as modeled too closely upon those in his plays" (Carhart 73). Setting aside such bias,[5] Carhart's assertion provides a valuable insight into Baillie's revision of Ophelia, demonstrating that not only was Baillie familiar with Shakespeare's work but that she was also actively engaged in refashioning his themes and characters for her Romantic world.

While Baillie endeavored to revise Shakespeare through the lens of Romanticism, the overlapping Gothic focus on the irrational subject also emerged. Publishing after the success of early Gothic writers such as Horace Walpole, Ann Radcliffe, and Matthew Lewis, Baillie also wrote in response to her Gothic predecessors. Indeed, Jeffery Cox asserts that she is "central to a discussion of the Gothic because her plays offer a self-conscious examination of some of the fundamental conventions of the Gothic and their implications for the construction of the feminine" (51). Working both with and against traditional representations of madwomen, Baillie's plays provide a performative space for non-normative perspectives on Enlightenment thought and the ways in which those ideas influence perceptions of femininity. Baillie's work, therefore, reconsiders the role of mental illness as a safe expression of non-normative, non–Enlightenment femininity in nineteenth-century Gothic literature.

Baillie's plays, *Orra* (1812) and *Witchcraft* (1836) both feature women — Orra and Grizeld Bane respectively — who use their non-normative marginalized identities as cover in order to open up a marginalized perspective and to subvert the patriarchal construction of their world. Unlike Ophelia whose oppressed femininity leads to her fatal plunge into a muddy pond, Orra and Grizeld Bane use their "deviance" to control the way in which they are perceived by the dominant society. Both Orra and Grizeld Bane engage in an autobiographical rewriting of their lives undertaken to combat social circumscriptions and definitions of their gender: Orra's madness allows her to opt-out of the marriage market while Grizeld Bane manipulates the stereotypical representation of the female as marginalized Other to gain power over her oppressors. Baillie thus revises the image of Shakespeare's madwoman: her appropriation of the figure results in madwomen who utilize their madness to appropriate their own stories.

Before becoming her own *author*ity, Orra is portrayed as a woman in danger; like Ophelia, she is at the mercy of her incompetent male protectors. Yet she is also a witty, creative woman with a vibrant imagination that inclines her to stories of the supernatural. The ghosts and skeletons that inhabit these narratives excite within her a "joy in fear" (II.ii.242). Ironically, her male protectors exploit Orra's affinity for Gothic literature in order to dominate her, staging a Gothic drama for her benefit: Orra's guardian confines her to a Gothic castle in an attempt to force her to marry his son; the watchman attempts to manipulate her fears in order to drive her into his arms; Orra's intended dresses up as the feared hunter-knight to gain access to her bedroom. Orra had envisioned a future where she could become the benevolent matriarch of society's outcasts: "In short, I would, without another's leave, / Improve the low condition of my peasants, / And cherish them in peace" (II.i.240). Yet Orra's matriarchal vision is ultimately thwarted by the desires of the male characters who wish to marry her (and her money).

Ultimately, Orra turns the weapon of the Gothic against her enemies: she ultimately escapes the confines of their prison and their narrative through the Gothic route of madness. The stage directions paint Orra as the very portrait of a madwoman, literally frightened out of her wits by her costumed lover. She has become: "Orra, with her hair and dress disordered, and the appearance of wild distraction in her gait and countenance" (V.ii.257). The stage directions echo the traditional portrait of Ophelia's disordered female body, threatening only in that is breaches courtly norms. Yet unlike the final "mermaid-like" pose of Ophelia — dead and inhuman — Orra's final posture is one of vibrant and humanly heroic rebellion: she "holds her clenched hands over her head with an air of grandeur and defiance" (V.ii.258). Once terrified, Orra now becomes terrible. In her madness she becomes a horrifying spectacle of female power, agency and subversion.

Orra's madness is indeed dangerous and destructive, consuming both of the men who attempt to confine her. The play concludes with Orra "dragging them back with her in all the wild strength of frantic horror, while the curtain drops" (V.ii.259). Orra's final action in the play is thus a complete inversion of social hierarchies and, indeed an erasure of Enlightenment reason, and the emblematic rational male: "Speech and sight are presented as useless in the last image of the play, as two male figures, one a symbol of present patriarchal authority, one a symbol of future authority, are pulled back into that epistemic darkness" (Eliot 99). Orra's madness thus empowers her to oppose the patriarchal oppression that would confine and exclude her because of deviance from the Enlightenment norm.

Grizeld Bane, the madwoman who terrorizes *Witchcraft*, likewise authors her own narrative, and revises the stereotypical construction of femininity, thereby threatening the normative structures of her society. In her note on the tragedy, Baillie credits Sir Walter Scott's *The Bride of Lammermoor* as the inspiration for her drama. Baillie was taken especially by the scene in *Lammermoor* in which several poor, elderly women question why Satan has not requested their services in return for a share of his power. Accurately understanding the gender and social implications of the scene, Baillie attempted to persuade Scott to expand the episode, suggesting he came "within one step" of the potentiality of these characters (Appendix 483). After Scott's refusal, Baillie undertook the project herself and created the drama, *Witchcraft*. In this play she transforms Scott's disenfranchised, powerless aged women into a socially powerful witch, once again, revising the figure of the madwoman to examine the horrifying intersection of femininity and madness.

Grizeld Bane's physical body is marked by a variety of signs of the non-normative: age, gender, class, and disability. Her marginality, and her social invisibility, allow her to assume the role of witch and to create a narrative for herself, in which her marginalized body assumes new-found supernatural power. While the Sheriff voices the Enlightenment reality that witches are socially powerless — "Are not witches always old and poor?" (IV.i.630) — Baillie's witch is powerful indeed. Indeed, the potency of her power is enhanced by her socially invisibility which is partially a product of her marginalization. Her invisible power allows Grizeld to revise the dominant, narrative about "old and poor" women as she transforms herself from "some old haggard beldame, with an ill name" into the most powerful woman in Renfrewshire (IV.i.631).

Grizeld Bane thus manipulates the stereotypes of her society to reframe her life story, as a narrative in which she is the central, powerful and visible character. We learn that before the opening of the play she was nobody: "a miserable woman whose husband was hanged for murder, at Inverness, some years ago, and who thereupon became distracted" (V.ii.642). But from the opening lines, Grizeld Bane is presented as a commanding agent. In Grizeld Bane's auto-biographical narrative, she is one of Satan's mortal proxies and a member of his infernal and subversive court. Consequently, she actively engages in inverting the dominant social hierarchy, wherein the poor become courtiers and criminals are honored guests. In her madness, Grizeld liberates her executed husband. He appears to her in the Satanic world: "my own mate is there, and the cord about his neck changed into a chain of rubies" (IV.ii.634). Grizeld Bane frees herself from the burdensome "truth" of rationality by irrationally recasting herself as the powerful inhabitant of a supernatural world. In doing so, Grizeld liberates and empowers herself. Through this self-liberation, she forces her audience to question whether the confining truth of reason is any more desirable that the liberating truth of madness.

Taking Baillie's lead, female Gothic writers in the nineteenth century continued to re-appropriate the image of the madwoman for their own liberating social purposes. Charlotte Brontë's Bertha Mason Rochester, who burns down the house in which her husband has imprisoned her, is another example of a insane and untamed woman who exerts the power of her madness,[6] as is the heroine of Charlotte Perkins Gilman's "The Yellow Wallpaper"—who drives her husband to a breakdown through her commitment to the reality of her own hallucination. By destroying the symbol of patriarchal confinement, or the patriarch himself, the dangerous "madwoman" effectively liberates herself. The subversive insanity of Orra and Grizeld Bane, then, prefigures the actions of their successors, suggesting perhaps, that for a woman living in a world structured by the supposed rational dominance of men, escape into madness is the only chance for change.

NOTES

1. I would like to thank Laura Engel and Maggie Q. Hannan for their invaluable feedback during the composition of this essay.

2. Throughout, I employ the term "mad" with full knowledge of its problematic theoretical and social implications. However, in keeping with eighteenth-century representations of madness, I have adopted the contemporary parlance.

3. The madman Ward encounters requires his audience to be reflective: what is "the truth" and what is its connection to madness? For more on the development of the notion of madness in western Culture, see Michel Foucault's *Madness and Civilization*.

4. Baillie came from a family of medical doctors, not the least of whom was her brother, Dr. Matthew Baillie, who authored the immensely popular book *The Morbid Anatomy of Some of the Most Important Parts of the Human Body*. In her *Introductory Dis-*

course she describes the theoretical purpose informing her dramas: "There is, perhaps, no employment which the human mind will with so much avidity pursue, as the discovery of concealed passion, as the tracing the varieties and progress of a perturbed soul" (*Introductory Discourse* 4).

5. While Baillie's critics were largely positive in their reviews, there were certainly some critiques meant to discount her contribution to the English dramatic tradition. Even in praise of Baillie, Lord Byron wonders if a female writer could be capable of producing her art: "When Voltaire was asked why no woman has ever written even a tolerable tragedy? 'Ah (said the Patriarch) the composition of a tragedy requires *testicles.'*— If this be true Lord knows what Joanna Baillie does — I suppose she borrows them" (203).

6. Of course this pattern is first discovered by Sandra Gilbert and Susan Gubar in *The Madwoman in the Attic*.

WORKS CITED

Baillie, Joanna. Appendix. *Dramas*. vol. 3. London, 1836.

_____. Introductory Discourse. *The Dramatic and Poetical Works of Joanna Baillie*. 2nd ed. London, 1853.

_____. *Orra: The Dramatic and Poetical Works of Joanna Baillie*. 2nd ed. London, 1853.

_____. *Witchcraft: The Dramatic and Poetical Works of Joanna Baillie*. 2nd ed. London, 1853.

Byron, Lord. *Byron's Letters and Journals*. vol. 5. Ed. Leslie Marchand. Cambridge: Harvard University Press, 1976.

Carhart, Margaret S. *The Life and Works of Joanna Baillie*. New Haven: Archon Books, 1970.

Coleridge, Samuel Taylor. *Coleridge's Shakespearean Criticism*. Ed. Thomas M. Raysor. Cambridge: Harvard University Press, 1960.

Collier, Jeremy. *A Short View of the Immorality and Profaneness of the English Stage: Together with the Sense of Antiquity Upon this Argument*. 1st ed. London, 1698.

Cox, Jeffery. Introduction. *Seven Gothic Dramas, 1789–1825*. Athens: Ohio University Press, 1992.

Elliott, Nathan. "'Unball'd Sockets' and 'The Mockery of Speech': Diagnostic Anxiety and the Theater of Joanna Baillie." *European Romantic Review* 18.1 (January 2007): 83–103.

Foucault, Michel. *Madness and Civilization: A History of Insanity in the Age of Reason*. 2nd ed. London: Routledge, 2001.

Gilbert, Sandra M., and Sandra Gubar. *The Madwoman in the Attic: The Woman Writer in the Nineteenth-Century Literary Imagination*. 2nd ed. New Haven: Yale University Press, 2000.

Hazlitt, William. *Characters of Shakespear's Plays*. London, 1817.

Johnson, Samuel. Afterword. *Hamlet, Prince of Denmark*. By William Shakespeare. *The Plays of William Shakespeare*. Vol. 8. London, 1765.

Porter, Roy. *Madness: A Brief History*. Oxford: Oxford University Press, 2002.

_____. *A Social History of Madness: The World Through the Eyes of the Insane*. New York: Weidenfeld and Nicolson, 1987.

Ward, Edward. *The London Spy*. Ed. Paul Hyland. East Lansing, MI: East Lansing Colleagues Press, 1993.

The Case of the Malnourished Vampyre: The Perils of Passion in John Cleland's *Memoirs of a Coxcomb*

CAROLYN D. WILLIAMS

Eighteenth-century England was a land of lost opportunity, so far as the horrifying representation of sickly, deformed, and otherwise non-standard bodies was concerned. Deviant bodies were frequently represented in ways that encouraged readers and audiences to laugh, weep, or indulge their curiosity, but few representations of the non-normative body were geared to turn stomachs or to set hair on end. Any terrifying fictions about diabolical creatures in some macabre approximation to human form would look archaic and superstitious to the modern and rational eighteenth-century audience. The neglect of the fear-provoking potential of the non-normative body in the eighteenth-century — even on the part of the Gothic mode which revels in demonizing difference — demonstrates a great deal about the cultural context of sensibilities. In the popular culture of our time an ominous ambience is often intensified by the display of a grotesque human body, for example the dangerous albino in Dan Brown's *The Da Vinci Code*. These expectations have been raised by performances like those of Béla Lugosi as Ygor in *Son of Frankenstein* (1939), and Charles Laughton as Quasimodo in *The Hunchback of Notre Dame* (1939). They saw things differently in the eighteenth century: Simon Dickie's study of printed jests, staged performances, and practical jokes has brought him to the conclusion that "any deformity or incapacity was infallibly, almost instinctively, amusing" (16). Three actors of the period made a living by exploiting their physical difference: Henry Norris, "a tiny man with odd face and voice"; the one-eyed James Spiller; and John Hippisley, "disfigured by a great burn scar" (16). They all achieved success as comics: their deformities were seen as a subject of mirth rather than pity or horror.

Although a taste for callous ridicule appeared at all social levels in the period, it was not universal (Dickie 3–5). The growing fashion of the sentimental inspired a resistance to cruel ridicule, and a more sympathetic response. Laurence Sterne displays this reaction in his semi-autobiographical novel, *A Sentimental Journey through France and Italy* (1768). On observing an unexpectedly high proportion of dwarves in Paris, his narrative persona, Yorick, muses on "the unaccountable sport of nature in forming such numbers of dwarfs — No doubt, she sports at certain times in almost every corner of the ... world; but in Paris, there is no end to her amusements — The goddess seems almost as merry as she is wise" (1:111). Yet Yorick moves from wit to the sentiments of pity and even empathy:

> So many miserable, by force of accidents driven out of their own proper class into the very verge of another, which is gives me pain to write down — every third man a pigmy! — some by rickety heads and hump backs — others by bandy legs — a third set arrested by the hand of Nature in the sixth and seventh years of their growth — a fourth, in their perfect and natural state, like dwarf apple-trees; from the first rudiments and stamina of their existence, never meant to grow higher [1:112].

This carefully compiled list of pathologies, representing all people with short stature as victims of some material cause beyond their control, invites readers to grieve with Yorick for their plight. Yorick follows these musings with an anecdote describing his successive indignation and delight when a dwarf is mocked by one man, then treated kindly by another (114–16). Thus, physical abnormality inspires laughter or pity in the mid-eighteenth century, but not terror.

The growing influence of Enlightenment thinking — the move from the religious and superstitious notions that disability and disease were expressions of divine wrath toward more scientific explanations — also played a part in the changing responses to physical difference: from theological horror, to relieved laughter, to a more empathetic sympathy, and then to scientific horror.[1] The emergence of medical theories based on Enlightenment principles of reason and science dictated that few educated writers would dare to draw connections between malformed bodies and the supernatural: doing so would imperil their pretensions to intelligence and up-to-date education, would ally them with the masses, who had not yet been exposed to Enlightenment thinking. However, modern writers could enliven their style, and appeal to the popular (and female) imagination of their audiences by invoking the supernatural in allusions and imagery. In doing so, they could also gesture to Enlightenment ideology that was in the process of asserting that the human who deviated from the scientific ideal of the normative body was a new rational kind of monster.

The Supernatural Link Between Immorality and Disability

Yet it was hard to sustain a rational tone when forging a link between immoral behavior and non-normative disability. This link could lead the writer from the scientific and enlightened back to the territory of the supernatural and theological. This tendency appears in the attack by a contemporary critic, John Dennis, on the poet Alexander Pope, who suffered from serious curvature of the spine, short stature and malformation of his ribs as a result of Pott's disease that he developed in adolescence.[2] Still smarting from a 1713 pamphlet in which Pope had claimed he was mad, Dennis jumped on the opportunity offered in 1716 when Pope tricked the shady bookseller Edmund Curll into drinking a dose of emetic.[3] To provide justification for his virulent attack, Dennis connected Pope's malformed body to his somewhat twisted behavior. In his pamphlet, *A True Character of Mr. Pope* (1716), Dennis describes an inhuman and uniquely evil "little Monster" (4). Dennis proposes that Pope's physical abnormality is a congenital expression of his evil character, and that both, therefore, are legitimate targets for a moral critique. Any reader who might sympathize with Pope's "Natural Deformity" and connect it with the general disease and misfortune that all "Mankind are liable to" is warned: "the Deformity of this Libeller is Visible, Present, Lasting, Unalterable, and Peculiar to himself. 'Tis the mark of God and Nature upon him, to give us warning, that we should hold no Society with him, as a Creature not of our Original, nor of our Species" (4). In fact, not only is Pope monstrously and uniquely inhuman, he is the progeny of that solitary evil figure, Satan: "By his constant and malicious Lying, and by that Angel Face and Form of his, 'tis plain that he wants nothing but Horns and Tail, to be the exact Resemblance, both in Shape and Mind, of his Infernal Father" (5). Thus, despite the completely reasonable justification for Dennis's attack, his strategies transform Pope, and his own text, into an extreme example of proto-Gothic monstrosity.

The Psychological Link Between Immorality and Disability

A less supernatural and more psychological representation of the link between the deformed body and moral evil appears in *The Twin-Rivals* (1703), a comedy by George Farquhar. Farquhar provides a psychological explanation for the behavior of Benjamin Wou'dbee, the bad twin. He is a hunch-back who is rejected by society: he would like to be a great seducer, but the only women willing to offer him sexual gratification are prostitutes. He complains, "This confounded Hump of mine is such a Burthen at my Back, that it presses me down here in the Dirt and Diseases of *Covent-Garden*" (1.1.74–76). He envies the normal physique of his brother, whom he blames for his own condition: "'twas his crouding me that spoil'd my Shape" (1.1.89–90). Benjamin's theory is discounted by the fact that the father of the twins was also a hunchback, thereby suggesting a more scientific explanation for his fate. Moreover, the father is referred to as a man of excellent character, which suggests that Benjamin's bitterness regarding his disability — he plots to ruin his brother — is an individual response to disability rather than proof of an inevitable link. The model for this psychological, if not sympathetic, accounting for the causal relationship between disability and immorality is Richard III, the iconic Shakespearean character whose twisted body represents his twisted morality. Shortly before acting in Farquhar's comedy, the actor Colley Cibber had aroused audiences to "Terror and Detestation" (Cibber *Apology* 131) in the title role of his production of *Richard*. As Burnett notes, Richard's opening soliloquy presents "bodily difference and a damaged moral outlook" as "mutually constitutive" (66). Yet Shakespeare's play also suggests that cruel exclusion on the part of his family is a contributing factor to Richard's malevolence. Cibber's awareness of the complex interactions between mind and body may likely have informed his interpretation of Benjamin Wou'dbee, but the subtext of *The Twin-Rivals* clearly illustrates that disability automatically denotes evil.

An Early Medical Link Between Immorality and Disability: Cleland's Gothic Narrative

John Cleland continues to tease out the causal relationship between the disabled body and defective morality by introducing a character whose debility arises directly from his own bad conduct. In doing so, he points to the figure of Enlightenment horror — the figure who inspires fear because it does not fit neatly into scientific Enlightenment categories of the norm. In 1751, two years after publishing his notorious pornographic novel, *Memoirs of a Woman of Pleasure* (1749), Cleland produced *Memoirs of a Coxcomb*, the tale of a young rake's sexual adventures. The latter book presents a somewhat biological explanation for the physical manifestation of depravity, depicting hideous ugliness as a consequence of immoral and non-normative sexual behavior.

Sir William Delamore, the narrator of *Memoirs of a Coxcomb* recalls his youthful affair with a sophisticated older woman, whose sexual expertise was enhanced by a variety of exotic charms: "Lady Travers, who joined to the charms of her person, a consummation in all the mysteries and science of voluptuousness ... united in herself the profound fire of the Spanish, the sentimental tenderness of the French, and the elegant neatness of the English women. She was alone a seraglio of beauties" (310). Enjoying high social status, and freedom from family ties, Lady Travers lives openly in sin and invites William to appear with her in public; she thus reverses the normative gender roles by treating him much as a high-ranking gentleman of the time might have treated a mistress. She also indulges in literary pursuits, dabbles in politics, and states her views with a frankness that violates contemporary gender boundaries. Sir William notes this as an unattractive flaw: "too knowing an air in women only gives them a masculine look, which becomes them no better than whiskers and jack-boots would do" (295).

While Lady Travers's sexual, economic and intellectual powers lead to an independence that masculinizes her in the lights of conventional society, William's unmanly dependence upon her leads to a weakness that feminizes him. He becomes "absorbed in this ruling passion" (310), so dependent on Lady Travers that when he makes love to other women, he obsessively returns to her, "more desire-drunk than ever" (311). Consequently, William begins to show visible marks of decay: "my constitution, overdrawn upon by the fierceness of my desires, and even by the vanity I took in the pleasure I gave, began to give signs of suffering.... All my sprightliness, vigour, and florid freshness, the native attendants of healthy youth, began to give shew of drooping, and flagged under the violence of the heat, with which the constancy of fire in my imagination melted me down into current love" (310–12).

Cleland thus suggests a causal connection between morally unhealthy sexual activities and the physically unhealthy body. The scientific plausibility of the causal connection is further emphasized when William hides in Lady Travers's bedchamber, planning to jump out and surprise her; it is he who experiences the surprise. After settling himself in a "dark closet which gave both sight and hearing fair-play, through the interstices" (313), he witnesses the return of Lady Travers. After ordering her servant to admit no one, she sends for Buralt, a character not previously mentioned to the reader, although he is known to William. When Buralt enters, his illness is obvious. He is "leaning upon Mrs. Vergers, with his knees knocking together, [displaying] a wildish stare, and all the symptoms of debility and pallid faintness" (316), before collapsing onto the bed. He is accompanied by "a plain, modest-looking country-woman" (316), hired as Buralt's wet-nurse, since he is too weak to digest anything but human milk. But after a good look at her client, she recoiled with visible horror, and affright; nor without reason; for it is hardly possible to figure to one's self a more ghastly spectre than what this wretch exhibited, wrapped in a kind of blue coat, that sat on him yet less loosely than his skin, which was of a dun sallow hue. His eyes goggled from sockets appearing sunk inwards, by the retreat of the flesh round them, which likewise added to the protuberance of his cheek-bones. A napkin in the shape of a night cap covered all his hair, (except a platted queue of it, and some lank side-locks) the dull dingy black of which, by its shade, raised, and added to, the hideousness of his grim meagre visage [316–17].

Cleland shrewdly heightens the horror by presenting Buralt from the perspective of the nurse, since William's shock is diluted by jealousy and anger. The nurse's horrified response is conveyed by the gothicism of the language of this passage: this is not a man, but a skeletal "ghastly spectre." The horror remains and even expands when the man takes on the status of an infant: "with her face averted, she gave him her breast, which he fastened upon, and looked more like a sucking demon, or a *vampyre* escaped from his grave, than a human creature" (317). Thus the debility of the man reduces him to an inhuman monster, transgressing supposedly fixed categories: he is a living vampire, an adult infant. Sir William realizes that Buralt is also his double (another destabilizing Gothic trope), representing his future self if he continues in his unhealthy sexual relationship with Lady Travers, a relationship that is clearly medically as well as morally unhealthy. Buralt thereby plays the classic role of the monster: the spectacle of his body serves as a warning to prevent young William from going down the path that will lead him to be enfeebled, infantilized and vampirized.

Cleland thus introduces the Gothic into his predominantly realistic, satiric text, describing a world in which danger presents itself in well-lit chambers as well as dark closets. Indeed, even when he has escaped the closet and the house of Lady Travers, some of her draining, emasculating power remains: "I was however so faint, and overcome with all the agitations, and conflicts which I had just undergone, that I threw myself on a chair ... 'till I could recover a little breath" (320).

Cleland's Gothic Vampyre

In the course of setting up Buralt as an early model of the Gothic monster, Cleland deploys a word was something of a novelty in 1751; he describes him as a "*vampyre*" (317). The earliest citation for this word in the *Oxford English Dictionary* is dated 1734: "These Vampyres are supposed to be the Bodies of deceased Persons, animated by evil Spirits, which come out of the Graves, in the Night-time, suck the Blood of many of the Living, and thereby destroy them." As late as 1792, it was considered necessary to annotate the word when it appeared in print (Trumbull 113). Certainly the concept preceded the appearance of the word in English: according to an article which first appeared in the March 3, 1732 edition of the Franco–Dutch journal *Le Glaneur,* and was later translated into English, the inhabitants of "a certain Canton of *Hungary* ... also a Part of *Transilvania,*" believe that "certain dead persons, whom they call Vampires, suck the Blood of the Living, insomuch that these People appear like Skeletons, while the dead Bodies of the Suckers are so full of Blood, that it runs out at all the Passages of their Bodies, and even at their very Pores" (Boyer 4:124). Although enlightened gentlemen regarded vampires as figments of a foolish exotic superstition, they were happy to use them as rhetorical devices to condemn various forms of unjust exploitation. In 1762, Oliver Goldsmith warned that "a corrupt magistrate" will degenerate until he "at last sucks blood like a vampyre" (2:66). The American satirical poet John Trumbull, writing in 1792, claimed that a corrupt and cruel commissioner of prisoners, who profited by failing to feed his charges properly, "thriv'd, like a Vampyre, on their blood" (Trumbull 112). The commissioner's few surviving prisoners were reduced to "moving skeletons" (113).

In terms of the figure of the vampire, then, Buralt is clearly victim and prey. Although he quite gruesomely sucks the life-giving milk from the wet-nurse, he remains a skeleton himself. Cleland thus suggests Lady Travers is the primary vampire who has vampirized Buralt through her insatiable sexual appetite, and who is on the path to effecting the same change in William.

The Female Vampire at the Intersection of Science and the Gothic

Lady Travers's identification as the supernatural vampire of myth is paralleled by her definition as the female vampire of science. In fact, the primacy of Lady Travers's monstrosity in Cleland's novel — her horrifying ability to transform men into monsters — can be traced back to the theory of ancient Greek medicine that all female bodies were monstrous, by virtue of deviating from the normative male body. In *The Generation of Animals* Aristotle asserts that the female body merely nourishes the offspring to which the male had conferred the spark of life (Aristotle 387).[4] Aristotle's notion of the relation between the genders and his concept of the power of semen, indicate a bridge to the later concept of the vampire. Aristotle describes semen as a refined form of blood, which is itself derived from food, so in consequence the loss of semen is a serious depletion for the male body:

semen is certainly a residue from that nourishment which is in the form of blood and which, as being the final form of nourishment, is distributed to the various parts of the body. This, of course, is the reason why the semen has great potency — the loss of it from the system is just as exhausting as the loss of pure healthy blood [Aristotle 91].[5]

The quasi-scientific theory that the loss of semen threatened the health of the male survived for thousands of years. William Salmon laments around the turn of the eighteenth century: "many who have been too much addicted to that pleasure, have killed themselves in the very act" (*The Complete and Experienced Midwife* 130). Even those who no longer subscribed to the traditional belief that women were perpetually obsessed by rapacious lust still agreed that frequent copulation was dangerous for men.[6]

Ultimately, then, both the scientific theories of Aristotle, and the irrational theories of the Gothic converge: the source of life-threatening debility is Lady Travers. Her insatiable and unnatural sexuality sickens her partners by draining them of their life force, their semen. Like a vampire, she is capable of engendering others like her: Buralt, who drains the wet-nurse of her life force, her mother's milk[7] and William whose debility indicates that he is on his way to sharing Buralt's fate. The symptoms of William and Buralt, thus reflect the continuing influence of Aristotelian medical theory[8] as well as the powerful influence of Gothic horror. But what is most startling is that they demonstrate that the line between science and the Gothic is permeable indeed. The medical diagnosis of Buralt's wasting symptoms is closely aligned with the Gothic interpretation: both agree that the sexual woman depletes the body of the man, although only Cleland uses the language of the Gothic — "vampire." Additionally the narrative role that Buralt plays suggests that he truly is a Gothic monster, serving to warn through spectacle. William responds to this warning by avoiding Lady Travers, thereby saving himself from biological depletion or vampirism, depending upon the diagnostic perspective.

NOTES

1. As Katharine Park and Lorraine J. Daston have shown, the eighteenth century witnessed the continuation of a process beginning in the early sixteenth century: at first, monsters were generally viewed as "divine prodigies" expressing God's reaction to contemporary political and religious developments, and warning of future upheavals; they gradually came to be regarded as "natural wonders"; by the end of the seventeenth century they had been "integrated into the medical disciplines of comparative anatomy and embryology" (23). The pace of change, of course, varied in different levels of society: "literate culture evolved far more rapidly than the traditional culture of the less-educated classes" (24).

2. For a detailed case history, see Nicolson, Marjorie and G. S. Rousseau, *"This Long Disease, My Life"* (7–22).

3. See "The Narrative of Dr. Robert Norris," and "A Further Account of the Most

Deplorable Condition of Mr. Edmund Curll," in Alexander Pope, *Miscellanies in Verse and Prose* (5–19, 20–27, 28–39).

    4. In other words, "a male is male in virtue of a particular ability, and a female female in virtue of a particular inability" (Aristotle *Generation of Animals* 391). Aristotle is quick to equate this difference with monstrosity:

> anyone who does not take after his parents is really in a way a monstrosity, since in these cases Nature has in a way strayed from the generic type. The first beginning of this deviation is when a female is formed instead of a male,
>
> though this indeed is a necessity required by Nature [Aristotle *Generation* 401].

Necessary or not, he concludes that "we should look upon the female state as being as it were a deformity" (Aristotle 461).

    5. Hippocrates (c. 460–377 B.C.) and his followers, including Galen (A.D. 129–200/217), thought women did produce fertile seed, but agreed with Aristotle about the value of male sperm: "The evidence that it is the most potent part which is secreted is the fact that even thought the actual amount we emit in intercourse is very small, we are weakened by its loss" (Hippocrates "The Seed" in *Hippocratic Writings* 1.317).

    6. For accounts of traditional and innovative theories in the period, see Boucé's *Sexuality in Eighteenth-Century Britain*.

    7. In fact, since milk, like semen, was believed to be directly derived from blood, Buralt and Mrs. Travers, quite literally drain their victims' life's blood. The seventeenth-century midwife Jane Sharp believed that menstrual blood makes the child grow in the womb, and, "when the Child is delivered, then it returns to the Breasts to make Milk" (61). The use of milk as a cure for tabes dorsalis makes sense in this context: it substitutes one blood-derived fluid for another.

    8. In *The Œconomy of Love*, John Armstrong, an eighteenth-century physician and poet, warns young men to ration copulation in order to preserve health: "Husband your Vigour well" (line 545); men who force their constitutions, especially by the use of aphrodisiacs, will suffer "*Tabes,* and gaunt *Marasmus*" (line 562).

WORKS CITED

Aristotle. *Generation of Animals.* Ed. and Trans. A. L. Peck. Cambridge: Harvard University Press, 1943.

_____. *The Whole of Aristotle's Works, Complete.* London: Sold for the Booksellers, 1782. This comprises *Aristotle's Compleat Master-Piece,* 32nd ed.; [William Salmon]. *Aristotle's Complete and Experienced Midwife.* 14th ed.; *Aristotle's Book of Problems.* 31st ed.; *Aristotle's Last Legacy.* All separately paginated.

Armstrong, John. *The Œconomy of Love: A Poetical Essay.* 3rd ed. London: T. Cooper, 1739.

Boucé, Paul-Gabriel, ed. *Sexuality in Eighteenth-Century Britain.* Manchester: Manchester University Press, 1982.

Boyer, Jean Baptistse de, Marquis d'Argens. *The Jewish Spy: Being a Philosophical, Historical and Critical Correspondence, by Letters Which Lately Pass'd Between Certain Jews in Turkey, Italy, France, Spain, etc. Translated from the Originals into French, by the Marquis d'Argens, And Now Done Into English.* 5 Vols. London: D. Browne and R. Hett, 1739–40.

Burnett, Mark Thornton. *Constructing "Monsters" in Shakespearean Drama and Early Modern Culture.* Houndmills, Basingstoke: Palgrave Macmillan, 2002.

Cibber, Colley. *An Apology for the Life of Mr. Colley Cibber, Comedian, and Late Patentee of the Theater-Royal.* Dublin: George Faulkner, 1740.

_____. *The Tragical History of King Richard III. As it is Acted at the Theatre Royal.* London: B. Lintot and A. Bettesworth [1700].

Cleland, John. *Memoirs of a Coxcomb*. London: R. Griffiths, 1751.

Dennis, John. *A True Character of Mr. Pope. The Second Edition. Miscellanies upon Several Subjects; Occasionally Written. By Mr. Joseph Gay*. Ed. John Breval. Loddon [*sic*]: [E. Curll], 1719.

Dickie, Simon. "Hilarity and Pitilessness in the Mid-Eighteenth Century: English Jestbook Humor." *Eighteenth-Century Studies* 37.1 (2003): 1–22.

Farquhar, George. *The Twin-Rivals: A Comedy*. London: Bernard Lintott, 1703.

Goldsmith, Oliver. *The Citizen of the World: or Letters from a Chinese Philosopher, Residing in London, to His Friends in the East*. 2 Vols. London: J. Newbery and W. Bristow, 1762.

Hippocrates. *Hippocratic Writings*. Ed. G. E. R. Lloyd. Trans. J. Chadwick. Harmondsworth: Penguin, 1987.

The Narrative of Dr. Robert Norris, Concerning The Strange and Deplorable Frenzy of Mr. J — N D — IS, A Full and True Account of a Horrid and Barbarous Revenge by Poison, on the Body of Mr. Edmund Curll, and *A Further Account of the Most Deplorable Condition of Mr. Edmund Curll. Alexander Pope, Miscellanies in Verse and Prose*. London: John Thomas, 1744.

Nicolson, Marjorie, and G. S. Rousseau. *"This Long Disease, My Life": Alexander Pope and the Sciences*. Princeton, New Jersey: Princeton University Press, 1968.

Park, Katharine, and Lorraine J. Daston. "Unnatural Conceptions: The Study of Monsters in Sixteenth- and Seventeenth-Century France and England." *Past and Present* 92 (August 1981): 20–54.

Shakespeare, William. *Complete Works*. Ed. W. J. Craig. London: Oxford University Press, 1943.

Sharp, Jane. *The Complete Midwife's Companion: Or, The Art of Midwifry Impov'd*. 4th ed. London: John Marsall [*sic*], 1721.

Shelley, Mary. *Frankenstein: Or, The Modern Prometheus*. 1818. Ed. D. L. Macdonald and Kathleen Scherf. Peterborough, Ontario: Broadview, 1994.

Sterne, Laurence. *A Sentimental Journey through France and Italy*. 2 Vols. London: G. Faulkner, J. Hoey, Sen., J. Exshaw, H. Saunders, 1768.

Trumbull, John. *M'Fingal: A Modern Epic Poem in Four Cantos*. 5th Ed. London: Chapman, 1792.

"The Monster Vice": Masturbation, Malady, and Monstrosity in *Frankenstein*

CHRISTINE M. CROCKETT

In 1757, the renowned French physician Samuel-August Tissot, famed for his care of the Swiss court at Lausanne, visited a young watchmaker who had reputedly masturbated daily from the time he was seventeen. Having heard of the young man's deteriorating physical condition, Tissot sought to lend him a hand, so to speak, in curing him of the "deplorable habit" of self pollution.[1] Tissot's anti-masturbation text, *Onanism*, was first published in Latin in 1758, then in his native French in 1760, and finally the first English edition was translated and published in 1766, almost ten years after his encounter with the watchmaker. In *Onanism*, Tissot explains that the habitual masturbation performed by the young man, identified only as "L.D.," had disabled him both physically and professionally. We are told by Tissot that "[h]e entirely lost his strength and was obliged to give up his profession, being altogether incapacitated" (25). The patient's repeated practice of the so-called "solitary vice" eventually escalated to the point that he experienced unbidden and uncontrollable ejaculations leading, finally, to a dramatic hemorrhage of vital spirits which put an end to his life.

The figure of the masturbating watchmaker merits an extended description, and Tissot is more than willing to present what he calls a "portrait of terror." L.D. is part of a larger narrative strategy that Tissot deploys in his medical examination of masturbation. Tissot portrays the most horrifying cases of masturbators in order to frighten his readers and thereby cure them of their habitual solitary sexual practices. In *Masturbation: The History of a Great Terror*, Jean Stengers and Ann Van Neck note this strategy deployed in eighteenth- and nineteenth-century anti-masturbatory treatises, and in Tissot's work in particular: "The most effective course of action in tearing the unfortunate masturbator from his deplorable habits remained the drawing of a 'portrait of danger.' One should — one must — bring him face to face with the 'terrifying image, and that will make him shrink back in horror'" (74). It was, as Stengers and Van Neck put it, "cure by terror" (74).[2]

Tissot, therefore, holds nothing back when he writes of L.D. Drawing upon Gothic tropes, he describes his encounter: "I found a being that less resembled a living creature, than a corpse ... reduced almost to a skeleton.... Far below the brute creation, he was a spectacle, the horrible sight of which cannot be conceived, and it was difficult to discover, that he had formerly made part of the human species" (25). This passage is striking in its insistence upon masturbation as a self-willed sexual practice that eventually makes monstrous a once healthy body. Who would choose such a fate? Tissot seems to ask his reader; yet, this cautionary tale also suggests that one cannot *but* succumb to the seductive practice of solitary sex. L.D.'s case suggests that anyone (and possibly everyone) might lack the force of will necessary to resist such urges.

His inability to control basic bodily functions manifests a more traumatic truth: in willfully indulging in a sexual practice that was deemed both a sin and a disease, L.D. has lost autonomous control of his mind as well as of his body. More a "corpse" than living creature, L.D. now exists only insofar as he is an object for the horrified gaze of an onlooker. He has un-made himself as a human being and as an autonomous subject by repeatedly indulging in self-abuse. Tissot's model was both popular and influential. Nearly a century after his revision of *Onania*, Samuel Gregory M.D. drew his readers' attentions to what he called the "monster vice" (25) in his 1845 sexological text, *Facts and Important Information for Young Women on the Subject of Masturbation*. Gregory's work is unique in its direct acknowledgement of female masturbation, but otherwise conforms to the strategies employed by earlier anti-masturbation texts, pointing to the debilitating and dehumanizing consequences of the deviant practice.

"The Wreck of Manhood": Eighteenth-Century Depictions of Masturbation and Disability

Sometime between 1708 and 1712, nearly half a century before Tissot's masturbation manifesto, the first edition of an epistolary anti-masturbatory tract was published in London by an anonymous editor.[3] *Onania, or, the Heinous Sin of Self-Pollution, and All its Frightful Consequences, in both Sexes, consider'd* purports to be a didactic text, meant to expose the "youth of the nation" to the risks they would run were they to indulge in the "heinous sin of self-pollution."[4] This collection of first-hand accounts from victims of the solitary vice, interspersed with medical and moral advice from the editor, documents a range of maladies that ensue upon the commencement of masturbation. These accounts paint masturbation as a self-inflicted disease which would inevitably, and completely, disable body and mind. Masturbation appears as a particularly disturbing practice in *Onania* (named for Onan, the biblical character punished for this sin) because it is debilitating. Euphemistic references to masturbation as "self abuse" or "self pollution" speak to this concern, for it was believed that the dysfunctional will would, contrary to nature, abuse or pollute the body.

Even worse, such immoral and destructive sexual activities would precipitate the appearance of physical ailments that essentially made the act visible upon the body. *Onania's* editor warns his readers, for instance, that "these Self-Defilements do rot and weaken the body" (6), then follows this generalized preview with increasingly graphic examples of the fate awaiting male bodies specifically. "In the first place," we read, "[masturbation] manifestly hinders the Growth" (17) and "many young Men, who were strong and lusty before they gave themselves over to this Vice, have been worn out by it" (18). Thus pointed attention is paid to impaired masculine ideals: the masturbating boy will not grow as tall as his more continent brothers, and might even, once pubescent, retard or even reverse his progress towards (sexual) maturity, potentially unto death.[5] What follows are detailed physiological accounts of unattractive and ultimately impotent masturbating men whose "meagre Jaws, and pale Looks, with feeble Hams, and Legs without Calves, their Generative Faculties weaken'd, if not destroy'd in the Prime of their Years" the editor tells us, mark them as "[a] Jest to others, and a Torment to themselves" (19). Such "licentious Masturbators," described in a way that emphasizes their undeveloped secondary sexual characteristics ("meagre Jaws," "pale Looks," "feeble Hams," "Legs without Calves") are especially ghastly because they visibly diverge from the ideal eighteenth-century British male. The hyperbole emphasizes the spectacular consequences of this secret behavior. The unsettling admonitions stress that private sexual practice would become embarrassingly public, through the visible deterioration of the body. This rhetorical strategy is, of course, an excellent way to police private practice. The editor laments that this damage occurs in the very "[p]rime" of the victims' lives. Thus masturbation derails the progress of healthy bodily maturation, and can likewise destroy a young man's ability to procreate, at the very stage of life where the proper functioning of both body and mind should work in tandem to create the ideal, morally upright British citizen, physically capable of populating the nation with his progeny. Such descriptions highlight a concern with how a physical deviation from the norm may be perceived in the social realm, and how its visibility might affect the onlookers. Because masturbators will be mocked by others, they will also be "a Torment to themselves." Thus, while self-abuse can lead to private physical suffering this editor suggests that it will also lead to public social "torment," engendered by the shame the masturbator will experience as a result of the publicly physical spectacle of his private sexual transgression.

As Michel Foucault writes in *Abnormal*, his discussion of the development of "abnormal" identities, masturbation like other taboo, non-normative sexual acts, "superimposes on the visible causes that can be localized in the body a sort of historical etiology in which the patient is responsible for his own illness: If you are ill, it is because you willed it, if your body is afflicted by illness, it is because you touched it" (241). The masturbator's body, therefore, manifests a failure of will in the concomitant failure of the body itself to exhibit the physical characteristics which mark a body as being properly male. The terrifying reality at the heart of this discourse is that the wasting male body can be taken as a symptom of a deeper moral, unmanly weakness which *cannot* be hidden; private sexual practice inevitably becomes horrifyingly public. Of course, the seeming inevitability of the masturbation narrative, while shocking, might also generate a paradoxical sensation of confidence for an Enlightenment populace. There is something to be said about the comforting illusion that physical appearance expresses inner vice, making it easier for the observer to use the visible mark of deviant otherness[6] in order to make social judgments.

The Enlightenment Creation of the Masturbating Monster

With the Enlightenment valorization of rationality, the ability to reason, to make well-thought-out, willful decisions became linked, via the discourse of a rising medical complex, to the healthy and hale English-person's body. Moreover, this healthy English body, the product of rational decisions, was linked to dominant social categories of identity such as race, class, and gender. Those who did not fall into the deceptively neat category of "healthy" and "rational" became encoded as Other, as non–English and therefore, in many respects, not human. A study of the suppression and demonization of the practitioners of non-normative sexual behavior is enriched by examinations of cultural depictions of otherness: specifically by drawing our attention to those bodies which were labeled as disabled or pathological by medical texts of the eighteenth century. At the intersection between the discourses of disability and monstrosity lies the figure of the masturbator, product and manifestation of eighteenth-century anxieties regarding what, exactly, separated the healthy human from the pathological monster.

The spectacular figure of the masturbator's gothicized and horrifying body that was created by medical discourse, the physical embodiment of the "masturbation panic" which swept Enlightenment-era Europe, would have been an inviting image for Mary Shelley. The monster that she created in *Frankenstein* (1818) is clearly kin to the monstrous masturbator. L.D., the monster portrayed by Tissot, is evoked by Mary Shelley's description of her creature with his tightly stretched, fading skin, brilliant white teeth, and dark black hair as they stand in "horrid contrast with his watery eyes, that seemed almost of the same color as the dun white sockets in which they were set, his shriveled complexion, and straight black lips" (34). As in the case of L.D., the creature's body is measured by its distance from the "normal" human body. It is not that Frankenstein's creature is lacking any human attribute; rather each part is different from its human counterpart. It is precisely that sublimely "horrid contrast" between the human and the deviant which marks both L.D. and the creature as monstrous.

But it seems likely that the real masturbator, secreted in Shelley's text is her eponymous protagonist. Victor calls Shelley's abomination of nature "the work of [his] own *hands*" (48, italics mine); like Tissot's watchmaker who transforms himself into a monster, Victor, the solipsistic and solitary scientist, uses his own hands to produce a creature that is horrible to behold. As Judith Halberstam has noted, the creature is a new kind of monster: "*Frankenstein* ... demands a rethinking of the entire Gothic genre in terms of *who* rather than *what* is the object of terror. By focusing upon the body as the locus of fear, Shelley's novel suggests that it is people (or at least bodies) who terrify people" (28). Indeed, the uncannily inhuman body of the monster provides the horror in *Frankenstein* as it does in the anti-masturbation narratives.

The spectacle of the monstrous bodies of Victor and his "hideous progeny" troubles a core binary of Enlightenment humanism: the distinction between the human body — normative healthy, reasoning, European male — and the inhuman body, unhealthy, unreasoning. This binary was the foundation of the sexological rhetoric of the eighteenth century and the Romantic age which sought to construct an opposition between the body of the wasting masturbator and the healthy normative body. The non-normative bodies of creator and creature in Shelley's novel challenges the conventional binary, destabilizing the comforting set of categories through the failure of Victor's body, which becomes increasingly disabled by his choice to create the monster, and by the physical power of the creature's hale body that merely bears the external marks of aesthetic difference.

The deterioration of Victor's body and mind thus challenges the stability of the healthy body in the health/disease binary. His physical decay almost directly maps the narratives of masturbators depicted by sexological texts such as *Onania* and *Onanism*. These accounts, like other contemporary tales of bodily decay and dysfunction, demonstrate the idea that disability is a process which occurs gradually over time. Moreover, the accounts of masturbators suggest that an individual's inability to exert reason and will, could determine his momentary placement in the frighteningly dynamic binary of health and illness. Victor, like the masturbator, chooses immoral and un(re)productive behavior that results in his physical decline which challenges the notion that to be humanly healthy or non-humanly diseased is a permanent and stable category of identity. Conversely, Victor's monster challenges the stability of the other half of the binary: the state of diseased otherness. He bears only the aesthetically objectionable markings of the non-human body, without the concomitant moral and psychological impairment which sexological texts suggested would accompany such physical markings of difference. Thus, Shelley's novel interrogates a social binary constructed to enforce social norms, such as the prohibition against masturbation.

"Filthy Creation": Mary Shelley and the Masturbating Scientist

Anti-masturbation texts of the eighteenth and early nineteenth centuries often described universities as hotbeds of sexual vice. Dedicated, self-absorbing study was believed not only to weaken the body by excessive and concentrated time spent on one subject, but was also considered to be, much like reading itself, an activity which, either by inflaming or, conversely, dulling the mind (a hypothesis which varied from text to text), allowed for the imagination's indulgence in a fantasy life which would then lead to masturbation.[7] Parents, teachers, and doctors were cautioned to be on the lookout for reclusive behavior and a morbid attraction to solitude for, as Tissot warns, "[n]othing is more pernicious to people inclinable to be devoted to a single idea, than idleness and inactivity.... They cannot too assiduously avoid laziness and solitude." To drive home his point, he repeats "[they] should never be left entirely alone" and finally issues the rather unreasonable (and certainly impractical) blanket statement "they should not be allowed to meditate, to read, or any way occupy the mind" (129).[8] To focus for any extended period on one given subject was seen to indicate not only a dangerous self-absorption, but also a proclivity for returning repeatedly to a favorite topic — a scholarly addiction.

It is striking, then, that while a student at the University of Ingolstat,

Victor increasingly resorts to solitude in order to do his extracurricular reading and experimentation. On his first night at the University, he tells Walton, he was "conducted to [his] solitary apartment, to spend the evening as [he] pleased" (26), while the next few days are "spent almost in solitude" (27) during which time he is occupied by studies. Victor's solipsism has already been discussed by many critics, and has been read by some to be an indictment of the self-absorbed Romantic poet. However, viewing Victor's solitary and self-absorbed study habits through the lens of autoerotic discourse reveals other interpretations of Victor's behavior, and of his language. He declares at various times that he is "ardent," in his pursuit of such knowledge, "eager" in his studies, reading "with ardour" (29), and these powerful adjectives serve to situate Victor's behavior on the verge of sexual addiction. His emotions have trumped his will, and these highly charged signifying phrases indicate an indulgence in dangerously excessive emotion, a kind of emotional ejaculation, which sexological texts suggested would sap the strength and vitality of a once healthy body.

Shelley pointedly echoes some of the language of Tissot when talking about her solitary scholar. Tissot writes: "Although exhausted by perpetual fatigue, they are seized with all the disorders incident of the brain, melancholy, catalepsy, epilepsy, imbecility, the loss of sensation, weakness of the nervous system, and a variety of similar disorders" (75). Tissot's language suggests a link between the physically draining compulsive activity of masturbation and the mentally draining compulsive work of the scholar. His depiction of the masturbator is uncannily anticipatory of Victor's description of his pursuits, and their effect upon his body: "Who shall conceive the horrors of my secret toil[?].... My limbs now tremble, and my eyes swim with the remembrance; but then a resistless, and almost frantic impulse, urged me forward; I seemed to have lost all soul or sensation but for this one pursuit" (Shelley 32). This "resistless," "almost frantic impulse" fixed upon "one pursuit" is remarkable in its proximity to accounts of masturbatory self-absorption and compulsion. Indeed, it is precisely such monomaniacal obsession which most concerns anti-masturbation texts for such pursuits would ultimately remove the subject from commerce with his fellow man (and woman).[9] Notice too, the link between muscle reflex and exhaustion here. As long as the suggestive "unnatural stimulus" holds Victor's attention, he remains engaged with his solitary obsession. Like his favorite natural philosophers, he "dabbles" with what he should leave alone. Like Tissot's watchmaker, his vision is troubled, tellingly, by the imagined memory of his acts, and his body's unbidden and uncontrollable trembling also reminds us of the accounts of masturbators whose trembling not only stands in for orgasmic spasms, but also for a complete physical and mental breakdown.

Victor's description of the process of experimentation, whereby he learns to (quite literally) single-handedly create life, furthers the reading of his practice as masturbatory: "I collected bones from charnel houses; and disturbed, with profane fingers, the tremendous secrets of the human frame. In a solitary chamber, or rather cell, at the top of the house, and separated from all the other apartments by a gallery and staircase, I kept my workshop of filthy creation." (32). As an addition to the titillating manual pleasure of "dabbling" we now read that his "profane fingers" operate in a solitude that is trebly insisted upon ("solitary chamber," "top of the house," "separated from all the other apartments") where he works upon his "filthy creation." The proliferation of such signifying terms[10] is further inflected by Victor's simultaneous account of his personal health which begins to fail him at this time.

> My cheek had grown pale with study, and my person had become emaciated with confinement.... I appeared rather like one doomed by slavery to toil in the mines, or any other unwholesome trade, than the artist occupied by his favourite employment. Every night I was oppressed by a slow fever, and I became nervous to a most painful degree; a disease that I regretted the more because I had hitherto enjoyed most excellent health [32–33].[11]

Victor's increasing mental exertion, which saps his physical strength, creates in his body a kind of class transvestism. Because he has masturbated, this elite young man has essentially reduced himself to the social level of a lowly worker, a slave. Victor is no longer the healthy, reasoning, and free citizen and scholar that he once was; instead, he has been enslaved by his passionate pursuit.

Moreover, this description is absolutely in keeping with early nineteenth-century popular sexological tracts. Using newly professionalized medical language that effectively replaced the memoir-like Enlightenment narratives of masturbators, the writers of these sexological texts effectually regulated the earlier untidy first-person accounts of masturbation. For instance, John Robertson's *On Diseases of the Generative System*, a popular medical text published in 1812, just six years before the first edition of *Frankenstein*, systematically and scientifically describes the familiar progression from masturbation, to addiction, to eventual physical debility as follows: "The face becomes pale and cadaverous, and the body flabby or emaciated, with coldness in the extremities ... all attempts at [sleep] are interrupted by the most frightful dreams ... the patient becomes terrified to go to bed, lest sudden death should be his fate" (qtd. in Hunt 597). The words resonate with the language used by Victor, himself a scientist. He talks of having "grown pale with study" and "emaciated with confinement." In the pages that follow the climactic creation scene, Victor adds to his list of symptoms, complaining "I was disturbed by the wildest dreams" (34), "I started from my sleep with horror; a cold dew covered my forehead, my teeth chattered, and every limb became convulsed"

(35), and "My heart palpitated in the sickness of fear" (35).[12] Although Victor cannot bring himself to describe his activities, his illness is noticed by Clerval who declares in wonderment, "how very ill you appear; so thin and pale" (36). Victor's health quickly deteriorates, as he explains, "[t]his was the commencement of a nervous fever which confined me for several months" (37). As he reflects back to his sufferings at that time, Victor's self-diagnosis is compellingly close to the clinical descriptions of the medical texts: "[t]his state of mind preyed upon my health." Tellingly, he admits further that, "solitude was my only consolation — deep, dark, death-like solitude" (59). Of course, this decline has also been precipitated by the creation of the monster and the subsequent murders of William and Clerval. Yet the course of the decline and the description of symptoms faithfully follows the path of the sexological narrative. As in the narratives, once the warning signs become apparent in Victor, friends and family members notice the visible symptoms of his invisible vice.

Predictably, Victor's father is exceedingly concerned with what he perceives as Victor's excessive, self-indulgent behavior, the failure of his *will* in allowing himself to decline. The father attributes his son's physical deterioration to a hyper-indulged grief over the loss of his friend, Clerval, and tries to "reason with me [Victor] on the folly of giving way to immoderate grief." Significantly, the fatherly advice is couched in language which forges a linguistic connection between the healthy body and manly duty: "excessive sorrow prevents improvement or enjoyment, or even the discharge of daily usefulness, without which no man is fit for society" (59). Not surprisingly, the elder Frankenstein is alarmed only after his son's psychic struggle becomes physically apparent, when the secret vice is exposed through marks of illness on the body, and when Victor is at risk from moving from the normative healthy male to the non-normative, and effeminate, invalid.[13] In fact the concern of Victor's father and his friends is heightened because of his impending marriage to Elizabeth. Thus, the father's advice is driven by an insistence that Victor be able to perform his manly procreative duties for the sake of the British empire,[14] as well as for the patriarchy that has engendered him.

Ultimately, Victor's decay is so explicitly visible that it is apparent to a complete stranger. The bodily dysfunction catalogued by Walton once he meets Victor emphasizes the horrifyingly and spectacular nature of his disability.[15] Before Walton learns of Victor's past, he is struck by the sight of his corruption: "His limbs were nearly frozen, and his body dreadfully emaciated by fatigue and suffering," writes the troubled Walton to his sister; "I never saw a man in so wretched a condition" (14), he laments. Walton's emphatic "never" suggests that the wretchedness which Victor's body displays has placed the young scientist outside the bounds of Walton's understanding of what it means to be a man. The distance between Victor and the rest of mankind is further dramatized when Walton tells his sister that he is, in fact, fascinated: "I never saw a more interesting creature," he writes, further separating Victor from the realm of the human. Walton adds, "his eyes have generally an expression of wildness, and even madness ... he is generally melancholy and despairing; and sometimes he gnashes his teeth" (14). Yet, although Victor is clearly not fully human here — he is like a wild animal — Walton finds him fascinating and pathetic, rather than horrifying.

"A being like myself": A Monster Better Than Myself

In Shelley's novel, Gothic horror is reserved for responses to the official monster, the creature whose existence transgresses the clean lines of anti-masturbatory narrative while also challenging our understanding of masculine ability. Paradoxes are at the heart of descriptions of the monster throughout the novel. Victor refers to him as "lifeless matter," "lifeless clay," and a "lifeless thing" which, once living, is a "demoniacal corpse" and a "mummy ... endued with animation" (33). The monster is both living and dead, a former subject (a "corpse" and "mummy") that is now object ("matter," "clay," "thing"). Shelley contrasts Victor's description of the creature with his recollection of his earlier vision of the monster. "His limbs were in proportion, and I had selected his features as beautiful. Beautiful! — Great God!" (34), Victor exclaims, before cataloguing the grotesque physical details which make the living creature what he later calls "the filthy mass that moved and talked" (99).

In fact, the monstrosity of the creature derives from his ability to surpass the human norm. Unlike his creator, the monster is physically robust, exhibiting what Victor calls a "gigantic stature" (49), a "stature ... [which] seemed to exceed that of a man" (65), and a body which, according to the monster, Victor has "made ... more powerful than thyself; my height is superior to thine; my joints more supple" (66). Moreover, Victor witnesses the monster perform nearly impossible physical feats such as quickly climbing up icy precipices, moving at "superhuman speed," and surviving in even the most inhospitable environments, while the monster himself describes surviving a gunshot wound to the shoulder (65). The creature is thus, a "monster" because he deviates from the norm, not in being inferior but in being superior — demonstrating the dangerous limits of the norm, and also demonstrating why his monstrousness horrifies while Victor's arouses compassion.

The monster is also socially and narratively horrifying because he, unlike Victor, resists the conventions of the masturbation narrative with his horrifyingly vital body. The monster bears the external marks of his creator's moral failing, but the absence of any physical deterioration troubles the narratives that link moral and physical debility. Like those masturbators who had come before him, Victor eventually dies as a result of his ill-advised, passionate and (improperly) willful pursuit of his single-minded project. In keeping with those normative narratives of autoerotic debility, Victor's body must pay the price for his over-indulged sensibilities. The monster, however, the surprisingly successful outcome of Victor's deviant practices, fares better. It is the monster who retains his strength and vigor until the very end of the novel: his non-normative endurance a reproach to Enlightenment standards that ultimately limit the possibilities of the human.

NOTES

1. Other equally colorful euphemisms for the practice of masturbation include: "the deed of personal enjoyment" (*A Short Treatise on Onanism*), "secret and excessive venery," "filthy practice," "vile manoeuvre," "manual pollution," "solitary debauch" and predating, by four years, Rousseau's similar description of masturbation as "the dangerous supplement" in *The Confessions* (1770), the "horrid supplement" (*Onanism*). In fact, as Thomas Laqueur points out in *Solitary Sex*, Tissot and Rousseau became correspondents shortly after Tissot sent the French novelist a copy of *Onanism*, having approved of Rousseau's take on the solitary vice.

2. See Stengers and Van Neck *Masturbation: The History of a Great Terror* for one of the first investigations of masturbation as discussed in medical discourse. Stengers and Van Neck credit Tissot as the first to promote the theory that terror could cure a patient of masturbation.

3. This author has been "outed" by Thomas Laqueur as the publisher John Marten. See *Solitary Sex*.

4. Especially useful for anyone interested in the cultural history of masturbation is Thomas Laqueur's study *Solitary Sex* (2003). His analyses of *Onania* as well as of Tissot's *Onanism* are particularly compelling.

5. Because it was seen to waste vital fluids, upon which the body depended in order to survive, masturbation was popularly considered by contemporary texts as a suicidal vice. See Barker-Benefield "The Spermatic Economy: A Nineteenth Century View of Sexuality" for a consideration of the economic metaphor inherent in medical accounts of masturbation as well as Thomas Laqueur "Masturbation, Credit, and the Novel During the Long Eighteenth Century" which complicates Benefield's original thesis regarding the discourse of spermatic scarcity.

6. Some eighteenth-century texts do express a skepticism regarding the ability of a body to accurately depict the vagaries of the individual mind. Fittingly, Mary Shelley's mother, Mary Wollstonecraft, resists this linkage in *A Vindication of the Rights of Woman*. It should be noted, however, that Wollstonecraft assisted in the translation of a text which condemned the practice of masturbation, and that she is part of a tradition of authors who decry the practice (see *Solitary Sex*). Wollstonecraft's condemnation suggests that the more "dangerous ... deformity" is not that which is visible but, rather, the unseen vices which could be concealed under the misleading mantle of exterior polish and ornament. It is precisely this uneasy balance between "deformity" and normalcy which the discourse of masturbation had sought, earlier in the century, to clarify.

7. Tissot's text, *An Essay on Diseases Incidental to Literary and Sedentary Persons*, warns young men of the ill effects of study: "studious men ... grow pale with poring over books ... the first symptom is languor, and a love of indolence; then the understanding begins to grow dull, the memory to flag; they become sleepy, stupid, and often continue a long time in that state before their death" (39 n).

8. Nearly a century later the concern that excess study enabled masturbation continued to appear in medical texts. The famous doctor William Acton, who supported the Contagious Diseases Act, wrote of "Hard study ... as predisposing to this condition" (272).

9. G. Barker-Benefield has written about what he has called "the spermatic economy" in his study *The Horrors of the Half-Known Life*.

10. In *Sex Scandal* William Cohen suggests that sexual transgressions are often inserted into seemingly neutral texts via "signifying practices," or euphemistic language which skirts outright depictions of sexuality. See especially his chapter "Manual Conduct in *Great Expectations*."

11. The graphic description of Victor's failing health not only links solitary practices to physical ailment, but is further complicated by the discourse of both class and race when he likens his suffering to that he would experience under the yolk of slavery, performing manual labor in mines. Tissot's linkage of self-subjection to slavery appears in *Diseases Incidental to Literary and Sedentary Persons*: "a constant habit is real slavery ... minds seemed to be chained to ... bodies, which is the most shameful sort of servitude" (76).

12. A late nineteenth-century example of this discourse may be found in Joseph Howe's medical text *Excessive Venery, Masturbation, and Continence* (1887) wherein Howe explains that a masturbator is easily obsessed by one idea, and that this repetitive fantasy is precisely at the center of his disease. "His mind continually dwells on his affliction," Howe explains, "and he is unable to concentrate his attention on any other subject. All the minutae of the dreams are continually before him.... He is restless at night and troubled with frequent nightmares" (210).

13. A concern with the idealized male body has been examined by cultural historians such as G. Barker-Benfield and Thomas Laqueur. Their early excavations into the realm of masculinity have paved the way for more recent explorations of male health and the discourse of nationhood, many of which consider how the ability, or inability, of a male to properly (physically and mentally) function is a central concern.

14. In "Time is Sick and Out of Joint" Cindy Lacom suggests that the body's potential to work, or its failure to do so, was an important distinguishing factor for Victorians who were increasingly concerned with the economic progress and prowess of the British Empire. Gesturing towards Victor's monster as an example of an individual with a disability, Lacom posits that the negative public reaction the monster experiences is "prompted not by his physical monstrousness but by his resistance to an economic and colonial enterprise, a resistance that alienates him from human communion because he will not or cannot participate in a marketplace economy that commodifies human bodies and subjectivity" (548). What Lacom seems to suggest here is that it is not the markers of physical difference which keep the monster from becoming an active (and, it follows, productive) masculine member of society, but rather the social difference that is indicated by his insistence on providing anonymous assistance to the De Lacey family. By refusing to take part in an economy which demands that he benefit at the cost of others and that he, in turn, work for sustenance, Lacom suggests, the monster dis-ables himself socially.

15. It is telling that even when Walton imagines the young, healthy Victor, he continues to use the term "creature." to describe Victor, a term which Victor himself uses to categorize his monstrous creation. Walton echoes this sentiment and language after hearing Victor's tale, imagining that the now-dying scientist had been "a glorious creature ... in the days of his prosperity, when he is so noble and godlike in ruin" (147). What is espe-

cially meaningful about Walton's conclusion is that he draws upon the standard binary of illness and health. Seeing the ill form of the man, he fills in the blank in the binary to imagine the same man in a state of health.

WORKS CITED

Acton, William. *The Functions and Disorders of the Reproductive Organs*. London, 1871.

Barker-Benfield, G. "The Spermatic Economy: A Nineteenth Century View of Sexuality." *Feminist Studies* 1 (1972): 45–74.

Foucault, Michel. *Abnormal*. New York: Picador, 2003.

Gregory, Samuel. *Facts and Important Information for Young Women, on the Subject of Masturbation; with its Causes, Prevention, and Cure*. 1845. *The Secret Vice Exposed! Some Arguments Against Masturbation*. Ed. Charles Rosenberg and Carroll Smith-Rosenberg. New York: Arno Press, 1974.

Halberstam, Judith. *Skin Shows: Gothic Horror and the Technology of Monsters*. Durham: Duke University Press, 1995.

Hunt, Alan. "The Great Masturbation Panic and the Discourses of Moral Regulation in Nineteenth- And Early Twentieth-Century Britain." *The Journal of the History of Sexuality* 8 (1998): 575–615.

Lacom, Cindy. "'The Time Is Sick and Out of Joint': Physical Disability in Victorian England." *PMLA* 120 (2005): 547–542.

Laqueur, Thomas. "Masturbation, Credit, and the Novel During the Long Eighteenth Century." *Qui Parle* 9 (1995): 1–19.

_____. *Solitary Sex*. New York: Zone Books, 2003.

Onania; or the Heinous Sin of Self-Pollution. New York: Garland, 1986.

Shelley, Mary. *Frankenstein*. New York: Norton Critical Edition, 1996.

Stengers, Jean, and Anne Van Neck. *Masturbation: The History of a Great Terror*. Trans. Kathryn A. Hoffman. New York: Palgrave, 2001.

Tissot, Samuel August. *Onanism, or, a Treatise Upon the Disorders Produced by Masturbation: or, the Dangerous Effects of Secret and Excessive Venery*. 1766. Trans. A. Hume. Garland: New York, 1985.

Wollstonecraft, Mary. *A Vindication of the Rights of Women*. New York: Norton, 1988.

Invasion and Contagion: The Spectacle of the Diseased Indian in Poe's "The Masque of the Red Death"

RUTH BIENSTOCK ANOLIK

"I Bring Death": The Disappearance of the Native American

Saynday,[1] the trickster figure of Kiowa[2] folk-tales returns to his Native American village to discover that it has changed: "white-faced" cattle have replaced the buffalo; "the clear water was soggy with red mud; gone are the deer and antelope, and the tipis." This change, of course, is the result of the white settlers whose "soddies dented the hillsides and the creek banks" ("I Bring Death" 51). However this degeneration and destruction is just the prelude for an even greater threat that is on the way. On the horizon, Saynday sees a "dark spot" advancing from the east. As the spot gets closer, Saynday sees that it is a man on a black horse, wearing a black suit and "a high hat, like a missionary's." Red dust "spotted" both man and horse. Saynday can see that beneath the dust, "the man's face was pitted with terrible scars" (51). Lest there be any uncertainty regarding the man's identify, he announces to Saynday:

> I'm Smallpox.... I come from far away, across the Eastern Ocean.... I am one with the white men — they are my people.... I bring death.... My breath causes children to wither like young plants in spring snow. I bring destruction. No matter how beautiful a woman is, once she has looked at me she becomes as ugly as death. And to men I bring not death alone, but the destruction of their children and the blighting of their wives [52].

The personified Smallpox thus vividly details what the devastation wreaked by smallpox, and by the settlers who spread it, looked like from the Native American point of view.

The clinical accuracy of the description of the disease is notable. The red spots on man and horse allude to "the characteristic smallpox rash ... flat, red spots (lesions)" <MayoClinic.Com>. The personified Smallpox comes from across the Atlantic, and then continues to travel westward with the white missionaries; since missionaries were often the precursor of the settlers, and for many Native Americans the first whites to whom they were exposed, and since smallpox did, indeed, travel over the ocean from Europe, the theory of the legend, that the missionary is the source of the disease, is ironic, but quite plausible. Additionally the tale informs us that the personified Smallpox is attracted to a bigger population because he can kill more people: "I can do my best work when people are crowded together" (53)—a clinical reality of all plagues.

The accuracy of these details attests to the long and intimate experience of the Kiowa people — and other Native Americans — with smallpox. As Calloway explains in his notes, the legend "is clearly a creation of the late nineteenth century by which time the Kiowas had had plenty of experience with the disease" (50). This experience probably began as early as 1779[3] reaching a climax in the late 1830s. Robertson notes that "Among the Kiowas December 1839 through February 1840 is remembered as *T·dalkop Sia*—the smallpox winter" (281). This was the last outbreak of the great epidemic that decimated many Native American Tribes in 1837. The "smallpox winter" is memorialized by the Kiowas in the calendar pictograph for Winter 1839–40.[4] This pictograph (which may be found in Mooney 274) displays, in the conventions of the genre, a simple stylized representation of the major event of the period: a single image stands for the long verbal narrative of an entire year of events. The main figure is a man, portrayed by a simple line drawing; he is covered from head to toe with spots. The simple visual figure of the pictograph, like the single figure in the tale suggests that in Kiowa culture both the pictorial tradition and the oral tradition depend upon a common strategy of synecdoche, concentrating much meaning within a single representative figure. Both the image and the tale of smallpox emblematize the disease with great economy: a single figure bearing red spots represents the menacing, pervasive and invisible danger, distilled and projected onto a single figure. Similarly, the single ill figure in the pictograph elides the great number of Kiowas who were subject to the plague.[5]

In fact, the number of Native Americans from many tribes killed by the "High plains smallpox epidemic of 1837" (Brown 2) was overwhelming. Mooney records: "the great smallpox epidemic which began on the upper Missouri in the summer of 1837 and swept the whole plains north and south, destroying probably a third, if not more of the native inhabitants, some whole tribes being nearly exterminated" (274). Ironically, the spread of the disease

was probably exacerbated by the movement of wandering Indian tribes, resulting from forced migrations. The period of Indian Removal, when Native
Americans were forcibly relocated from their ancestral lands, lasted from
approximately 1824 until 1850. The Indian Removal Act passed by Congress
in 1830, legitimized this exile, leading to killings and forced marches, although
Mooney (writing in 1898) blithely describes this exile as Indian tribes "emi-
grating" to "Indian Territory in the spring of 1838" (275). As the history of
the Kiowas indicates, the great epidemic of the later 1830's was only one of
many waves to sweep away the Native American population and culture.
Indeed, most contemporary historians acknowledge that it was smallpox and
other disease rather than military force that ultimately worked to defeat the
Native American people. The consequence was that the Native American was,
to use a term drawn from more recent cataclysm, "disappeared."

We Bring Death: White Guilt and Its Repressions

While the Native Americans were being literally erased from the land,
they were simultaneously being erased from the cultural artifacts of white
American Society. As Lucy Maddox asserts in *Removals*, the removal of the
native population from American territory was paralleled by their exile from
nineteenth-century American literature. Perhaps the Native Americans were
disappearing from the American text, or perhaps they remained, invisible and
repressed. Traces of repressed anxiety and guilt about the atrocities being carried out for the purpose of national expansion are certainly evident in nineteenth-century narratives. The wide proliferation of smallpox blanket stories,
none of which stand up to scrutiny, may be explained by the phenomenon
of white guilt. One of the earliest and most prevalent of these legends, now
discredited by most historians, centers on the supposed order given by the
British Commander Amherst in 1763 to "infect Indians by presenting them
with blankets used by smallpox victims" (Mayor 57). Later versions tend to
invert the story and to displace the blame onto the Native American. Mayor
argues in the section of her essay entitled "Identifying with the Poisoner;
Blaming the Victim," that many "efforts to explain, deflect, or minimize the
colonists' guilt are prominent in historical accounts of smallpox" (68). The
strategy of these stories, as Mayor indicates, is to blame the victim instead of
the perpetrator. The thieving Native American, coveting blankets he does not
own, is responsible for the spread of disease, rather than the invading and
infected white settler who conquers Indian land. Mayor adds, "compassion
for victims is tinged with hints about their ... duplicity" (69). This strategy
is visible in a poison blanket narrative that places the blame for the "High

plains smallpox epidemic of 1837" (Brown 2) upon the Native Americans. "Historians agreed that smallpox was brought to the High Plains in 1837 aboard the steamboat *St Peter's* as it made its annual voyage up the Missouri River" (2). Brown records eye-witness accounts of Indians stealing infected blankets off the ship. Robertson disputes the St. Louis story, calling the accounts "rumors" that might be attributed to "white guilt" (300). The historical veracity of these stories may be difficult to prove, but they are undeniably important in demonstrating the level of white guilt and anxiety within the white American population. Edwin J. McCallister uncovers a fascinating instance of the development of this displacement and repression of white guilt in "Smallpox, Opium, and Invasion: Chinese Invasion, and Native American Displacement...." McCallister describes the cover illustration on a February 1879 *Harper's Weekly*, showing a "Chinese man and a Native American man looking over a poster featuring [an] Irish-American labor leader." The slogan reads: "'The Chinese Must Go!' The Native American observes to the Chinese man, 'Pale face 'fraid you crowd him out as he did to me'" (143). McCallister asserts that the poster "exposes anxieties among white middle-class America" that a new wave of immigrants would replace them, as they replaced the native peoples, and connects this fear to "the white guilt regarding the displacement of Native Americans" (145), a guilt that was itself displaced and repressed.[6]

Scholarly Repression

The erasure of the figure of the Native American from the land, the record of history and the record of literature — as well as the repression of expressions of white guilt — is reflected and perpetuated in the repression of the Native American from scholarly accounts of nineteenth-century literature. As Maddox asserts, "the one significant blind spot in *most* readings of nineteenth-century American literature has been the failure to take seriously the presence of the American Indians as a factor in the shaping of the literature" (173). It is possible that this blind spot is a consequence of the shadow cast by the powerful influence of Toni Morrison's essay, "Romancing the Shadow" (1992), which makes the cogent, and for its time revolutionary, argument that the darkness of American literature, particularly Poe, encodes the presence of a dark enslaved people who help Americans define themselves in opposition as free men. Yet Morrison's tight focus leads her to repress and to displace the figure of the Native American, reading the Indian as a code for the "primary" racial Other, the African American.[7] The full force of Morrison's elision comes at the moment when she appears to open the door to the figure of the Native American: "Why is it [the American land] seen as raw and savage. Because it is peopled by a nonwhite indigenous population? Perhaps. But certainly because there is ready to hand a bound and unfree, rebellious but serviceable, black population" (45).[8] With that dismissive "perhaps," with that absolute "certainly," the figure of the Native American disappears from the essay and consequently from the work of other critics influenced by Morrison.[9]

This critical lacuna is filled by scholars like Justin D. Edwards, who recognizes that the Gothic Native American in American literature is not necessarily a code for another people, but instead represents a real people with a real history. Although Edward's consideration of Poe's novel *Pym* calls attention "to the anxieties of potential bloody conflicts between blacks and whites, slaves and masters" (3), he quickly moves to a reading that allows for the presence of the Native American, and others, in the text. Focusing on Poe's language, Edwards observes that the "savage" Tsalal natives "have the ordinary 'stature of Europeans or Indians'.... Native American imagery, moreover, is present in their garments and possessions: they wore 'skins of an ... animal' ... and they possess canoes" (Edwards 10). Thus, as Edwards concludes, the Tsasals are "a confused racial farrago" (10), including the Native American in their mix. Perhaps a critical influence for Edwards is Leslie Fiedler whose *Return of the Vanishing American*, contains a discussion of *Pym* that emphasizes Dirk Peters's status as a Native American. In fact Fiedler reads *Pym* as "an account of the opening of the West, though Pym is heading *South*" (130). In Fiedler's reading, Pym's relationship with Peters "is as close as Poe is ever to come to the essential myth of male companionship triumphing over hostility between the races" (131).

From Repression to Spectralization and Demonization

As Renée L. Bergland argues in *The National Uncanny*, a literary consequence of repression is spectralization. Bergland's book proposes to "examine one specific discursive technique of Indian removal — describing them as insubstantial, disembodied, and finally spectral beings" (3). Bergland explains: "During the removal, Native Americans were described as 'vanished' far more often than they were described as vanquished" (149). In fact, "during the nineteenth century ... American national discourse insisted that Native Americans were extinct, that they did not exist, or that they existed as representatives of the past.... The same discourse denied Indians political existence....In 1831 ... the Supreme Court opined that the Cherokee people ... had no American civil identity" (15) — the Native American was thus, like the slave, a non-person. Because the Native American has been erased and repressed from history and from culture, "for more than three hundred years, American literature has been haunted by ghostly Indians ...When European Americans speak of Native Americans, they always use the language of ghostliness" (1). Bergland's insights are, of course, anticipated by D. H. Lawrence's invocation of the spirits of "the Red Man" (40), "the unappeased ghosts of the dead Indians" (41). Although the Native American remains, he remains as an invisible, haunting ghost.

When the Native American did actually make an active appearance in American literature,[10] he was represented as a monster. Goddu's discussion of the non-canonical John Neal's *Logan* (1822), illustrates the demonized — spectacularly and materially horrifying — Indian. Neal describes his Indian character as a "bloodthirsty demon," a "savage" (Goddu 67) as well as "the unappeased ghost of the American landscape" (68). As Goddu notes, Neal also uses the gothicized language of spectacular horror in a short story, "Otter-Bag, the Oneida Chief" (1829), in which, as Goddu observes, "The Indian is only present as a trace: 'a skeleton of a race that is no more'" (58).

Red Death

Previous readings of "The Masque of the Red Death" (1842) by Edgar Allan Poe exemplify the invisibility of the Native American in nineteenth century literature and criticism. There is much evidence that Red Death is the emblem of both the Native American, and the disease that wiped him out — thus echoing the economy of the Kiowa imagery.[11] The critical neglect of this evidence suggests another example of the guilty repression of the Native American from studies of nineteenth-century literature.[12] A reading of "Red Death" that is attuned to the presence of the Red Indian, reveals the return of the repressed and diseased red man, and opens up possibilities of shedding light on this shadowy figure. While Neal's "Otter-Bag" imagines the skeletal Indian as the dead remnant of a living body, Poe reanimates that skeleton. His narrative thus taps into his favorite Gothic trope: the return of the dead.

The critical debate surrounding the diagnosis of Poe's plague attests to the invisibility of the Native American in this story; critical diagnoses range from cholera to bubonic plague but the diagnosis of smallpox has not yet appeared.[13] The various posited diagnoses point to an act of critical repression, considering that Poe's story was published in 1842, and that smallpox raged among the Indians in the 1830's. Of course, Poe encourages this confusion, through the ambiguity and even the impossibility of the symptoms of the plague — the symptom of immediate death does not have a clinical corollary, an indication perhaps that the story itself works to repress the diagnosis of smallpox. It is, however, possible to posit a diagnosis for this mysterious plague, and thereby identify the figure of Red Death, by reading "The Masque of the Red Death" side by side with "I Bring Death," a story that presents smallpox and its spread in no uncertain terms. This comparison does not in any way suggest that the stories have any relationship with each other beyond an uncanny mirrored resemblance. Each text responds to the same historical phenomenon: the death of countless Indians from the smallpox spread by the whites, although the Kiowa's despairing legend comes from the perspective of the victim and Poe's anxious story from the perspective of the perpetuator. When the two texts are read together, significant parallels appear. Both stories spend much narrative energy describing the emblem of small-pox. The economy of both stories, and of the Kiowa pictograph, results in a single concentrated emblem that expresses the full import of innumerable deaths. In fact, Poe's single image is the more efficient, in that it signifies the *disease* portrayed by Smallpox in the Kiowa story, and the *diseased*, portrayed by the figure in the Kiowa calendar pictograph. In Poe's "Masque," as in the Kiowa legend what little narrative energy that remains is expended on a sin-gle act: the movement of the emblem of smallpox from east to west.

    That both texts concentrate upon a single overpowering figure that emblematizes the disease is not particularly surprising or significant; the visi-ble personification of an invisible source of horror and death is a common strat-egy in narratives of infectious disease and other invisible dangers. It is psychologically comforting to visualize and thereby localize and contain invis-ible danger. Of greater significance is the correspondence between the Kiowa description of Smallpox, encroaching upon Kiowa land and Poe's costumed party-crasher. Both invasions of space gesture to the biological movement of smallpox as it invades the body. Poe's specter appears uninvited at the "masked ball" that Prince Prospero stages for his aristocratic friends which allows Poe to point to the duplicitous nature of invisible contagion. Before symptoms appear disease appears in the guise of a healthy person. Only after the contagious period passes do the symptoms emerge, belatedly identifying the sufferer as a source of contagion.[14] The ball is held within a "castellated abbey," to which the "thou-sand friends," have fled, in retreat from the "Red Death," the "fatal" and "hideous" plague that is wiping out the population of the prince's dominions. As for his subjects, outside the abbey walls, "the external world could take care of itself" (461). Prospero attempts to avert the invasion of his body by disease by setting up a "wall [that] had gates of iron" (461), their bolts welded shut.

    The costume which the Red Death wears to the masquerade — a masked "visage" which resembles "the countenance of a stiffened corpse" (464), "the habiliments of the grave" (463) — transgresses the very fluid code of the ball: "In truth the masquerade license of the night was nearly unlimited; but the figure in question had out–Heroded Herod, and gone beyond the bounds of

even the prince's indefinite decorum (463). The shockingly transgressive costume evokes "disapprobation and surprise" and finally "terror, or horror, and
... disgust" (463) because the figure enacts the scandalous return of that which
the prince and his courtiers are trying to repress: the plague that lurks outside the abbey walls. Red Death's transgressive "costume" recalls the major
features of the Kiowa description of Smallpox: redness and red spots, upon
a black background. The redness of the Kiowa Smallpox is highlighted by the
dark backdrop of the missionary's suit and black horse. Poe's Red Death is
also provided with the black background of death: the black room, in which
Red Death eventually begins his killing. In fact the horror of the room is
derived from the intermingling of the red (of blood? of smallpox?) with the
black of death. Although the room is hung and furnished all in black, "the
panes here were scarlet — a deep blood color." Torches in the hall outside send
their light through the red panes into the room, creating an effect "that was
ghastly in the extreme" (462).

More significantly the figure of Red Death bears the spotted symptoms
that characterize the Kiowa Smallpox. What frightens the revelers most is that
"his vesture was dabbled blood"— and his "face was besprinkled with the scarlet horror" (464). The dabbled blood and the scarlet horror sprinkled on the
face suggest the red spots that typify smallpox, both clinically and in the Kiowa
tale. Thus it is possible to see the redness of Poe's plague as encoding not blood,
but the blood-red spots of smallpox. Admittedly the opening description of the
Red Death focuses on the image of blood: "Blood was its Avatar and its seal —
the redness and the horror of blood." Yet, as the sentence indicates, the fearful
signs of the plague are not blood itself but the "redness" and the "horror"— the
signs of smallpox. The narrator continues "the scarlet stains upon the body and
especially on the face of the victim were the pest ban which shut him out" (461),
a sentence that suggests the social response to the overt signs of smallpox. Even
the most horrifying symptom: "profuse bleeding at the pores" (461)— could
be read as an excessively graphic metaphor for the red spots of the disease.

The Movement of the Red Death

The great care with which Poe describes the setting of his story, and his
attentive delineation of the cardinal directions of the rooms of Prospero's suite
provide additional evidence for the identification of Poe's plague as smallpox,
especially when contextualized with the significance of the points of direction
in the Kiowa legend. Certainly there are many spectacular details in the description of Prospero's decadently lush suite that are worthy of close consideration:
the famous colored rooms, lit by torchlight shining through their interior win-

dows, "the ebony clock" that stands in the "black chamber" which lies at the end of Prospero's colorful labyrinth in which "the apartments were "irregularly disposed....There was a sharp turn at every twenty or thirty yards" (462). Yet these details ultimately create a sense of what du Plessis calls "deliberate chaos" (41): the colors resist attempts to discover deeper meanings. They do not represent the days of the week (Malbott), or the seven ages of man, or the seven deadly sins. They signify nothing more than "the author's desire to represent aesthetic chaos and disorder" (du Plessix 41), the fevered dream of delirium.

What is exact and meaningful is the specification of the cardinal points of the suite. We are reminded more than once that Prospero's colorful labyrinth extends from east to west.[15] The narrator observes that "the eastern extremity was hung ... in blue," evoking the blue sky of sunrise, contrasting with the "western or black chamber" (462), hung in the colors of black night. The very specific movement of the Red Death — no ambiguity here — is identical to the movement of the Kiowa Smallpox, and of the disease smallpox, from east to west. This directional emphasis provides additional information that works to support the diagnosis of Poe's plague. In the Kiowa legend, both Saynday and Smallpox himself comment upon the movement of smallpox from the east, movement that was directly linked to the geographically invasive spread of the disease. Saynday wonders about this fact. When he sees a "dark spot coming toward him from the east," he thinks to himself: "That's strange.... The East is the place of birth and of new life" (51). Not, of course, in the case of smallpox, that as the Kiowa author(s) knew, also moved from east to west. Poe's narrator emphasizes the direction of the movement from east to west: "it was in the eastern or blue chamber in which stood the Prince Prospero" that he first glimpses the red specter. On his part, the Red Death moves with a "deliberate and stately step" through the blue chamber to the purple," through all the colored chambers — moving thus from east to west — until he attains the western "extremity of the velvet apartment" where Propero, also moving from east to west, encounters him and meets his death. The grand movement of Prospero and the Red Death, really the only movement in a story taken up by the description of the rooms and of the revels, so closely follows the pattern of geographical movement of Smallpox in the Kiowa tale, and smallpox in American and Native American history, that it is hard to imagine a more satisfying diagnosis for Poe's plague.

The Return of the Red Indian

As the similarity between the Kiowa representations of the disease in the legend and the victim in the pictograph indicates, only a short conceptual step is required to move from figuring the illness to figuring the sufferer. As Susan Sontag argues, this slippage leads to the misconception that the person with the disease is, like the disease itself, an inhuman enemy. In discussing her objection to the war metaphor applied to the treatment of disease, Sontag notes: "The metaphor implements the way particularly dreaded diseases are envisaged as an alien 'other,' as enemies are in modern war; and the move from the demonization of the illness to the attribution of fault to the patient is an inevitable one" (99). Thus the sufferer of the disease becomes the dangerous Other, the cause rather than the victim of the disease — a process evident in the smallpox blanket narratives. The demonization of the sick could be explained as a protective measure, keeping the healthy from the sick who *may* be a source of infection. Yet since many infectious diseases are not readily communicated by contact with a symptomatic individual, the othering of the victim works mostly in a magical way, creating a distinct boundary between diseased Other and the observer, to secure the location of the observer on the healthy side of the health/illness binary.[16]

Poe's Red Death is thus, not only the Red Disease but also the diseased Red Indian. His costume — the shroud, the death mask — references not just the fatal consequences of the disease, but also the current situation of the Indian, a people that was already consider dead and gone. As Bergland observes, "the Red Death is the ultimate Indian ghost, the disembodied phantom of inescapable racial hatred" (118). He is, indeed, ghostly, in that his costume is "untenanted by any tangible form," evoking "unutterable horror" (464) in the revelers who discover this. But in addition to being an insubstantial, though powerful ghost, he also takes on a visibly monstrous form[17]: a killer wearing a blood-splashed shroud and a cadaverous mask.

"Masque" is, then, another instance of anxious displacement, like the blanket stories, in which the Other is also associated with the origins of the disease. Like the Kiowa tale — in which Smallpox is (accurately) displaced onto the Other, the invading missionary, "Masque" displaces the responsibility for smallpox onto the Native American, the Other of white America. Thus Poe's story reveals a guilty fear of just revenge, a fear that the dead and diseased Indian will rise from the grave — emerge from repression — to wreak spectacular vengeance, an appropriately "wild justice" (to borrow from Francis Bacon), for a supposedly wild and savage people. This is, then, not merely the return of the repressed; it is the uprising of the repressed.

The Joyous Return of the Repressed

At the conclusion of Poe's story, we are told that "Darkness and Decay and the Red Death held illimitable dominion over all" (464) — but this is the understanding of events from the perspective of the previously dominant Prince Prospero and his courtiers, the European Americans. A reading of Poe's story as the revenge of the Native American indicates that there is a sort of subversive joy to be found in the story, though not perhaps for Poe and for his nineteenth-century American readers. One source of this joy is apparent when we consider another Poe story of disability and vengeance, "Hop Frog" (1849) as well as the Kiowa "I Bring Death." In each of these stories, the abject and repressed wreak their wild justice, to a satisfyingly happy effect. The Kiowa legend ends with a revenge fantasy. Kiowa sends Smallpox off to the Pawnee — a richer, bigger enemy — encircling his own village with protective fire to prevent the return of the now-abjected disease: "'Perhaps I can still be some good to my people after all,' Sayday said to himself feeling better." The narrator concludes: "And that's the way it was, and that's the way it is, to this good day" (53). Poe's "Hop-Frog," also presents an unambiguous account of just revenge: the title character, a misshapen dwarf (who is also dehumanized by the narrative voice — he is at various moments, a frog, a squirrel and a monkey, a creature with "powerful and very repulsive teeth" [265]), takes a horrible revenge on a tyrannical king, a "monster" (265), and on his equally cruel advisors, who enslave and torture him because he is a foreigner and a dwarf.[18] Although the dwarf is clearly the figure of the grotesque and the inhuman Other — at his triumph, there emerges a grating sound from the "fang-like teeth of the dwarf, who ground them and gnashed them as he foamed at the mouth and glared, with an expression of maniacal rage" (267) — there is a sense of narrative joy when the dwarf escapes, presumably back to his home. The joy is amplified when we remember that in an earlier scene the narrator has informed us that the dwarf misses his "absent friends" (264), especially on this day, his birthday.

Even a superficial reading of "Masque," locates it in the paradigm developed by the other two stories: the just revenge of the oppressed. The thoughtlessly evil aristocrats who abandon their people to the plague, are killed by the very same disease. This reading would certainly appeal to the young America that was still working through its trauma with the old English aristocracy and trying to avoid falling into a new American aristocratic system. A reading of the Red Death as the unfairly injured Native American also results in a sense of readerly satisfaction on the part of modern readers. This satisfying reading of the monstrous Red Death aligns with Cixous's joyous reading of the powerful monster, emerging from repression and invisibility, in "The Laugh of the Medusa" (1976), and with Gilbert and Gubar's reading of the monster as the emblem of uncontained liberation in *The Madwoman in the Attic* (1979). These women were writing in the 1970s about the joyous and subversive power that feminist critics were discovering in the newly visible female writers and their characters. Their insights apply to the newly visible Native American in Poe's story. Here is the historically, culturally and critically repressed Native American — rendered as Other because of his foreign and diseased status — reversing the process of invasion and death, "stalk[ing] to and fro" (464), in the halls of his oppressor, avenging the deaths of his people: a fantastic moment of wild justice that could only occur in the transgressive and liberated space of the Gothic, the genre that sheds its garish light on the invisible and on the repressed.

NOTES

1. Parsons explains that there are many stories about this trickster: "Sendeh is a medicine-man and is called upon to revive the moribund." To the Kiowa, "Sendeh was the first person in the world. He is our human prototype" (Parsons xvi).

2. The Kiowas are a Native American tribe of the southern Plains. They probably "left the Montana high country of the Yellowstone after 1682.... By this time they had acquired horses and moved out into the Great Plains.... According to legend, the Kiowas journeyed eastward into the Black Hills of South Dakota. From here they ventured southward into Wyoming ... moving to Kansas, Colorado and Oklahoma, staying and settling in the Southern Plains [in the nineteenth century]" (Palmer 3–4).

3. Calloway speculates that the Kiowas "could not have escaped the epidemic of 1779–81 on the plains" (50). They were also badly hurt by the smallpox epidemic of 1801–02. As Robertson notes, they lost culture and "social order" (194), as well as people: "traditional crafts and cultural links with the past disappeared amid fevers and blistered skin" (194–195). There were likely other epidemics in 1816 and 1819, "probably communicated from Spanish settlements" (Mooney 168). The greatest was the epidemic of 1839–40. "Smallpox continued to plague the Kiowas as late as 1899–1901" (Calloway 50), at which time the United States government instituted smallpox vaccinations for Plains Indians, including the Kiowas, "to protect them from the smallpox which had recently decimated them" (Mooney 177).

4. Mooney further describes the graphic documentation of Kiowa history: "the pictograph record covering periods of from sixty to perhaps two hundred years or more ... compiled by the priests and preserved with sacred care through all the shifting vicissitudes of savage [sic] life until lost or destroyed in the ruin that overwhelmed the native governments at the coming of the white man" (Mooney 141). At the time Mooney wrote "the Dakota calendars and the Kiowa calendars here reproduced are the only ones yet discovered among the prairie tribes" (143). Another smallpox pictograph, for another smallpox winter, 1861–62, may also be found in Mooney (311).

5. In writing of the contemporary Kiowa writer N. Scott Momaday, William M. Clements notes that the calendar pictographs demonstrate the Kiowa tendency to link word and image, so that word and image exist in an "aesthetic symbiosis" (142), with the image used to "stimulate the literary imagination" 141). For more on strategies of Kiowa tales see Palmer.

6. McCallister argues that guilt is then displaced from the white subject to the Chinese object. White America, in fearing Chinese invasion and significantly, the smallpox invasion that might follow, "began to imagine the same kind of racial holocaust happening to them, the sins of the fathers being visited on the sons" (147). McCallister adds that "the fear of Chinese using opium to seduce and destroy whites ... helped to displace white guilt over the sale of alcohol to Native Americans" (151). It is also possible to see the ves-

tiges of the old tale of smallpox-infested blankets in a story McCallister cites, "The Canton Shawl," appearing in *Overland Monthly Magazine* in 1914. In this story a white American infects his Spanish lover with smallpox by presenting her with a shawl given to him by a Chinese courtesan (148). The resemblance of this tale to Hawthorne's story, "Lady Eleanore's Mantle" (1838) reveals the power these myths had over the American imagination. The date of Hawthorne's story invites a closer look at this response to the Native American smallpox epidemic.

7. This repression is noticeable when Morrison reads the whiteness and blackness in Edgar Allan Poe's *The Narrative of Arthur Gordon Pym*, as encoding racial whiteness and blackness in America, without considering the presence of redness. In ignoring the figure of the Native Americans, Morrison participates in the cultural erasure of this group. Discussing the goals of the white European settlers, she ironically imagines their notion of the new world as lacking history, "a blank page waiting to be inscribed" (18), without noting what or who had been erased to make the page blank. Comparing William Dunbar to Faulkner's William Sutpen in *Absalom! Absalom!* Morison argues that both settlers "built an estate where before there had been nothing but trees and uncultivated soil" (40). The Native American had also been there but Morrison neglects to mention this detail.

8. Morrison's comment reveals a certain tone-deafness here. As Goddu demonstrates the word "savage" was directly related to the Indian: "savagism argued that in the wake of progress's inevitable forward movement Indians were doomed to extinction" (55).

9. The title of Kennedy and Weissberg's collection, *Romancing the Shadow: Poe and Race*, (alluding, of course, to the essay of the same name in Morrison's *Playing in the Dark*), illustrates the powerful influence of Toni Morrison on racial critiques of nineteenth-century American literature. The editors frankly acknowledge that the "volume is indebted to Toni Morrison's reflections on American literature and received its instigation from her book, *Playing in the Dark*" (Acknowledgements v). As a consequence, a majority of the essays in the collection focus on Poe's representation of the African American, although a more heterogeneous approach is suggested by the subtitle. This lends a poignant power to the suggestion to broaden scholarly investigation of Poe and race and to include Poe and the Native American that appears in John Carlos Rowe's essay, "Poe's Imperial Fantasy and the American Frontier." Rowe points to "the similarities between the Southern colonization of Africans and more general U.S. efforts to colonize the frontier by subjugating its native peoples" (77). In considering Dirk Peters, the (deformed) Native American character in *The Narrative of Arthur Gordon Pym of Nantucket* (the first chapters of which were published in early 1837), Rowe initially acknowledge that Pym represents Native Americans, but then he wavers, arguing that Peters "shares physical characters [of deformity] with Poe's black characters" (85), and that he illustrates a racial confusion common to the period, that placed all non-white races in the same catch-all category of Other. Teresa Goddu follows a similar pattern in her chapter entitled "The Ghost of Race: Edgar Allan Poe and the Southern Gothic" that appears in her seminal work, *Gothic America*. Goddu expresses her indebtedness to Morrison: "this chapter takes up Morrison's call" (75), persuasively documenting Poe's racism as a "proslavery Southerner" (78) and criticizes his "racial politics" (78), meaning in this case, his attitude towards slavery. Even when Goddu asserts that "to historicize *Pym* merely in terms of slavery is to miss its engagement with larger nineteenth-century racial ideologies" (82), she turns to other cultural projects and racial ideologies, neglecting the racial ideologies that supported the displacement and murder of Native Americans. Mentioning only briefly that Pym is a "half-breed" (91), Goddu argues that "*Pym* continues to collapse the categories of black and white" (89).

10. As for the appearance of the Indian in the work of Fenimore Cooper, I accede to the majority of scholars who argue that the actual Indian does not appear in Cooper, that he exists only as the disappearing foil for the encroaching White American.

11. The reading of Red Death as indicating a specific referrant does suggest that

despite his famous rejection of Hawthorne's use of allegory, Poe resorts to the strategy in this story.

12. Poe's own personal sense of guilt and anxiety is the subject of mild critical debate. Although Betsy Erkkila, suggests that Poe's poem "Tamerlane" (1827) reflects Poe's own historical resistance to the ... rhetoric of Western conquest and imperial advance" (46) as well as American discomfort and concern regarding imperialism and the displacement of the Native American, other critics find Poe to be less morally sensitive. Rowe notes that Poe's literary accounts "stress the warlike qualities of ... North American tribes ... for the sake of justifying U.S. removal and destruction of native peoples" (88). Poe thus displaces "the violence of Euro-American colonizes onto the 'inherent' tribal violence of 'primitive' native peoples" (88), as he displaces the fatal contagion of the whites onto the figure of the Native American.

13. Susan Sontag depends on the dominant critical reading when she writes that "The Masque of the Red Death" (1842) [was] inspired by an account of a ball held in Paris during the cholera epidemic of 1832" (141).

14. This terrifying reality is exhibited in the illustration of "Fracastoro's poem *Syphillis,* that is reprinted in Gilman's *Disease and Representation* (257). In the drawing a young man kneels before a young woman. All he sees is the beautiful face she presents to him; the viewer also sees that the face is a mask, held by the young woman to shield her skeletal face.

15. Vanderbilt notes the east-west movement but aesthetizes rather than politicizes his observation; connecting the arrangement to the order of nature, he observes that Prospero's suite is "arranged from east to west ... [connoting] the daily cycle of nature" (381)

16. Sontag also notes that the demonization of the ill victim is often solidified by the association of the disease and the sufferer with other forms of otherness, foreignness: "there is a link between imagining disease and imagining foreignness" (136). As Sontag notes, the link between disease and foreignness often has a historical foundation, as in the case of the Indians; plagues do often arrive from foreign countries, attacking people who have little or no immunity to a new invading disease. But often the historical reality results in a demonization of the foreign source, as the illness is linked with the originating country. We most recently saw this in the early days of the H1N1 virus, called for a while the "Mexican flu," amplifying the fear of the invading virus by linking it to the pre-existing American fear of the invading Mexican.

17. The two aspects of Red Death, one invisible and the other visible, invert the two corresponding stages of infectious disease. Invisible at first, disease gradually becomes visible through its symptoms. In the biological model, the invisibility of the disease is what makes it most dangerous because it cannot be averted or battled, and indeed, in Poe's story, the courtiers completely lose heart when they discover the emptiness behind the costume.

18. The monsters are all, significantly, "large, corpulent, oily men" (263). Hop-Frog, the name imposed upon the dwarf by the tyrant, contrives to have them tarred and covered in flax and then sets them on fire. This moment of revenge also occurs at a masquerade and revolves around the idea of the mask — the villains accede to the tar and flax because they believe that they are adopting the costume of "'the Eight Chained Ourang-Outangs'" (265).

WORKS CITED

Bergland, Renée L. *The National Uncanny: Indian Ghosts and American Subjects.* Hanover, NH: University Press of New England, 2000.
Brown, Thomas. "Did the U.S. Army Distribute Smallpox Blankets to Indians?: Fabrication and Falsification in Ward Churchill's Genocide Rhetoric." *Plagiary: Cross-Disciplinary Studies in Plagiarism, Fabrication and Falsification* 1 (9): 1–30.

Cixous, Héléne. "The Laugh of the Medusa." *Signs* 11 (1976): 875–893.

Clements, William M. "'Image and Word Cannot Be Divided': N. Scott Momaday and Kiowa Ekphrasis." *Western American Literature* 36.2 (2001): 134–52.

Edwards, Justin D. *Gothic Passages: Racial Ambiguity and the American Gothic.* Iowa City: University of Iowa Press, 2003.

Erkkila, Betsy "The Poetics of Whiteness: Poe and Racial Imagery." *Romancing the Shadow: Poe and Race.* Ed. J. Gerald Kennedy and Liliane Weissberg. Oxford: Oxford University Press, 2001

Fiedler, Leslie A. *The Return of the Vanishing American.* New York: Stein and Day, 1968.

Goddu, Teresa A. *Gothic America: Narrative, History, and Nation.* New York: Columbia University Press, 1997.

Hawthorne, Nathaniel. "Lady Eleanore's Mantle." *Nathaniel Hawthorne: Selected Tales and Sketches.* San Francisco: Rineheart, 1970.

"I Bring Death." *Our Hearts Fell to the Ground: Plains Indian Views of How the West Was Lost.* Ed by Colin G. Calloway. Boston: Bedford/St. Martin's, 1996.

Kennedy, J. Gerald, and Liliane Weissberg. *Romancing the Shadow: Poe and Race.* Oxford: Oxford University Press, 2001.

Lawrence, D. H. "Fenimore Cooper's White Novels." *Studies in Classic American Literature.* By D. H. Lawrence. 1923. New York: Penguin, 1977.

Maddox, Lucy. *Removals: Nineteenth-Century American Literature and the Politics of Indian Affairs.* New York: Oxford University Press, 1991.

Mayor, Adrienne. "The Nessus Shirt in the New World: Smallpox Blankets in History and Legend." *The Journal of American Folklore.* 108.427 (Winter 1995): 54–77.

McCallister, Edwin J. "Smallpox, Opium, and Invasion: Chinese Invasion, and Native American Displacement in Late Nineteenth- and Early Twentieth-Century American Fiction." *Complicating Constructions: Race, Ethnicity, and Hybridity in American Texts.* Ed. David S. Goldstein and Audrey B. Thacker. Seattle: University of Washington Press, 2007

Mooney, James. *Calendar History of the Kiowa Indians.* 1898. Washington, D.C.: Smithsonian Institution Press, 1979.

Morrison, Toni "Romancing the Shadow." *Playing in the Dark: Whiteness and the Literary Imagination.* New York: Vintage Books, 1993.

Palmer, Gus. *Telling Stories the Kiowa Way.* Tucson: University of Arizona Press, 2003.

Parsons, Elsie Clews. *Kiowa Tales.* 1929. New York: Kraus, 1969.

Plessis, Eric H. du. "Deliberate Chaos: Poe's Use of Colors in 'The Masque of the Red Death.'" *Poe Studies/Dark Romanticism: History, Theory, Interpretation* 34.1–2 (2001): 40–42.

Poe, Edgar Allan. "Hop-Frog." *The Short Fiction of Edgar Allan Poe.* Ed. Stuart Levine and Susan Levine. Urbana: University of Illinois Press, 1990.

_____. "The Masque of the Red Death." *The Short Fiction of Edgar Allan Poe.* Ed. Stuart Levine and Susan Levine. Urbana: University of Illinois Press, 1990.

Robertson, R. G. *Rotting Face: Smallpox and the American Indian.* Caldwell, Idaho: Caxton, 2001

Rowe, John Carlos. "Poe's Imperial Fantasy and the American Frontier." *Romancing the Shadow: Poe and Race.* Ed. J. Gerald Kennedy and Liliane Weissberg. Oxford: Oxford University Press, 2001

Sontag, Susan. "AIDS and Its Metaphors." *Illness as Metaphor and AIDS and Its Metaphors.* New York: Doubleday, 1990.

Vanderbilt, Kermit. "Art and Nature in 'The Masque of the Red Death.'" *Nineteenth Century Fiction* 22. 4 (March 1968) 379–89.

Knights of the Seal: Mad Doctors and Maniacs in A. J. H. Duganne's Romance of Reform

Lisa M. Hermsen

To His Friend, John Glover Drew and to The Glorious Phalanx, Who, Beholding the Crimes and the Miseries of the Present, Strive for a Better and Purer State of Society, This Romance is Respectfully Dedicated by The Author [Duganne "Dedication"].

A. J. H. Duganne's *Knights of the Seal; or the Mysteries of Three Cities, A Romance of Men's Hearts and Habits* (1845) was published in Philadelphia just as the sensational genre of American Gothic literature was gaining popularity through the expanding American press.[1] Duganne's novel has been placed both within the American Gothic tradition of Charles Brockden Brown's *Wieland*[2] and within the tradition of the sensationalist city mysteries exemplified by George Lippard's *The Quaker City, or the Monks of Monk Hall*.[3] The *Knights of the Seal* is an especially significant work because Duganne aligns the Gothic fear of madness and the supernatural with horror in response to reform movements that he believed were a threat to a rational and enlightened republic.[4]

In fact, Duganne insists that his narrative is based upon events that could be documented in public sources which readers might discover if they simply looked for themselves. He prefaces *Knights of the Seal*: "In this Book, Reader — has been written down the unpunished crimes of the three cities! Look on the Records of the Courts, and you will find this true!" Duganne marshals Gothic elements to build a world subject to criminal activity, public vices, and private corruptions. Villainous murderers lurk; heroines are compromised, and virtuous citizens fall too easily into corruption. Interest-

157

ingly, while other critics[5] have drawn attention to Duganne's writing on various reform movements — including anti-slavery, temperance, poverty, labor, land, prostitution, and prison — none has yet noted the significance of lunacy or asylum reform as a leading motif in *Knights of the Seal*, his most popular text.[6] This is an unfortunate oversight because Duganne's literature strongly opposes — through the irrationality of the Gothic — the rationale of asylum reformers. Duganne uses his unruly Gothic fiction to counter the hierarchical authority to diagnose madness that empowered the reformers and their allies.

Horrifying Dangers of Social Reform

In fact, Duganne's novel participates in an early[7] turn to the American Gothic tradition in order to expose the horrors of the dark and decrepit world of antebellum America, as well as the dangers of dark republican reforms.[8] The tradition of American Gothic suits Duganne's purpose since it is a literature in which many critics note a surprising paradox: the dominance of gloom and darkness in the literature of a land that pretends to be bright and sunny. For Duganne, "reform" was a ghoulish practice. In the nineteenth century, the relationship between capital and crime resulted in a market economy that was linked to the unfortunate degradation of society, and to the consequent necessity of social reform. In Duganne's mystery, the agency of corruption and the agency of reform are one and the same.

The novel's villains, powerful "libertines" who pursue pleasure and lack virtue, are professionals, statesmen, and merchants, who move freely about the gloomy city. They mingle in the doubled worlds of commerce and crime, hypocritically producing institutions to serve the poor. These spectacles of institutional reforms — the monstrous architecture of the almshouse, penitentiary, and asylum — in fact, perpetuate rather than alleviate the tortures of the poor. For Duganne, reform frenzy is thus more frightening than supernatural events: asylum corridors are more horrifying than haunted castles; raging mad doctors are more dangerous than uncanny phantasmal visions.

Duganne's anxieties about reform can be traced in the details with which the nineteenth-century Quaker asylum in Philadelphia is voyeuristically described in *Knights of the Seal*. Duganne's Gothic treatment of reform is a response to the abundance of print material — public letters of appeal, annual institutional reports, and physician treatises — articulating a rational advocacy for asylum reform. The unifying message of this rhetoric is that insanity is a condition caused by social pressures to rapidly civilize, cultivate and refine the population in post-revolutionary American society. Those who resisted such social pressure, the insane, were treated as outcasts and criminals, confined and chained in cold dungeons, where they were neglected and abused, left to their solitary ravings. Nineteenth-century appeals, reports, and treatises argued for moral and scientific treatment in the new asylums, often turning to the contemporary faith in a rationalizing democracy as a potential cure for madness.[9] Duganne, however, uses a competing approach. In a sensationally subversive attack on the rhetoric of asylum reform, he satirizes the reliance on reason, exposing the destabilizing connections between madness and reason. He critiques the stereotypical "maniac" as a stock cultural representation, and a distraction from comprehending the actual experience of insanity.

Asylum Reform in America

Asylum reform in America was infused with the optimism of revolutionary reform. In the new American republic, reformers mythologized the symbolic breaking of chains to highlight democratic freedoms of all types. For Americans, the asylum was symbolic: no longer would America's citizenry be caged and abandoned in madness; they would be free to live as part of a rational republic. The image of Philippe Pinel freeing the insane from their chains and from their dungeon cells at the Bicêtre and Salpêtrière hospitals in France in 1794 — after the French Revolution — held obvious meaning. The Philadelphia committee for public asylum reform, in its *Appeal to the People of Pennsylvania on the Subject of an Asylum for the Insane Poor*, refers explicitly to the "learned French physician" (19), Pinel, in its argument that maniacs be placed in institutions only for the purpose of treatment and cure of insanity. By the date of the publication of this appeal in 1838, the story of Pinel releasing the maniacs from their chains, the "myth de Pinel," had been widely cited as support for American asylum reform. In the mythic narrative, Pinel removes the shackles of fifty-three inmates, resulting in an unexpected transformation: wild inmates become calm; violent inmates reject their destructiveness; inmates who had resisted clothing and hygiene embrace these marks of civilization. In fact, the entire institution is transformed into a calm and peaceful place. The *Appeal* describes a similar scene at an American asylum, Worcester State Asylum, supervised by an American physician, Doctor Samuel Woodward:

> [an] assembly of the insane, a large proportion of whom have been incarcerated for years in prisons and dungeons, or confined with chains and manacles, the objects of terror and dread to all around them ... convened

> on the Sabbath for public worship, all decently clad, and respectable in
> appearance, calm and self-possessed, listening with apparent attention to
> the messages of truth, uniting in the devotions, and joining in songs of
> praise, all going and returning from the chapel with order and decorum
> [15].

The work of Pinel and Woodward was praised for its moral as well as practical success. *The Report of the Boston Lunatic Hospital at South Boston* concludes: "In the management of our patients we have endeavored to adopt those principles of physical and moral treatment, which, first presented by Pinel, have been so happily illustrated and effectively applied by Tuke, Woodward, and other eminent men, who at the head of Lunatic Hospitals in Europe and America, have done so much for the amendment and recovery of the Insane " (13).

Throughout *Knights of the Seal*, Duganne plays with two iconic myths that supported the birth of asylum reform: the liberation of the "maniacs," and the moral restraining gaze of the physician. The myth of liberation was exemplified by Pinel's freeing of the insane. The notion of the powerful gaze of the physician was developed in the description of "moral treatment" by William Tuke at the York Retreat in England in 1796. These mythic tales, as Michele Foucault argues, had been widely transmitted and claimed as founding truths by healers of the nineteenth century, who claimed them to "organize the world of the asylum, the methods of cure, and the concrete experience of madness" (Foucault 481). These myths circulated widely beyond professional asylum practice even in America, from popular magazines like the *North American Review* to public documents like the Annual Reports written by Asylum Superintendents and distributed to benefactors, legislators, and the public (sometimes reprinted in periodicals like the *New American Review*). So many sources and resources on the subject were offered that, as David J. Rothman assures, these concepts of asylum reform were "well within the comprehension of the ordinary public" (109). Thus, Duganne would no doubt have been aware of the ongoing discussions of "Lunacy Reform" as he was writing his novel about the plight of the mentally ill in American.

The Gothic Asylum

In *Knights of the Seal*, Duganne invites his readers to travel with him to three eastern cities: Boston ("city of churches, temples, and Pharisees"),[10] New York ("city of the merchant-princes"),[11] and Philadelphia (the "dreadful city"). When Duganne turns his attention to Philadelphia, the Quaker City, he focuses his attention upon the "mad house," which was associated with the city's Quaker community. Philadelphia was a particular apt setting for Duganne's critique of asylum reform. Duganne's fictional Quaker Asylum in Philadelphia was inspired by the private Friends Asylum for the Relief of Persons Deprived of the Use of Their Reason, near Philadelphia — which was, in turn, modeled after the York Retreat in England. In *A Description of the Retreat, an Institution Near York for the Insane Persons of the Society of Friends*, Samuel Tuke describes the conviction and desire that results in *proper* care for those suffering from "the loss of reason" (19). The document was republished in Philadelphia in 1813 and was widely circulated thereafter as a description of a model management, without the use of restraints or punishments. Given its direct lineage to the York Retreat, the Friends Asylum was considered to be one of the most progressive institutions in America.

The Friends Asylum, now considered to be the "historiographically defined institutional embodiment of nineteenth-century cultural authority over madness" (D'Antonio 15), was established years prior to the public appeal for asylum reform. The Friends Asylum opened in 1817 as one of the first private insane asylums in the United States. By the time the 1838 *Appeal* for a public insane asylum in Philadelphia was published, the Friends Asylum was already citing historical practice and claiming successful reform. The 1838 *Annual Report from Philadelphia on the State of the Asylum for the Relief of Persons Derived of the Use of their Reason* describes the older practices in the treatment of the insane:

> unhappy subjects were remorselessly consigned, hopeless of cure, to chains and a loathsome cell: there to exhaust their remaining energies in unheeded ravings; or cut off from all the sympathies and kindness which render life desirable, to drag out a wretched existence sunk in deplorable idiocy; it is no wonder that with the thought of a mad-house were associated the feelings of horror and dismay [13].

The report contrasts this with the transformed asylum: "under the influence of an enlightened philanthropy," the asylum has been "radically and totally changed" (13).

In Duganne's novel, the reader is quickly introduced to Doctor Palmarin's gothicized asylum, where "there sounds a shriek as if of mortal agony — the last gasp of hopeless desperation." As the reader is lured into asylum, "the place grows wild with horrible cries — laughter that curdles the blood, — low plaintive moans of misery — curses and prayers" (7). The asylum is fitted only with "trembling light" inadequate to "dissipate the thick blackness of the place" (10). Here is a melancholic old wild man, called "Western," who "once was a man" but is now a madman. He is confined, chained around his waist and arms, restrained by an iron ring that allows "but scanty room to walk his narrow floor" (44). Another inmate, a maniac, described over and again as "furious" and "raving" is kept in a cage with barred windows, more fit for a "wild beast" (7). His violent nature allows him the superhuman strength to break his chains and bend the bars of his dungeon cell. Another inmate is a harmless idiot boy who is not confined to a cell although he is beaten regularly. Doctor Palmarin, the asylum superintendent, reigns with absolute power over his inmates. Thus early in Duganne's novel, the asylum emerges as a decrepit and diseased Gothic structure, peopled with dangerously inhuman madmen and endangered innocents. As an unreformed institution, it is a place of Gothic "horror and dismay," rather than the site of restored reason.

The Devilish Madman; the Humanized Madman

Duganne certainly draws on stereotypical descriptions of demonic mania in his depiction of the inmates of the asylum. Mania, as opposed to the less threatening state of melancholy,[12] was defined as furious and frenzied overexcitement. The *American Medical Lexicon* (1811) describes:

> raving or furious madness ... characterized by a conception of false relations, and an erroneous judgment, arising from imaginary perceptions or recollections, exciting the passions, and producing unreasonable actions or emotion, with a hurry of mind in pursuing a train of thought, and in running from one train of thought to another; attended with incoherent speech, called raving, and violent impatience.

The sufferer of mania reverts to delirium and furor, becomes insensitive and dangerous, and finally irrational, like a wild beast or brute. When manical passions are acutely excited, according to William Sweester, writing in the very popular text, *Mental Hygiene, or an Examination of the Intellect and Passions* (1843), the visage of the maniac will often turn pale, the limbs tremble, and in extreme cases, convulsions, hysterics, madness, temporary ecstasy, or catalepsy, and even instant death may ensue (88).

Duganne's furious maniac — wild man, frantic devil — glares with bloodshot eyes, gnashes his teeth, and curses furiously. He is described most vividly and horridly with "red eye-balls," "white foam on his lips," and "long talon fingers." His "nostrils opened and closed like those of a war-steed at the trumpet blast" (45); he is a wretched figure, an animal to be caged and chained, an inhuman, devilish Other who cannot be comprehended by the rational mind. Duganne thus incorporates cultural anxieties and the conventional modes of Gothic description in delineating his mad characters. The presentation of these characters appears to tap into the model of the insane as threatening figures of unreason, degeneration, degradation and deviltry.

Yet, ultimately, Duganne resists the tendency to demonize the madman.

When the melancholic Western is rescued from the madhouse and happily restored to his family and friends, he weeps quite rationally for his fate (202). Even the supposedly murderous maniac shows his humanity. When the idiot boy is cast into his cage, the maniac soon shifts from a "bloody purpose" to a "strange sympathy" (55). Escaping the cell, the naked maniac, with matted hair, carries the boy to safety. Covering his eyes, he clasps the boy with his torn and bloodied hands: "Rocking himself to and fro. And gazing earnestly on the boy's white face, and kissing franticly the marble forehead, while the hot tears gushed from his red, bloodshot eyes" (54). Duganne reminds his readers: "Verily! There is reason in the mad we know not of" (55)

The Demonic Doctor

In fact, Duganne ultimately asserts that the true source of danger is Doctor Palmarin the "maniac physician," mad doctor, who holds the medical and social power to define (diagnose) madness, to "prescribe" an insanely Gothic treatment of the insane, and to interpret any notions of reform by the lights of his own irrational and evil approaches.

Perhaps one of the most benign exercises of power that Doctor Palmarin deploys is the power of the physician's gaze, to use Foucault's terminology. Foucault cites a narrative that appears in Tuke's *A Description of the Retreat, an Institution Near York* to argue that the superintendent of the institute exerted the power of the gaze to determine the distinction between reason and madness, and to impose reason. Tuke describes this strategy as a "mild," rather than "terrific ... means of management," as it involves exertion of power without resorting to physical brutality. Tuke describes an encounter between a superintendent and a maniac who is experiencing a fit of violence:

> The maniac retired a few paces and seized a large stone, which he immediately held up, as in the act of throwing at his companion. The superintendent, in no degree ruffled, fixed his eye upon the patient, and in a resolute tone of voice, at the same time advancing, commanded him to lay down the stone.... He then submitted to be quietly led to his apartment.

According to Foucault "the full force of authority," the underpinning for the power of the gaze, was invested in the superintendent "by the fact of his not being mad" (488).

Duganne captures the hierarchical power of the physician's gaze when he tells of the "furious maniac," described as a bloodthirsty wild dog, who twice threatens to escape. On the first occasion, "the glittering and unblenching glance of the Doctor" fixes upon the maniac's eyeballs. The maniac trembles and flees to his cell with a cry of fear. Doctor Palmarin follows the

maniac—"his eye quailing not"—and motions toward the door of the cell for
the maniac to enter (19). Thus, writes Duganne, does Doctor Palmarin tame
the "raving maniac" (19), with the power of his controlling gaze. When the
maniac attempts a second escape, "the Doctor sought to catch his fiery eye."
The maniac grasps the throat of the Doctor and with "super-human strength,"
lifts him off the ground and prepares to throw him across the room. But when
the Doctor "fixed his eye upon him" (55), the maniac quails; the Doctor ties
his wrists and leads him to his cell.

Yet, Doctor Palmarin does not limit his imposition of power to the relatively subtle power of the gaze. His rage leads him to more primitive and
spectacular modes of control, as delineated by Foucault: the control derived
from the spectacle of the tortured body. When the "hag" cook offends him
by threatening to reveal the atrocities of the asylum, the Doctor, "the spirit
of Revenge" (204), strikes her with a violent blow. Watching his unconscious
victim, "his livid face bore the impress of the strong passions that were seething
in his heart" (122). As his eyes fix upon the woman "he presented a horrible
picture of rage" (122).

Doctor Palmarin's rage requires no rationale. The unoffending inmates
of the asylum bear the brunt of his wrath. When the Doctor meets the idiot
boy in the asylum corridors, he warns him with a "savage voice" that if the
boy speaks to the maniac, he will be flayed alive. "Within the space of a
minute," the doctor's irrational rage overtakes him—his face "grew fearful to
behold" (45). As his eyes become livid and his nostrils twitch, the Doctor
lifts the boy by the throat and throws him into the maniac's cell, presumably
to be torn apart by the wild man. The consequence of this irrational act, the
humanity of the maniac described above, explicitly indicates where madness
lies.

In fact, in Duganne's asylum, the physician is the monstrous source of
torment rather than cure; his behavior provokes insanity rather than healing.
A series of interchanges between the Doctor and Western suggest that the Doctor is far more devilish than his mentally ill patients. In an early exchange,
the Doctor assures Western that: "Doomed you are! Never shall you breathe
the free air of heaven again! I tell you, you are dead in this living world!" (19).
The following dialogue reinforces the sense of the Doctor's deviltry:

> "Again!" cried [Western], "So soon come to torment me?"
>
> "Now and forever," hissed the voiced of the [Doctor] in his ear—"Till the
> last drop of blood is dried within your veins, or till mine can feel no more
> the luxury of tormenting you!" [44].

This passage provocatively illustrates Duganne's suggestion that the Doctor, and not his devilishly wild inmates, is the true demon in this institution.

Doctor Palmarin's senseless anger at the innocents he persecutes, his threat of doom and the loss of heaven, his hissing voice and his threat of eternal torment — all suggest Satan himself, inflicting torture upon his prisoners, causing one under his control to howl "with the wail of a lost soul" (19).[13]

Thus we find, as the narrative unfolds, that the mad doctor's power, sanctioned by a rational society, is more dangerous, less human, and more demonic, than the enraged ravings of the imprisoned maniac. Duganne thus articulates a concern that any institution based on an inequitable distribution of power is doomed to immoral chaos, and that any individual who has complete power over others is fated to perpetuate mad suffering. In his view, the problem with the asylum reform movement was that asylum reformers, despite the best intentions, ultimately disempowered the inmates. The power held by of the Doctor, and the asylum reformers — allowing them to dictate the categorical division between reason and unreason, and to pathologize and demonize deviance from the "norm" — allowed them to subjectively and willfully cast fellow human beings into prisons from where there was no hope of escape. Reform might mollify the conditions of imprisonment but it did not radically affect the distribution of power within the institution. Thus the anxious dark system that Duganne depicts in his novel is not only a problem of public health; the real problem is the creation of an undemocratic system of arbitrary imprisonment in the new American democracy.

Duganne's Radical Model of Reform

Duganne's *Knights of the Seal* thus exhibits a horrified response to the notion of institutional reform that did not radically dismantle the hierarchy of the institution. Duganne unveils the immorality of moral treatment imposed upon a specific class of people; the novel reveals a democratic revulsion toward unilateral power, even when that power is motivated by the seemingly benevolent forces of reform. Ultimately, Duganne condemns the progress of urban industrialization which he sees as the root cause of mental illness. Without the culture of industrialized capitalism there would be no need for asylums and no need for asylum reform. Duganne thus resist the notion of the asylum as a symbol of liberty or enlightenment and counters the idea that a confining institution with a hierarchy of power can be adequately transformed into a place of moral healing. Anticipating Foucault, Duganne suggests that the unilateral exertion of any power — including the power of the physician — cannot lead to health and morality. Thus the ultimate source of horror is not the mad man. True horror comes from the enlightened culture that cannot accommodate deviance from the enforced norm, and from the physician, who diagnoses and pathologizes deviance from the norm, and who imposes inhumane imprisonment as the cure for pathologic deviance. Thus Duganne suggests that asylum reform only treats the symptom of social dysfunction; systematic social reform is the only possible cure for the social roots of madness.

In fact, Duganne endorsed and supported social reform projects that would improve the plight of the poor and the oppressed, projects that would keep the weak free from the reach of the rich and powerful.[14] Duganne supported the National Reform Association and the Industrial Congress, two of the most important American antebellum land reform and labor movements. His public writing and his politics earned him the title, "poet of National Reform" (Streeby 19). However, Duganne remained distrustful of the benevolence of banks and other capitalist structures, and of the institutions they supported: hospitals, asylums, schools, and orphanages.[15] The kind of reform Duganne trusted was the radical reform of the entire society. He promoted the creation of a democracy in which each human being could live freely, without the impositions of a norm determined by the rich and powerful. His novel illustrates the belief that a project which only worked to buttress the systems of power through institutional reform would result in the erection of a house of mad horrors, rather than the promised enlightened city of the new American democracy.

NOTES

1. The urban Gothic city mystery genre was wide-reaching and quite popular among a new mass audience. City mysteries like Duganne's, written for massive production by a new print industry, were first to achieve dominant success among a captivated working-class readership. After Eugène Sue's *Les Mystères de Paris* was serialized in Paris' *Journal Des Debats* and published internationally, the "city mystery" genre was imitated by writers in Great Britain and the United States, and proliferated in the literature of mass culture. The publication and popularity of the genre, as well as its influence in both popular and more "genteel" early American literary traditions, has now been well-documented. See David S. Reynolds, Michael Denning, Paul Joseph Erickson.

2. Charles Brockden Brown was one of the first American writers to adapt the Gothic to construct national narratives of industrial capitalism, exposing the darkness and degeneracy underneath an idealized cultural identity. See Goddu.

3. George Lippard was the leading American writer of sensationalist literature and the best-selling American author in the "mysteries of the city" genre, which unveiled the honest vice of labor and hypocritical virtue of capital. See Reynolds.

4. Paul Joseph Erickson acknowledges that Duganne's literary style lacks sophisticated plots and polished prose. In fact Erickson notes that Duganne's shortcoming was "as clear to antebellum critics as it is to us." (25). Nevertheless, Erickson argues that the work merits scholarly attention because it sheds light on politically-charged life in antebellum America

5. Duganne's Gothic has been referred to alternately as "subversive," "radical," and "dark" reform writing. It has been judged to be ineffective, limited, and ambiguous.

Reynolds finds, for example, that the voyeuristic narrative — by which author and reader participate in the lurid details of vice — registers an "ambiguity" and provokes a "divided response" so that his writings of dark reform "are mixed texts that resist straightforward interpretation" (59). For Denning, Streeby, and Erickson, Duganne's literary works are supportive of particular land and labor reform, more so than any general reform impulse. These critics note, however, that Duganne writes himself into far more difficult and entangled connections with the politics of class, race, and nation, and thus creates only more difficult, complicated, and contradictory visions for emancipatory reform practices.

6. Duganne's contribution to "reform," whatever it may be, is not easily traced, because it is not plainly inscribed. Historians of asylum reform David Rothman, Gerald Grob, Andrew Skull, and Nancy Tomes have written at length about the ways in which the asylum was rendered as a site of power for the social regulation of madness by the various strategies of therapists, capitalists and moralists.

7. David S. Reynolds's term is "preliterary."

8. Duganne's work, like much American Gothic literature of the period, is a response to the dizzying heterogeneity of reform efforts at work in antebellum America. Melville, Hawthorne, and Poe provide more recognizable treatments of imaginary reform in unruly literary expression. Yet the voices of less literary, more popular cultural voices, like Duganne's, echo the more canonical literature in using Gothic expressions to critique various reform impulses during the nineteenth century. The argument that popular literature of "dark reform" influenced other American literary traditions has been detailed convincingly by Reynolds.

9. See Jarvis, Chandler, Earle.

10. Boston is described as the city of religion and statehood, where the poor live in squalor. It is a "dark and dreary" place busy with sounds of "cursing and blasphemy" from cellars full of outcasts, thieves, and murderers.

11. New York, the "city of the merchant-princes," is portrayed as a scene of extravagant wealth, in startling contrast to Boston. Here is the reader visits a great mansion with marble staircases, a lofty hall, and a ball-room.

12. Within nineteenth-century classifications of insanity from professional textbooks to popular print, melancholy was understood and defined as a peculiar depression of the mind. Often, grief or loss were cited as its cause. A popular mental hygiene text, *Gunn's Domestic Medicine, or Poor Man's Friend*, offers this description: "This depressing affection of the mind, called a passion, when experienced in the extreme, sometimes degenerates into confirmed melancholy, despair and fatal insanity." Melancholy is sad and moribund. This is the affliction Western suffers. His face is described as mild and childlike, "though the face of an old man" (44). He once had the passions and pride of a man, and now "there was lines of suffering and sorrow borne with a patient heart" (44). He was once "a noble one of God's children, with a warm heart and trusting soul!" He has gone mad from grief because "he was robbed by his friend, betrayed by the wife of his heart, and deserted by the world" (7). Yet. this "crazy man" is kind to the idiot boy. While he sits most of the day pouring over his books, he also spends time reading to the boy. He is described as "kindly" and "the good pale gentleman" (20). Duganne draws explicitly upon public mental hygiene, which warned that the reasoning faculties of man have necessary limits, and when over tasked by sorrow, will result in melancholia, an excessive degeneration of the nervous system.

13. Duganne's "long, dark page of guilt and hypocrisy" (204) ends badly for Palmarin. All established boundaries between madness and reason are destroyed in the last frenzy of confusion, deception, and corruption within the labyrinth-like asylum. By the conclusion, Palmarin has attempted to murder the woman and the boy, and has threatened to murder the mad man, as well. Conspirators and enemies appear at the door of the

asylum, and any remaining order is fully lost. As Palmarin leans over to touch the body of the woman he presumes dead, her eyes open; Palmarin is struck by terror. After battling insanity for days, he awakes to even more chaos. After realizing the mistaken identities of his asylum inmates, his body "suddenly rose with a spasm,— then straightened out in the rigidity of death" (199). In the final chapter, Duganne asks the reader who has followed the mazes of crime: "have you yet the clue?" (203).

14. The dedication to *Knights of the Seal* is less Gothic than utopian. The dedication suggests a friendly relationship between Duganne and John Glover Drew, a well-placed member of the "industrial Council" within the Fourierist Phalanx at the Brook Farm Institute of Agriculture and Education. The Brook Farm, which was an attempt to build a utopian commune based on the principles established by Charles Fourier, promised to be a foundation of "genuine social progress." Duganne published *The Knights of the Seal* when the phalanx at Brook Farm remained optimistic about their experiment, just before its collapse in 1847. The farm's weekly publication, the *Harbinger*, of which Duganne is listed as contributor to volume one, outlined certain principles, including: devotion to radical, organic reform; relief for the toiling and down-trodden; advancement of all classes, pursuit of a democratic faith, and universal harmony on earth. The *Harbinger* principles also outlined disdain for false sentiment, and for hypocrisy, pretense, and duplicity. It exposed exclusive privilege in professional and social custom and "the falsehoods on which modern society is built" (Codman). Duganne's Gothic fiction works as the literary device by which Duganne is able to make a clear distinction between the utopian experiment that is Brook Farm and the urban reform project that is the Friends Asylum. There is a curious relationship between Duganne's *Knights of the Seal*, dedicated as it is to the Brook Farm experiment, and Nathanial Hawthorne's *Blithesdale Romance*, a critique of that very experiment. Duganne's work offers a powerful foundation for Hawthorne's more renowned book in that Duganne reveals that the "rational" republic no longer exists — if, in fact, it ever did exist.

15. The rise of capitalism emerged with social reform institutions like poor houses, Advocates for a "moral architecture" argued that these physical arrangements would then serve as a model for a healthier society as a whole. The advocates and known reformers, however, tended to be wealthy capitalists and paternal philanthropists. A single set of men, who met in Boston, New York, and Philadelphia to organize the first savings banks, were also the first founders of other social institutions. In Boston, statesmen John Quincy and William Phillips built the Provident Institution for Savings and advocated for poor-law reform and asylum reform. In New York, the first group to organize a savings bank included Cadwallader Colden, who founded the Asylum for the Insane, and Thomas Eddy, who founded the Newgate prison. And in Philadelphia, the Savings Fund Foundation was built by penal reformer Roberts Vaux. Furthermore the Quakers in Philadelphia were instrumental in organizing both mutual benefit societies and several charities, including the Friends Asylum. Duganne often and in print expressed his certainty of the threat from wealth accumulated without labor, especially that accumulated by "millionaires." In the *Knights of the Seal*, these millionaire men are described as "those who are 'good' at the bank-counter, and 'good' no where else" (47).

WORKS CITED

American Medical Lexicon on the Plan of Quincey's Lexicon. New York: T. and J. Swords, 1811.

Annual Report on the State of the Asylum for the Relief of Persons Deprived of the Use of Their Reason, Near Frankford, Pennsylvania. Philadelphia: Printed for Contributors, 1838.

An Appeal to the People of Pennsylvania on the Subject of an Asylum for the Insane Poor. Philadelphia: Printed for the Committee, 1838.

Chandler, George. *Reports of the Board of Visitors, of the Trustees, and of the Superintendent of the New Hampshire Asylum for the Insane.* Concord: Carroll & Baker, 1843.

Codman, Thomas. *Brook Farm* (Project Gutenberg, Released April 2005) [EBook#7932].

D'Antonio, Patricia. *Founding Friends.* Bethlehem: Lehigh University Press, 2006.

Denning, Michael. *Mechanic Accents: Dime Novels and Working-Class Culture in America.* New York: Verso, 1987.

Duganne, A. J. H. *The Knights of the Seal; or, the Mysteries of the Three Cities: A Romance of Men's Hearts and Habits.* Philadelphia: Colon and Adriance Arcade, 1845.

Earle, Pliny. *Twenty-fifth Annual Report of the Bloomingdale Asylum for the Insane.* New York, 1845.

Erickson, Paul Joseph. "Welcome to Sodom: The Cultural Work of City-Mysteries Fiction in Antebellum America." Diss. University of Texas at Austin, 2005.

Foucault, Michel. *History of Madness.* Ed. Jean Khalfa. Trans. Jonathan Murphy and Jean Khalfa. London: Routledge, 2006.

Goddu, Theresa A. *Gothic America: Narrative, History, and Nation.* New York: Columbia University Press, 1997.

Grob, Gerald. *Mental Institutions in America: Social Policy to 1875.* New York: Free Press, 1973.

Gunn, John. *Gunn's Domestic Medicine, or Poor Man's Friend.* 1830. Knoxville: University of Tennessee Press, 1986.

Jarvis, Edward, M. D. *Insanity and Insane Asylums.* Louisville: Prentice and Weissinger, 1841.

Pinel, Philippe. *A Treatise on Insanity: In Which Are Contained the Principles of a New and More Practical Nosology of Maniacal Disorders Than Has Yet Been Offered to the Public.* Sheffield, Printed by W. Todd for Cadell and Davies, 1806.

Report of the Superintendent of the Boston Lunatic Hospital and Physician of the Public Institution at South Boston. Boston: John H. Eastburn, 1840.

Reynolds, David S. *Beneath the American Renaissance: The Subversive Imagination in the Age of Emerson and Melville.* Cambridge, MA: Harvard University Press, 1988.

Rothman, David J. *The Discovery of the Asylum: Social Order and Disorder in the New Republic.* New York: Aldine, 2002.

Scull, Andrew. *The Museums of Madness: The Social Organization of Madness in Nineteenth-Century England.* London: St. Martin's, 1979.

Streeby, Shelley. *American Sensations: Class, Empire, and the Production of Popular Culture.* Berkeley: University of California Press, 2002.

Sweester, William M. D. *Mental Hygiene, or an Examination of the Intellect and Passions.* New York: Langley, 1843.

Tomes, Nancy. *A Generous Confidence: Thomas Story Kirkbride and the Art of Asylum Keeping, 1840–1883.* New York: Cambridge University Press, 1984.

Tuke, Samuel. *A Description of the Retreat: An Institution Near York for the Insane Persons of the Society of Friends.* Philadelphia: Isaac Pierce, 1813.

"The Secret of My Mother's Madness": Mary Elizabeth Braddon and Gothic Instability

CARLA T. KUNGL

Mary Elizabeth's Braddon's *Lady Audley's Secret* (1862), one of the best known of the Sensation fiction novels, clearly illustrates the relationship of the Sensation novel to the Gothic tradition. The novel features the Gothic tropes of secrecy, hidden lives, anxiety and madness, moving these motifs from the conventional Gothic setting into the upper-class home, where the innocent female protagonist is repositioned as an active villain, vaguely mad. Thirty years later, in the 1894 novel *Thou Art the Man*, Braddon returns again to the subject of psychological destabilization, this time focusing on Brandon Mountford, an epileptic framed for murder after a seizure and then sequestered away, not for his own recovery or safety — or for the good of society as in the case of Lady Audley — but to hide the identify of the true murderer. By depicting Brandon Mountford as confined and ill, Braddon transforms several conventional Gothic tropes: the illness (and confinement) is experienced by a man, not a woman; the illness is more visible and diagnosable — epilepsy as opposed to the ambiguous nature of Lady Audley's mental condition; and this novel concludes with neither rescue nor restitution, but a slow wasting away towards death.

In Braddon's novels, mental disability serves as a potent marker of the fearful Gothic Other who is clearly defined as inhumanly and monstrously different. This marker thus indicates the desire of the subject to make a clear distinction between the normative self and the non-normative Other. The fear of the different Other is further amplified by the otherness of gender. In *Though Art the Man*, Braddon inverts the typical representation of the "mad"

Other as female — as the title emphasizes, her central character is male. Braddon's substantial transformation of the trope of illness calls attention to the power of the abiding fear of the mentally different Other, indicating that the Gothic response to the mystery of madness is always fear, even when the object is the conventionally normative male.

The ambiguity of the veiled, inner mental condition in both *Lady Audley's Secret* and *Thou Art the Man* marks mental illness as the site of Gothic mystery. Judith Halberstam writes that the Gothic signifies a "preoccupation with boundaries and their collapse" (23); this was certainly true of the Victorian era, during which the maintenance of boundaries — between sexes, classes, races — was of particular concern in response to the looming breakdown of the old order. Lady Audley's actions, supposedly stemming from her invisible madness, make her dangerous: the madness empowers her to transgress the traditional boundaries that contain female behavior and to promote her very unladylike agenda. Brandon Mountford's mental condition, epilepsy, draws upon the uneasiness of the *fin de siècle*, highly charged with fears of mental and physical degeneration. The nature of the disease — it is only intermittently visible — also taps into social fears of contagion from the invisible Other, the figure who is perceived as enormously different, though appearing to be normative due to slight advances in social equality: the Jew, or the *arriviste*, for example.[1]

Lady Audley's Undefined Madness

> That invisible balance upon which the mind is always trembling. Mad to-day and sane to-morrow [*Lady Audley* 403].[2]

The plot of *Lady Audley's Secret* needs little review: Lady Audley "accidentally" commits bigamy, and then to cover up her crime, and retain her current status, resorts to various frauds and maneuverings, including the attempted murders of her first husband and of her second husband's nephew, Robert Audley. She declares herself a madwoman when she is finally caught, claiming she inherited the disease from her mother, and Robert Audley places her in an asylum in Belgium, locking her away supposedly for the good of society but also to protect the Audley family name. *Audley* is one of the first and best Sensation novels and the novel which, for better or worse, situated Braddon as a Sensation novelist; for the rest of her career she was known as the "Author of Lady Audley's Secret" and her ensuing writing was compared in some way with the Sensation novel formula she helped create.[3]

The nature of Lady Audley's madness has been the concern of most readers of the novel, who question both the extent of and existence of her malady. In one of the earliest feminist critiques of the novel, Elaine Showalter argues that Lady Audley's secret is that "she is *sane*, and moreover, representative" ("Desperate Remedies" 4). Her confession of madness is a ploy to hide the reality (if not normalcy) of female desire for agency and power. Jill Matus adds "Braddon suggests to the reader that Lucy is not deranged but desperate; not mad (insane) but mad (angry)" (344). Lynn Voskuil adroitly recasts the question of the legitimacy of Lady Audley's madness to discuss the difficulty of the diagnosis; she suggests that Lady Audley's theatrical performance of "madwoman" mystifies Dr Mosgrave's diagnostic abilities, and thus his pronouncement of madness becomes a way of reasserting male, scientific "middle-class authority" (634). Indeed, it is nearly impossible to discuss the book without trying to diagnose Lady Audley's disease. Braddon's authorial silence on the subject — her own inability or unwillingness to categorize it — adds to the ambiguity that fosters the fear engendered by the madness.

This sense of ambiguity occurs within the characters as well. No one seems quite sure how to categorize, or diagnose, Lady Audley's mental state, in part because it is inherently invisible, manifest only through its functional ramifications. Dr. Mosgrave, the fashionable doctor whom Robert Audley brings in as a consultant, first declares that she is not mad at all, stating several times that there is "no madness in anything she has done" (377). Rather, he asserts, she has used "intelligent means, and she carried out a conspiracy which required coolness and deliberation" (377). But after his interview with her, we hear several additional explanations: she is "not mad but she has the taint of heredity in her blood" (379); she has the "cunning of madness with the prudence of intelligence" (379); she has "latent insanity!" (377) which might only appear once or twice in a lifetime, and only under extreme mental pressure.

In Lady Audley's own telling, fits of madness overcome her during stressful times. Since the first has occurred after the birth of her child, it is possible to see a link between her madness and post-partum depression. Her own mother is described as losing her reason after giving birth, and it was certainly not an uncommon diagnosis; Showalter writes that "puerperal insanity" accounted for "about ten percent of female asylum admissions" during the Victorian era (323).[4] In her months of desperation following her husband's desertion, left with a tiny baby and father to support, she reports that "the hereditary taint" in her blood first manifested itself: "At this time I think my mind first lost its balance, and for the first time I crossed that invisible line which separates reason from madness. I have seen my father's eyes fixed on me in horror and alarm" (353).

Lady Audley's incarceration at the end of the novel is a forceful reinstatement of social suppression of non-normative female power. Her admittedly ambiguous behavior is easily diagnosed as madness by contemporary medical thinking. Lady Audley herself understands that after her confession that she will be labeled and confined as a madwoman. Perhaps aware of her role as Gothic heroine manqué, she romanticizes her situation: "she looked upon herself as a species of state prisoner, who would have to be taken good care of: a second Iron Mask who must be provided for in some comfortable place of confinement" (372–3). The Gothic trope of enclosure, first introduced in descriptions of Audley Court is more fully exploited in descriptions of Lady Audley's prison. Though it seems to have every comfort, Lady Audley soon realizes that the reality of her situation does not match her idealization of it. The lobby of her suite of apartments, which exudes a "dismal and cellarlike darkness," is followed by a saloon that has a "certain funereal splendour" and "gloomy velvet curtains" (388) and a coffin-like bed, "so wondrously made, as to appear to have no opening whatever in its coverings" (388–9). The room is lit by one candle, whose "solitary flame, pale and ghostlike in itself, was multiplied by paler phantoms of its ghostliness" (389).

Instead of living out her days in comfort, Lady Audley inherits the Gothic fate of live burial. As Dr Mosgrave describes her destiny: "'If you were to dig a grave for her in the nearest churchyard and bury her alive in it, you could not more safely shut her from the world'" (381).[5] Lady Audley's anti-climactic physical death, occurs only a year later, after a "long illness." It is only obliquely indicated by Robert Audley's receipt of a black-bordered envelope, but does underscore the effectiveness of her containment.

Enigmatic Epilepsy in "Thou Art the Man"

> Epilepsy is a mysterious and fearful affliction, an unsolved problem. It is a disorder of the borderland between body and soul [Sutter, qtd. in Lannon].

Written in 1894, Braddon's *Thou Art the Man* also contains sensational elements derived from the Gothic tradition. Braddon deliberately echoes her former works by including tropes of madness, secrets, imprisonment and criminality. Yet Braddon also complicates the conventions: the mental instability is transferred onto a male character, and is translated into a more readily diagnosed condition, epilepsy. The story opens with our introduction to the two main female characters: Lady Sibyl Penrith, whose secret past has resulted in a loveless marriage; and her niece through that marriage, Coralie Urquhart, whose boredom, combined with her father's urging, makes her determined to uncover Sibyl's secret. This secret, like Lady Audley's, also concerns madness, but not her own: ten years earlier, the man she loved, Brandon Mountford, was convicted of the murder of Sibyl's adopted sister, supposedly while he was in the grasp of an epileptic fit, a condition equated with insanity in the popular imagination and in the medical discourse of the late nineteenth century. In conjunction with her future brother-in-law, Hubert Urquhart (Cora's father), Sibyl has spirited Mountford away by boat during a storm. While the boat and all its passengers have been given up for lost, they survive. Before returning to society, Urquhart sequesters Mountford in a nearby house, where Mountford is held prisoner for ten years. The reason for this plot is that Urquhart is the real murderer, though he let Mountford take responsibility. While Cora's narration of her own activities weaves the present in with the past throughout the novel, most of the first volume is devoted to the past: Mountford's discovery of his "mad" mother, whose insanity first presented as epilepsy; his inheritance of the disease and its symptoms; his determination to keep the taint of his disease a secret from Sibyl and the world; the murder itself, which he and the rest of the community assume he has committed when they find out he is a "wretched epileptic" (2.19); the flight which seems to confirm his guilt.

Mountford's mental condition, like Lady Audley's, defies a fixed defining category. In fact, a dizzying variety of metaphors and adjectives are used to describe his affliction. Epilepsy is "a curse" (2.26), a "fatal tendency" (1.188), a "foul fiend" (1.185), a "hideous spectre" (1.218). Under its grip, Mountford is a "creature of demoniac impulses" (1.225), a "scourge and a horror to his fellow-men" (2.77). He is compared to a wild beast and to the tormented devil cast out by Jesus into a herd of swine (2.24); he is a "doomed wretch" (1.285). Although these labels indicate that the perception of the illness is consistently negative, and that the sufferer is inhuman, the sheer quantity of words deployed suggests a thwarted attempt to define and to classify on the part of the various speakers. The failure of language, coupled with the hideousness of the disease, creates a sense of Gothic horror that reverberates through the text.[6]

The presumption of Mountford's guilt is a reflection and indictment of the popular connection between epilepsy and madness. When he comes across the dead girl, after waking up from an attack, and gets her blood on him, all the characters conclude that he must have committed the crime. Sibyl's family doctor reproduces this faulty linkage most succinctly: "'I can believe anything of an epileptic sufferer, just as I can believe anything of a madman'" (3.99). Sibyl remembers Mountford describing "that inscrutable disease which can change sanity to madness, the sudden clouding over of the brain; the maniac's impulse towards evil" (2.76). Like Sibyl, the doctor moves from a quasi-scientific approach to a moral and even supernatural approach. He sounds more like a character in a Gothic novel than a man of science when he speaks of "the devil of epilepsy" that seizes Mountford, and explains that "as the fit passed it left him like the demoniac of old, panting with wild impulses, thirsting for blood." Ironically he adds: "I have thought it all out" (3.99–100). Certainly more superstition than thought has gone into this theory.

Mountford's internalization of the erroneous linkages — between epilepsy and madness, and between madness and evil — indicates the great power of this cultural misconception. In lamenting his fate to himself, Mountford says he is "worse than a leper, since with him [Mountford] physical malady might pass into moral delinquency — a creature beyond the pale of human love or friendship" (1. 285). The moral frame leads Mountford to consider his condition in terms, like the doctor's, that evoke the Gothic and its ongoing struggle between absolute good and absolute evil. He describes the "epileptic tendency" as "the irresistible impulse toward some act of blind violence — the rending and tearing of the fiend within, the devilish instinct to which murder or self-destruction becomes a necessity" (2.24). To be clear: no one in this text considers physical manifestations of epilepsy, like seizures, to be the worst symptom of the disease. The presumed tendency of the epileptic to lapse into uncontrollable homicidal behavior — to behave "'more like a lunatic than a man in his right senses'" (1.285) — is the quality that marks Mountford as a monster, even to himself.

In addition to illustrating the medical ambiguity surrounding epilepsy *Thou Art the Man* also illustrates the murky legal status of epileptics. If the sanity of the epileptic was in doubt, should he still be held responsible for a crime? Clark elaborates on the difficulties juries had in deciding what the court should do with an epileptic who had committed a crime. Writing in 1926 he notes "the tendency of juries to convict criminals who are proved to be epileptic — with the present status of the epileptic, what other way have they to protect the community? Occasionally, as a matter of expediency, the epileptic is held insane and is committed" (219).

It is the danger of incarceration in an asylum — a sentence that Mountford clearly does not merit — that leads his supporters to urge his flight from justice. Sibyl's desire to help Mountford run away, after he is convicted by a coroner's jury, is thus understandable. His own doctor advises escape rather than incarceration; he tells Mountford that his "best chance of warding off future attacks, and of outgrowing his malady, would be found in a free, adventurous life." Perhaps as a comment on the illogic of locking up fully sane epileptics, Braddon explicitly attributes Mountford's eventual descent into madness to his solitary confinement.

Gender and Madness

The fears of invisible disease present in *Lady Audley* and in *Thou Art the Man* indicate why madness becomes an apt sign for the Gothic preoccupation with the construction and breakdown of boundaries. The insane are dangerously apt to cross social borders, in committing murder, for example. As Michel Foucault argues in *Madness and Civilization* society creates the separate category of the insane and thereby the need to isolate the insane. In Braddon's two novels, fear that madness can also lead to the breakdown of gender constructs heightens this fear. So strong was the Victorian desire to contain and categorize by gender that gender-inappropriate behavior was sufficient evidence of a diagnosis of madness.

Though such a drastic verdict was not common, Peter McCandless, in "Liberty and Lunacy: The Victorians and Wrongful Confinement," discusses the diagnostic process that for many doctors meant noting aberrations from societal expectations: "the extent to which an individual deviated from the Victorian social and moral codes ... often became the measurement of his mental state" (341). He provides several examples of madness being diagnosed in men and women whose symptoms included resisting the gender expectations of their time.[7] Thus, the ways in which both Lady Audley and Brandon Mountford obfuscate typical gender norms becomes another indicator of their mad behavior, behavior that contributes to a horrifying breakdown of categories.

Lady Audley's Secret certainly questions the methods used to limit women to the narrow roles and the stereotypes that bind society. The novel illustrates the social strategy of marking a woman as mad if she exhibits the unfeminine traits of intelligence, self-assertion, and defiance.[8] In part, what Lady Audley suffers from is the curse of wanting to chart her own destiny outside of that which is socially acceptable and thus, medically acceptable. Dr. Mosgrave's attempt to define the exact nature of her malady indicates the strength of those established mores. To Chiara Briganti, in "Gothic Maidens and Sensation Women," Dr. Mosgrave's diagnosis of "latent insanity" means that "because she will not submit she must choose marginalization and madness, though there is no evidence of such madness" (206). But as McCandless points out, difference itself was seen as a marker of insanity. Lady Audley is feared because she is independent in a time where women's independence was not the norm: Victorian medical constructions represented defiance or nonconformity as derangement" (Matus 344). Lady Audley is "dangerous," as Robert Audley and Dr Mosgrave call her, not because she killed a man but because she threatens the world of men in general. Further, they fear the ramifications of her behavior on other women; Robert Audley says to himself after piecing together his evidence: "The more I see of this woman, the more reason I have to dread her influence upon others" (274).[9] Thus, when she is vindicated of murder, she is not freed from her prison but remains silently locked away; her release would "expose the failures of their definitions of womanliness" (Schroeder and Schroeder 57). As Briganti writes, "the diagnosis of insanity ends up erasing the individual woman to protect the myth of femininity" (205).

In *Thou Art the Man* Braddon illustrates that in the Victorian era, men were not exempt from social pressures to conform to gender-based expectations. Jane Wood discusses the need to "diagnose" a new kind of male hysteria: "stereotypes of masculinity were no less powerful and pervasive than their feminine equivalents and ... [i]n both cases, the terms of gender representation were unstable and the prescriptions for health and respectability were confused and contradictory" (63). The domestic ideology of separate spheres for masculine and feminine pursuits and lifestyles was enduring a new set of attacks in the 1890s. In the literary world, those who became known as Decadents, who preached "art for art's sake," and New Women, who dared to consider appropriating new freedoms for themselves, were seen as perpetuating dangerous life changes. Gender itself was in danger of becoming obfuscated: "Men became women. Women became men," wrote Karl Miller in his study of the doubling motif (qtd. in *Sexual Anarchy* 3). The "crisis" of masculinity, co-existing with a rise in women's suffragette activities, was reflected in fears of degeneracy appearing in previously robust men.[10] Periodicals were full of articles about the decline of the Empire and the "presumed degeneracy of the race and the startling increase in insanity" (Beckson xiv).

Against this background, Braddon invents an epileptic male — physically ill, unmarriageable, descending into madness. The decision to project illness onto a male subject was a clear inversion of a powerful Victorian trope. The motif of the sick woman in Victorian fiction is so common that Shirley Taylor opens her article on Braddon by stating, "In nineteenth-century fiction it seems that being female meant being ill" (88). Thus the epileptic eponymous "Man," Mountford, troubles two categorical binaries: sane/insane; male/female. As Joseph Kestner asserts in *Sherlock's Sisters*, the madness motif in this novel is "given an entirely different inflection" because the sufferer is male, placing the novel as "part of a larger legal/medical/detective debate about criminality and about masculinity" (63). Braddon emphasizes that Mountford's disease emasculates him. Like Lady Audley, he inherits the taint from his mother. He exhibits "feminine" anxiety, brooding on the implications of disease when he is young, consumed by his fear of the disease. Voraciously reading every book on the subject, he constantly looks for symptoms.

Gazing at himself in the mirror, he becomes wan and sickly, harming his health by worry. The attack that presumably concludes with the murder of Sibyl's sister, is precipitated by a "feminine" psychological state: depression caused by love trouble, his fear that he should not marry Sybil because of his condition. As in the case of Lady Audley, the non-normative gender behavior of Mountford contributes to the diagnosis of his presumed insanity. Mountford's weakness and illness mark him as too womanly. As Jane Wood explains, "despite the efforts of doctors to define and interpret male disease within constructs of masculinity, representation of male nervousness ... fashioned an image of an invalid feminized by the very nature of his disease" (60). It is the resistance to the comforting categories of gender, as much as his purported homicidal tendencies that mark Mountford as a threat to society and a candidate for the asylum.

A focus upon the madness of the two main characters in *Lady Audley* and *Thou Art the Man* thus reveals that together the two novels create a mirror effect, reflecting and inverting each other over the space of the thirty years that separate them. This focus also reveals that in addition to troubling the binaries of sane/insane, and male/female, the two novels trouble the binary of fantastic Gothic/realistic Sensation. In each novel, the modern and rational discourse of science and politics — discussions of the New Woman, contemporary scientific thinking — yields to the old irrational anxieties generated by invisibly transgressive mental illness. These anxieties, best expressed through the mode of Gothic horror, open the door to the irrational (though human) forces that filter into Braddon's Sensation novels. For despite the rational comfort offered by modern political movements and modern science, mental disease remains ambiguous and terrifying, a phenomenon more readily explained by Gothic tropes than by scientific theories.

NOTES

1. In his prologue to *London in the 1890s* Karl Beckson writes that "cultural trends" at this time were "moving in two simultaneously antithetical directions" (xiv). On the one hand, certainties about religion, politics, and morality which had largely united the Victorians gave way to despair about the future of humanity. On the other hand, "the rapid growth of such scientific disciplines as physics, astronomy, and chemistry transformed the nineteenth-century view of the world so dramatically that, by the *fin de siècle*, Victorians referred to their age as 'modern'" (xii). In *Literature and Culture at the Fin de Siecle*, Talia Schaffer describes this hopeful stance: "At the *fin de siècle*, it seemed possible to understand the body and the mind; to trace the medical, hereditary, sex-related and psychological factors shaping them; to ameliorate suffering in a new society, and to imagine the possibilities beyond" (300).

2. Braddon makes this statement not in reference to Lady Audley but to Robert Audley and his delicate hypochondriacal state of mind after hearing Lady Audley confess to pushing George Talboys into the well.

3. On the title page for *Thou Art the Man*, for instance, she is labeled this way.

4. According to Showalter, in the Victorian era, puerperal insanity was "widely accepted as a legitimate criminal defense, especially in cases of infanticide" ("Victorian Women and Insanity" 323).

5. Interestingly, the institution where Brandon Mountford's mother is held is described in a remarkably similar way. The novel is set in 1886, and Mountford's mother is put away shortly after his birth; assuming he is 30, Mrs, Mountford is put away in 1856 (a few years before Lady Audley). Mountford's mother lives and dies in rooms which are "brightly furnished, home-like, comfortable even to luxury" with a "spacious, old-fashioned garden, where the trees and shrubs and holly hedges had been growing for more than a century" (1.182–3). Despite the seeming comfort of the place, in Mountford's eyes, his mother was "no better off than a State prisoner" (1.183). The Gothic trope of enclosure is again prominently featured, as century-old holly hedges would most effectively serve as a barrier. While there is no way of knowing the severity of her epileptic condition, she is not encouraged to "outgrow" it like Mountford through a free adventurous life.

6. Despite the ambiguity of the character's language, the diagnosis of epilepsy was clearly defined at that moment in the history of medicine: by the 1860s scientist were beginning to recognize the condition as an actual physical malady. Researchers at London's newly established National Hospital for the Relief and Cure of the Paralysed and Epileptic had identified a physiological basis for epilepsy which countered the psychological explanation, the idea that personality and character, including immoral character, contributed to seizures. The discovery that phenobarbitol controlled epileptic seizures in many patients meant that "'hundreds of epileptics have been cured and are leading useful lives'" (Gowers, qtd. in Lannon 103). But as Susan Lannon points out in her article on the social control of epileptics during the latter half of the nineteenth century, findings about the physiological basis of epilepsy, as well as its successful cures and controls in the scientific community did not filter down to the general public. She writes: "people with epilepsy were still viewed by society and even by some physicians as lacking in moral character or as being physically and morally degenerate" (103).

7. Jill Matus argues that Lady Audley's "female-based" madness obscures cultural hegemony: "gender participates in the production of culture- and class-specific norms, which are then represented as natural" (334).

8. Men in *Lady Audley's Secret* are not exempt from categorization through gender expectations either: at the beginning of the book Robert Audley is presented as being unmanly, since he sits around reading French novels and is unwilling to take on a profession.

9. Nicole Fisk argues that she does influence the other three women in the novel (Clara Talboys, Alicia Audley, and Phoebe Marks) to live more independently.

10. The most famous of these is Max Nordau's *Degeneration*, which was translated into English in 1895. Lombroso's work *L'homme criminel* was also influential, and curiously, it addresses not just the nature of the criminal but of the epileptic as well.

WORKS CITED

Beckson, Karl. *London in the 1890s: A Cultural History.* New York: Norton, 1992.

Braddon, M. E. *Lady Audley's Secret.* 1862. New York: Oxford University Press, 2003.

_____. *Thou Art the Man.* 3 vols. London: Simpkin, Marshall, 1895.

Briganti, Chiara. "Gothic Maidens and Sensation Women: Lady Audley's Journey from the Ruined Mansion to the Madhouse." *Victorian Literature and Culture* 19 (1991): 189–211.

Clark, Pierce L. "A Critique of the Legal, Economic and Social Status of the Epileptic."
    Journal of the American Institute of Criminal Law and Criminology 17.2 (Aug 1926):
    218–233.
Fiske, Nicole. "Lady Audley as Sacrifice: Curing Female Disadvantage in *Lady Audley's
    Secret.*" *Victorian Newsletter* 105 (Spring 2004): 24–27.
Halberstam, Judith. *Skin Shows: Gothic Horror and the Technology of Monsters.* Durham:
    Duke University Press, 1995.
Kestner, Joseph A. *Sherlock's Sisters: The British Female Detective, 1864–1913.* Farnham, Sur-
    rey, UK: Ashgate, 2003.
Lannon, Susan. "Free Standing: Social Control and the Sane Epileptic, 1850–1950."
    Archives of Neurology 59.6 (June 2002): 1031–1037.
Matus, Jill L. "Disclosure as 'Cover Up': The Discourse of Madness in *Lady Audley's Secret.*"
    University of Toronto Quarterly 62.3 (1993): 334–55.
McCandless, Peter. "Liberty and Lunacy: The Victorians and Wrongful Confinement."
    *Madhouses, Mad-doctors, and Madmen: The Social History of Psychiatry in the Victo-
    rian Era.* Ed. Andrew Scull. Philadelphia: University of Pennsylvania Press, 1981.
Schaffer Talia. *Literature and Culture at the Fin de Siècle.* New York: Pearson Longman,
    2007.
Schroeder, Natalie, and Ronald A. Schroeder. *From Sensation to Society: Representations of
    Marriage in the Fiction of Mary Elizabeth Braddon 1862–1866.* Newark: University of
    Delaware Press, 2006.
Showalter, Elaine. "Desperate Remedies: Sensation Novels of the 1860s." *Victorian Newslet-
    ter* 49 (Spring 1976): 1–5.
_____. *Sexual Anarchy: Gender and Culture in the Fin de Siècle.* New York: Penguin, 1990.
_____. "Victorian Women and Insanity." *Madhouses, Mad-doctors, and Madmen: The
    Social History of Psychiatry in the Victorian Era.* Ed. Andrew Scull. Philadelphia: Uni-
    versity of Pennsylvania Press, 1981.
Voskuil, Lynn M. "Acts of Madness: Lady Audley and the Meanings of Victorian Femi-
    ninity." *Feminist Studies* 27.3 (Fall 2001): 611–39.
Wood, Jane. *Passion and Pathology in Victorian Fiction.* Oxford: Oxford University Press,
    2001.

"Don't Look Now": Disguised Danger and Disabled Women in Daphne du Maurier's Macabre Tales

Maria Purves

Daphne du Maurier's Gothic novels, such as *Rebecca, Jamaica Inn* and *My Cousin Rachel,* tend to receive much critical attention; yet it is in the later short stories that her formidable grasp of the Gothic can be truly felt. In these macabre, often shocking, tales written between 1951 and 1970, du Maurier demonstrates a mastery of the Gothic form, creating new ways of imagining and experiencing Gothic subjects. Du Maurier's aspiration in these Gothic tales often seems to be the brutalization of the reader. In this she follows the Gothic lead of Horace Walpole and Matthew Lewis, whose aim was to shock and horrify their eighteenth-century audience (initiating, as they did so, a new literary form). Du Maurier's connection to Walpole, Lewis and the "male Gothic,"[1] as their particular style has come to be termed, is in itself remarkable coming from a female writer of romantic novels. Yet, the macabre tales graphically present horrifying shock, eliciting fear in readers as successfully as did Walpole, Lewis and their other heirs.

The common Gothic theme of incest described in "A Borderline Case," for example, is not a vaguely-defined attraction between siblings or a relationship between distant relatives, but is treated glaringly, utterly: a teenage girl has a romantic and sexual liaison with a man who, horrifyingly, turns out to be her father. Likewise the supernatural of du Maurier's stories is neither explained away, in the realistic manner of Ann Radcliffe, the progenitor of the "female Gothic," nor displaced into the realm of the fantastic or the unconscious, as in much modern Gothic. Instead the source of danger in the stories is represented as a bewildering, literally maddening, combination of both the psychological *and* the genuinely weird.

The Female Gothic in Du Maurier's Novels

In her long fiction, du Maurier displays a variety of traits associated with the female Gothic. Her romances tend to approach Gothic subjects and motifs in a subtle, oblique and complex manner.[2] The novels demonstrate a delicacy of representation of otherness which is notably lacking in the tales. In *Rebecca* for example, as Avril Horner and Sue Zlosnik note, Rebecca's otherness is inflected merely "by the text's association of her with 'Jewishness'" (112), and by her association with "several characteristics that traditionally denote the vampire" or "the *femme fatale*" (111). Ultimately Rebecca's otherness is implied, rather than delineated with horrifying and shocking detail. *My Cousin Rachel* is similarly ambiguous. Although Rachel's Italian blood is made a cipher for her otherness, and she has the disturbing ability to infantilize men in the manner of the *femme fatale*, du Maurier's text is indefinite as to the authenticity of Rachel's otherness.[3] Neither narrator nor reader ever learns whether a stranger or monster really *does* lurk behind Rachel's attractive, comfortingly maternal and therefore *heimlich* exterior.

Du Maurier's attitude toward female disability is also gentler in the novels, where she tends to conform to the (perhaps uncomfortable) romantic stereotype of female illness as a form of containment for female independence. Nina Auerbach notes that in the novels "Du Maurier's most independent women" become either "paralyzed" or "devoured from within, usually by some variety of female cancer" (111). The crippled characters, such as Honor Harris in *The King's General*, suffer from having to "watch, immobilized, moved from place to place by others as men plunder, boast and kill" (110). In fact, "crippled or cancerous, du Maurier women are doomed, not because they are weak ... but because they are not really women ... they do not love enough, or well enough, or consistently enough, or at all" (112). According to Auerbach, uterine cancer is "a recurrent symptom ... of the refusal to love" (111). Auerbach points to Rebecca's posthumously diagnosed uterine cancer and "malformation of the uterus," and the uterine cancers of both the emotionally constrained mother in *The Parasites,* and Celia, her dutiful daughter, whose fibroid tumors prevent her from having the children she craves. This list could also include Françoise in *The Scapegoat* (1957), an emotionally fragile pregnant mother who is bedridden because of the danger of miscarriage. She is unable to deal with the needs of her young daughter, and is finally killed by a fall which also kills the unborn baby.

Gothic Horror in Du Maurier's Stories: The Monstrous Other

In du Maurier's short stories, however, there is no nuance, nor is there any sense of sympathy for female disability. In the stories, the starkly explicit use of Gothic motifs shapes the representation of the horrifying Other, specifically the monstrous Other, that often presents a very obvious physical difference. In her macabre tales, du Maurier returns time and again to disability, and particularly female disability, as a means of representation of grotesque otherness. In the collection *The Apple Tree* (1952), the evil, the monstrous and the uncanny are characterized by a "crippled" peasant woman, a "humped" and "freakish" tree embodying the spirit of an infertile wife, and a woman whose beauty is destroyed by leprosy. One critic described the tales as "all concerned with malformation" (Margaret Forster 260). The collections which followed, *The Breaking Point* (1959) and *Not After Midnight* (1971),[4] persist with the motif, which sees its climax, its horrifying apotheosis, in the dwarf murderess in "Don't Look Now." All of these characters (and more besides) mark an extraordinary leap in du Maurier's Gothic imagination from the subtle depiction of otherness in the novels to a more brutal, uncompromising account in the stories. The stories mark du Maurier's move from the female interpretation or vision of the Gothic, in which terror is implied without coming to fruition, to the masculine Gothic, which centers on the spectacle of shock and horror.

Du Maurier's affinity for the male Gothic tradition works to explain her focus on female disability in her creation of the monstrous Other. Although she displays a notable aversion to females and to female disability, this aversion does not appear in her attitude toward her male characters. In du Maurier's Gothic world, disability lends a man romantic interest, setting him apart in an attractive way. Nick, the anti-hero of "A Borderline Case" for example, has one eye. However rather than distancing him as the Other, his eye patch gives him a dashing, piratic air,[5] making him irresistibly seductive to an adventure-seeking teenage girl, Shelagh, who, shockingly, turns out to be his daughter. Similarly the albino vicar of Altarnun in *Jamaica Inn*, Francis Davey — a "freak of nature" (114) — is other-worldly, and somewhat charming rather than completely repellent. Initially he is actually appealing in a romantic sense: his white eyes instantly relax Mary Yellan, so much so that she allows herself to be taken back to his house after he finds her, distraught, on the moor. He and his peaceful abode seem like something from a fairytale, and like an infant responding to a fairytale Mary is soothed out of the fear which consumes her at Jamaica Inn. His voice "would compel her to admit every secret her heart possessed.... She could trust him; that at least was certain" (120). Even when we come to realize that his whiteness signifies a ghostly cold-bloodedness, this awareness does not detract from Davey's compelling qualities: indeed his grandiose mysticism rather adds fascination to his disability and vice versa.

Monstrous Female Disability

However in du Maurier's stories, a disabled woman is always instantly and completely repellent. "The Little Photographer," in the 1952 collection *The Apple Tree*,[6] provides a good example of du Maurier's differing representations of male and female disability. When a vacationing aristocratic Frenchwoman meets a "crippled" brother and sister who run a photography shop, she feels "a fascination" and later "a kind of compassion" for the brother's disability. However, she feels straightforward repulsion[7] for the sister's "grotesque" limp. The "lame" man is very sympathetic, beautiful even: "the face that looked out upon her from the open window was so unusual, so gentle, that it might have come straight from a stained-glass saint in a cathedral" (77). Indeed, the little photographer's look of the martyr anticipates the role he is to play. The bored Marquise, herself a monster, starts a sexual affair with him and, when the affair becomes too complicated, she pushes him over a cliff into the sea to his death. He dies as he lived, silently, without making a splash: a powerless, dispensible creature sacrificed to aristocratic ennui. The character of the crippled sister who provokes hysteria and repulsion in the Marquise, however, undergoes an interesting transformation. Just when the Marquise is thinking that she has gotten away with murder, the sister appears with some compromising photographs of the Marquise taken by her dead brother and, the glint in her eye rendering grotesque her veneer of peasant humility, demands lifelong financial recompense for his death. The woman's incapacitating disability, which earlier on in the tale had amused the Marquise so much, is proved to be a deceptive smoke-screen. The disability conceals a persona more cunning, ruthless, and capable than that of the monstrous Marquise herself. Once the crippled woman is thus empowered and the Marquise has become *her* stupid and trembling victim, it is impossible for the reader to pity the sister's disability. It is impossible, in fact, (because du Maurier is not subtle on this point[8]) to read the limp as anything other than a signifier of dishonesty and corruption — just as the brother's clubfoot signifies his vulnerability. Finally the disabled sister is unsettling — a figure of dis-ease. And it is her disability that lends her the power to provoke this dis-ease in others.

It is hard to avoid the whiff of misogyny in "The Little Photographer," and the other macabre tales. Unlike the case of the women in the novels, female disability in the stories does not work as a containment device for female power, although at first glance, the disabled women of the stories might appear to be as vulnerable as those of the novels. In the manner of Gothic masquerade, the dwarf woman of "Don't Look Now" initially appears (to the main character, John) to be a child needing protection: "It was a child, a little girl — she couldn't have been more than five or six — wearing a short coat over her minute skirt, a pixie hood covering her head" (*Classics of the Macabre* 31). Yet, the seeming vulnerability masks a grotesquely disabled and apparently mad woman, as we discover at the moment of John's senseless death, at the hands of the creature who turns out to be not a child but a gibbering "little thick-set woman dwarf ... with a great square adult head ... grinning" who throws a knife at John "with hideous strength" (*Classics of the Macabre* 69).[9]

The Dangerous Mask of Female Disability

Here as in *The Little Photographer* we can see du Maurier playing with the romantic concept of female illness which is a feature of her novels. The dwarf's disability makes her more powerful, not less. The disability allows her to appear vulnerable and to deceive her victims who follow her into a dark place out of a concern for her welfare, when she turns on them in order to act out an orgy of senseless violence. The disabled women in the stories have a similar effect on the audience. Typically, du Maurier's disabled women at first engage the reader's sympathy by provoking pity through their frailty or because of the repulsion expressed by the other characters. Yet eventually the disabled women transform into powerful creatures who mete out retribution on the very characters who belittled them. With that our sympathy is replaced by unease and herein — in the transformation from weak and pitiable creatures to powerful freaks — lies the horror, the epiphany of the uncanny.

Thus, du Maurier's disabled women are monstrous because they *appear* to be harmless and weak, when they are, in all cases, supremely — and brutally — powerful. Brutal, because they vanquish and kill those who threaten them — typically the sort of confident, controlling man or masculinized woman (as in the case of the Marquise in "The Little Photographer") who populates du Maurier's fiction. The disabled monsters also debase their victims in a spectacular manner. The dwarf whose senseless attack strips John of all purpose, dignity, and fight, humiliates him as she stabs him to death: "'Oh God' he thought, 'what a bloody silly way to die...'" (69). Du Maurier's disabled women act out the gendered revenge narratives of the Gothic with a fresh viciousness.

Here too, du Maurier troubles the categories of male and female Gothic. Gendered revenge narratives are (unsurprisingly) generally associated with the female Gothic. Diane Hoeveler argues that "the female Gothic novel represented women who ostensibly appear to be conforming to their acceptable roles within the patriarchy but who actually subvert the father's power at every possible occasion and then retreat to studied postures of conformity whenever they risk exposure to public censure." (6) However while Hoeveler's "Gothic feminist" masquerades passivity in order to thwart the actions of the predatory patriarch, the disabled women in du Maurier's tales play a far more active and spectacular role in his downfall. Indeed du Maurier's disabled women are much more remarkable than the Gothic feminists of Radcliffian fiction because they win their battles easily and their strongest weapon is not the physical perfection and fragility of the eighteenth-century heroine, but the disability that hides true power.

While du Maurier finds the stereotype of repulsive female disability to be valuable as a source of repellant horror, paradoxically, she puts female disability to good use: to subvert the world of patriarchal totality. Notably then, her disabled women are also Gothic feminists, of an entirely new and unique sort. Through them, du Maurier rewrites the Gothic paradigm, fusing the subtle narrative of female subversion in the female Gothic with the more brutal and overt destructive horror of the male Gothic.

Monstrous Feminism in the Stories

Before we interrogate further we should look more closely at these female types and the ways in which du Maurier both demonizes and empowers them. Mrs. Stoll in "Not After Midnight" is an excellent example: an unattractive deaf woman with hinted-at supernatural powers who takes revenge on her husband, and at the same time punishes the sexual sins of the bumptious male narrator in a uniquely macabre way. We should note that when it comes to sense-disability, du Maurier's representation shifts into a higher gear. Du Maurier is at her most uncanny when writing about blindness and deafness because she links them with clairvoyance, a concept which seems to have particularly preoccupied her during her turbulent middle years when the macabre stories were written.[10] Du Maurier endows blind, deaf, or sometimes "retarded" females with preternatural levels of perception, which not only compensates for their disabilities but makes them immensely powerful and vastly dangerous to the men around them.

In "Not After Midnight" the narrator Timothy Grey, is typical of du Maurier's male protagonists. Reflecting his name, he is rational, traditional, conservative (a classics teacher), stiff (he is a confirmed bachelor, although he had been engaged once), and solitary. Grey's foreign travel allows him to pretend on his annual holiday that he is not a dull, small-minded man who never had the courage to try for his ambitions: his passport falsely reads professor rather than teacher, because that title "arouses respect in the attitude of reception clerks" (*Classics* 238).

Grey takes a holiday in Crete which begins badly—he is not satisfied with his hotel room, imperiously demands another, and later at dinner finds out that his new room was last occupied by a guest who drowned. Emphasizing Grey's similarity to the late Mr. Gordon, du Maurier introduces the all-important Gothic trope of the double. Gordon is Grey's twin, and his death hints at the imminent death of Grey's *heimlich*, or known, self. Gordon had become friendly with the people in the chalet opposite, a Mr. and Mrs. Stoll, and Grey finds a card the Stolls had sent to the dead man inviting him to call on them, "not after midnight." Stoll is a heavy drinking, unpleasant American with an obsessive interest in archeology (indeed the hotel staff report that he brews his own beer from an ancient Cretan recipe); and Mrs. Stoll is his deaf, inhuman, automaton-like wife. When she speaks—only once, to invite Grey to call on them, "not after midnight," reinforcing the doubling of Grey and Gordon—she has "a voice without any expression."

As is usual with du Maurier's disabled women, Mrs. Stoll seems at first to be laughably unthreatening. She is impassive and tolerates her husband's bad behavior without embarrassment, leading Grey to dismiss her as "half-witted." However, he learns that actually, like the disabled sister in "The Little Photographer," the deaf Mrs. Stoll has furtive strengths. The Stolls are treasure hunters, illegally excavating an ancient wreck off the coast. In fact, Mrs. Stoll does all the excavating; Stoll, landlocked possibly by his alcoholism (yet another disability demonized in the story) struts about naked on the beach, drinking, and much resembling a hairy satyr. After Grey spies on their illegal archeological activities, Stoll tries to buy his silence in a threatening telephone call. Grey begins to suspect that Gordon did not drown accidentally. That night, he watches with horror from his darkened window as Mrs. Stoll swims over to his chalet. He pictures her in a black rubber suit, mask and flippers, and wonders if she treads water beneath his chalet every night while her husband lies drunk. The idea horrifies him and he waits in the silence and darkness for her arrival on his balcony.

The episode demonstrates du Maurier's mastery of the suspenseful Gothic moment. Mrs. Stoll is instantly invested with the dark eroticism of the Gothic *femme fatale*, the huntress. The eros and danger she suddenly displays combine to make her a sublimely sinister figure. Du Maurier has already set her up as a mysterious and impenetrable inhuman automaton, due to her deafness and the consequent robot-like quality of her voice and affect. This inhumanity, and its danger, is amplified when she is in the water. Du Maurier emphasizes her inhuman, seal-like nature with reference to her ease in the black water and her rubber-suited figure, sleek and black and dripping. The moment is one of pure horror, as Grey waits for Mrs. Stoll to penetrate his domicile:

> I could see nothing ... but the sounds came through the chinks in the shutters and I knew she was there ... even if I shouted, "What do you want?" she would not hear.... I sat there hunched on my bed ... full of foreboding, my dread of that sleek black figure increasing minute by minute so that all sense and reason seemed to desert me, and my dread was the more intense and irrational because the figure in the rubber suit was female [268–9].

Notably, even at the moment when his life is endangered by this inhuman creature, Grey still considers that he is being irrational in considering a woman to be dangerous. Grey is thus exposed by his reaction to Mrs. Stoll's transformation from pathetic lady to powerful female. We realize (if we had not already guessed) that for Grey, Mrs. Stoll's deafness is almost incidental — it is her femaleness which renders her as Other. Mrs. Stoll's unfeminine aggressive penetration is repulsive to him. "What did she want?" he asks, revealing himself to be innocent of what a woman could want, at midnight, rapping at his chalet door. The unknown and unconventional terrifies him. This woman is even more terrifying than most because of her empowering disability. The heightened powers of her sense of sight and touch allow her to move with ease in the darkness of night which renders the "normal" Grey blind. As in the case of most Gothic monsters (and many women), the male subject cannot communicate with her or reason with her. He must simply, passively, await the unknown violation with terror.

Gothic Encounter with the Unknown Self

The expected rape, when it comes, is a psychological sexual violation rather than a physical one, but no less damaging: the result is Grey's nervous breakdown. Mrs. Stoll leaves a priceless Greek jug shaped like a grotesque face and decorated with lewd satyrs. A card explains that it represents Silenos, Dionysus's tutor, who mistakenly brought up the infant Dionysus as a girl, since he was unable to distinguish truth from falsehood. Grey dismisses the gift and goes to bed where he dreams a disturbing dream. In the dream, he is back with his students:

> My boys ... wore vine-leaves in their hair, and had a strange, unearthly beauty both endearing and corrupt.... I put my arms about them, and the

pleasure they gave me was insidious and sweet ... the man who pranced in
their midst and played with them was not myself, not the self I knew, but a
demon shadow emerging from a jug. (270)

The sexual imagery is clear. Grey struggles to awaken to escape the experience which is of course the awakening of his true desires. Just as Silenos could
not see that the "girl" he was nurturing was in fact a boy, so Grey has neglected to identify the gender that he desires. The dangerous Mrs. Stoll, who
can navigate dark waters, pries open his subconscious, allowing him to recognize his suppression of Dionysus, repression of his own sexuality and his
desire for his own boys.

Notably the pederast in the dream is a self that has emerged "from a jug,"
reflecting Mrs. Stoll's gift, but also anticipating Grey's guilt-induced alcoholism which begins the next day when he tastes some of Stoll's homebrew
when it is offered to him by the barman of the hotel. The illness of alcoholism
also takes on Gothic undertones in this section of the story. The Gothic tendency to subvert notions of fixed and unified identity emerges as Grey's first
drink begins to erode his self-control and inhibition. As he continues to drink,
from the jug itself, he finds himself admiring its depiction of "pleasing, wanton joy" and pleasantly remembers his wanton dream. From that point on,
we witness Grey's rapid slide towards the total destruction of the rational and
normative person he thought he was. The Gothic horror of this disintegration is compounded when Grey finds the dead body of Stoll in the underwa-
ter wreck. Looking into the dead man's eyes he recognizes the "despair" and
"knowledge," including the self-knowledge, that he will soon encounter. The
seemingly passive and weakened Mrs. Stoll has destroyed them both. She
dominates even the landscape by the end of the narrative, as she stands on
the hills looking down at the two ruined men through glinting binoculars, a
symbol of her preternatural visionary powers.

Ancient Supernatural Powers of the Female: Blind Clairvoyance

Mrs. Stoll, like du Maurier's other sense-disabled women, thus tends to
embody the ancient and primitive power of the female. Mrs. Stoll is the powerful, all-seeing supernatural female. She dispenses death, is at one with the
nature of the Cretan landscape, is at home in its waters and is a domineer-
ing presence upon its hills. In her delivery of the jug to Grey, she embodies
Crete itself, offering up her history, mythology and mysteries in livid colors
to the dry-as-dust classics teacher, who has spent his life repressing the joys
to be found in the ancient cultures. Mrs. Stoll's gift of the jug and the dreams

it engenders shows Grey that Crete is also unknowable to such as he. Mrs. Stoll thus takes on the supernatural prophetic powers of the seer. Her access to mysteries — the mysteries of Crete, the mysteries of Grey's unconscious — allows her to hold a mirror up to Grey, forcing him to face himself for the first time. In this role her deafness is also an asset; it gives her the steeliness of the priestess-oracle who is emotionally cut off from the consequences of her truth-telling.[11]

The clairvoyant powers of a sense disabled women also provide a dangerous glimpse into unknown mysteries in du Maurier's best-known Gothic story, "Don't Look Now." In the story, a blind woman's visionary abilities emasculate the rational, confident protagonist John. John and his wife, Laura are on holiday in Venice after the death of their young daughter. Laura's grief is intense and debilitating and John feels that he is losing her to it. However a blind woman, holidaying in Venice with her twin sister,[12] sees the dead girl sitting next to the couple, smiling and happy — an incident which instantly offers Laura the comfort and relief which John is unable to provide.

In the typical du Maurier pattern, the sisters appear initially as pathetic and comical. Yet even at first encounter John recognizes them as a threat to his masculinity[13]: "He had seen the type on golf-courses and at dog-shows ... and if you came across them at a party in somebody's house they were quicker on the draw with a cigarette-lighter than he was himself, a mere male, with pocket matches" (31). John and Laura keep meeting the sisters in different places, and John is more and more angered and frustrated by their continuing power to comfort Laura. Under the influence of the blind sister, then, John and Laura trade emotional states, and, by implication, gender: for John has up until this point treated Laura's anguish as a feminine weakness, to be cured by a holiday and a good shopping expedition. The blind sister's intrusion forces John into a state of hysteria and paranoia, traditionally the peculiar domain of women. John also turns out to be psychic too, also representing his feminization at the hands of the seer-like blind woman. His clairvoyance comes as a surprise — cleverly implied early on in Nicholas Roeg's film version, but not in du Maurier's text. Ironically, John similarly possesses the "feminine" powers of compassion and indulgence, which could have brought back his wife, had he only acknowledged them.

However, John's male rationality (his blind spot) prevents him from recognizing the benevolent seeing powers of the blind woman. When she warns him that his daughter wants him to leave Venice, John is dismissive of the sisters' knowledge, although Laura takes this seriously and leaves to care for her ill son in England. When John sees a vaporetto on the Grand Canal, with Laura and the sisters on board, he discounts the possibilities of a supernatural meaning. It is, in fact, a vision of his own funeral but John assumes that the sisters are stealing Laura away. His wrong-headed decision to remain in Venice, to find Laura, and to bring the sisters to justice leads very quickly to his own senseless death at the hands of the dwarf. Admittedly, the plot is labyrinthine, like the cityscape of Venice, the perfect (and frequently used) setting for the Gothic, with its old associations of intrigue and horror, and with the masquerade, the principal source of the disabled woman's power.

The notion of physical blindness leading to a more powerful "second-sight," recurs in the story, "The Blue Lenses." Marda West acquires a stronger perception of herself and others after becoming temporarily blind. With her eyes bandaged after a recent operation, Marda experiences unfamiliar sensations: she experiences lesbian feelings for her night nurse, Nurse Ansel; she experiences an urge to fake her responses to the nurses and doctors, even to her loving husband whom she senses is patronizing her because she is sick. When the bandages are removed, Marda sees people "as they really are" — everyone bears an apt animal's head. To her horror, Nurse Ansel has the head of a snake; her husband is a vulture. Their animal movements betray their sexual relationship. Marda senses that they are planning to kill her for her money. She tries to run away and the world outside is also full of predators. Excessively sighted, she is less able than when she was blind. When Marda is captured and returned to the hospital, the doctors agree to replace the blue lenses with which she had been fitted. Finally the world looks normal again — that is, until she catches sight of herself in the mirror with the head of a timid doe, bowing in sacrifice. Here the disabled woman as protagonist and point-of-view character offers a new perspective on du Maurier's reading of the female condition.

With bandaged eyes, Marda looks inward and discovers new and exciting things about herself. With the veil of reality lifted she sees the uncivilized, nonhuman relationship that she, the innocent victim has with the others in her world. Clearly du Maurier is implying that conventional sight (and thinking) represents the true state of blindness.

This is the underlying theme of du Maurier's Gothic feminist narratives: for a woman, being blind and deaf to the demands of the world allows for the development of the powerful inner self, the ability to see and hear realities that are obscured by the conventional senses. Sense disability is thus an advantage for a woman, allowing her to hide and nurture her powers, be she a benevolent Marda or a predatory Mrs. Stoll.[14] Du Maurier's representation of self-fulfilled vicious and predatory women, like Mrs. Stoll, and even possibly like the dwarf in "Don't Look Now," complicates this reading. To understand the viciousness inherent in the motif it is necessary to interrogate du Maurier's strategies in coping with her own very real dis-ease.

The Uses of the Gothic Veil: Literature and Life

A comparative reading of the figure of the disabled woman in the novels and in the stories suggests that these two types correspond to two stages of du Maurier's life. In the novels, the passive, absent and silent woman, emblematized by the ill and spectral Rebecca, indicates a reading of the disabled woman as metaphor for the unhappy and angry wife, enduring her limited social role. The wife's limitations — symbolized by disability — include the enforced female silence and passivity that are recorded in the novels and reflective of the social era during which du Maurier herself was a devoted yet unhappy young wife whose husband had a tendency to stray.

On the other hand, the disability of the macabre woman in du Maurier's stories works as a veil that obscures real power, highlighting the social deviance — and danger — of the powerful and independent woman. The dwarf in "Don't Look Now," amplifies the dangerous deviance of the independent female. Like many of du Maurier's dangerous and macabre females, the dwarf capitalizes on her seeming weakness, the non-normative size that allows her to present herself in the guise of a small child, masking her true identity and thereby catching her victims off guard. Like the dwarf, Mrs. Stoll uses her disability as a sort of veil. Mrs. Stoll's deafness shields her from the ugliness and ineptitude of men, and obscures her own formidable strength. Her ability to silence the outside voices that command the imperatives of the gendered norm also contributes to her power. Mrs. Stoll thus represents the detachment and veiled secrecy necessary, in du Maurier's view at least, to female self-fulfillment and empowerment, in a world which continues to denigrate and demonize overt demonstrations of female power.

Du Maurier knew the value of such a veil. The pressures of her emotional and sexual desires were at odds with the masquerade of respectable married life that she was living. Du Maurier resented having to resume married life, and to relinquish sexual, emotional and spatial freedoms she had enjoyed during the war. The stress of leading a doubled, veiled life eventually led her to aspire to shut herself off from her emotions and "become blank, become withdrawn, in some strange inner life that might be entirely intellectual and spiritual, after enough work and discipline" (Letter to Ellen Doubleday, December 8, 1949).

However, it was du Maurier's tendency towards sexual experimentation, specifically the great love affairs she had with women throughout her life, which really created the need for a veil of obscurity drawn between the two halves of her doubled life. The conventional du Maurier believed that real women were dutiful wives and mothers, and that lesbians and other women who deviated from the norm — single women for example, or artists or divorcées — were to be pitied, and mocked.[15] Because of her unconventional self, hiding behind the veil, du Maurier experienced a self-loathing which went beyond self-chastisement, in print or otherwise. She saw herself, and often referred to herself, as an incomplete woman.[16] The term implies inadequacy, defectiveness, abnormality. In short du Maurier saw herself as disabled because her non-normative sexuality prevented her from being the sort of "healthy" woman that society prized. It is entirely plausible that du Maurier's image of herself as incomplete contributed greatly to her creation of the disabled women in her macabre tales. Feeling herself to be disabled by her sexuality it seems inevitable that she would write about female disability, and in an oblique way. Indeed, her demonization of disabled women seems entirely in keeping with the self-hatred and fear about her sexuality which she expresses in her letters. Yet the supreme power that du Maurier assigns to these women sets them apart from the sick, suffering, dying romance heroines and points to a yet more complex psychology behind the representation.

It should be noted that the first two collections of macabre tales were written in the 1950s. This was a decade which represents an absolute turning-point in du Maurier's life. In 1947 du Maurier had fallen deeply in love with the wife of her American publisher, Ellen Doubleday. Although criticism has acknowledged this relationship as an important one and crucial to the writing of *September Tide* and *My Cousin Rachel*, Doubleday's influence on the short stories has been overlooked, and yet it is remarkable.[17] Doubleday and du Maurier were emotionally very close from their first meeting, and before the death of Doubleday's husband there were the beginnings of a sexual relationship[18]; but during a romantic holiday *à deux* in Europe, Doubleday started to draw back from the physical side of their relationship. Du Maurier's letters to Doubleday at that time make clear that the macabre was starting to take root in du Maurier's imagination out of humiliation and anger. The letters to Doubleday show that there is a direct link between du Maurier's feelings of dis-ease and the conception and writing of the short stories. The macabre, disabled female characters emerge to reflect du Maurier's conflicted sense of herself. [19]

Through the short, sharp, dark and brutal macabre stories, then, du Maurier works to empower her own de-formed self—which could find neither expression nor acceptance in the real world. Moreover, the stories trace her transforming sense of self. From the outside, we see the disabled woman as inhumanly monstrous, and incomprehensible to the human subject. But we also get a glimpse of the subjectivity of the disabled woman who — humanly, understandably — uses her disability to hide from the world that rejects and to nurture her powers, often for revenge. The very brutality of the tales that shock and mock also encourage the reader to recoil with horror, to perceive du Maurier as a monstrous brutalizing author. By the time she wrote the final collection *Not After Midnight* in 1970,[20] du Maurier *was* almost totally cut off from social interchange. Thus the cruelty and superb horror in her final tales ultimately comes from du Maurier's own persona, rather than from her disabled women. She is like the grotesque dwarf in "Don't Look Now." Inhabiting a haunted Venice, which du Maurier associated with lesbianism, the dwarf provides the shocking climax that brutalizes the character, John, and the reader. The climax — a simple lashing out, a totally unforeseen flash of absurd violence — epitomizes perfectly du Maurier's exploitation of the Gothic as an antic fantasy in which she, the incomplete woman, can assert her power over her readers.

NOTES

1. Following the classification of a "female Gothic," as exemplified by Ann Radcliffe who, in part as a reaction to Lewis's explicit treatments of taboo subjects, handled common Gothic motifs with subtlety.

2. In *The Scapegoat* for example du Maurier uses the Gothic motif of the double to engage with complex psychological questions.

3. When fans would ask du Maurier whether or not Rachel was guilty, Du Maurier would always reply that she herself had never been able to make up her mind on the subject.

4. The U.S. edition was entitled *Don't Look Now*.

5. The "black patch ... suggested Moshe Dayan" on whom du Maurier admitted to having a huge crush (*Don't Look Now* 189).

6. Re-titled *Kiss Me Again Stranger* for the American edition.

7. Worrying that her children will laugh at "the ugly, shuffling, crippled woman" she hurries them out of the shop, but actually it is she who is on the point of "heartless laughter." This desire to laugh at the sister is twice recalled when she meets the brother in the following days and compares his disability to his sister's: his high-fitted boot "did not repel her nor bring her to nervous laughter, as it had done before when she had seen the sister"; and again "his limp was not so pronounced as the sister's, he did not walk with that lurching, jerky step that produced stifled hysteria in the watcher" (*Kiss Me Again*, 77–80).

8. The Marquise's husband terms the club-footedness which runs in families "a taint in the blood" (108).

9. The horror of this moment is matched by its irony: John's initial concern for the "little girl" is linked to his grief over the loss of his own very young daughter. Du Maurier's use of the motif of the double in this instance is quite heartless: another example of her dynamic manipulation of Gothic convention to brutal effect. However that may be the point. Although Horner and Zlosnik read in the figure of the dwarf avenging-daughter and avenging-mother narratives, as well as masculine revulsion for the ageing female body (181–6), she can also be read as part of a more complex narrative describing the pitilessness of foreign landscapes in times of personal grief. Venice, a city built for pleasure, does not care for John and Laura's pain: "the bright façade put on for show, glittering by sunlight" continues blithely, oblivious to their desolation.

10. During her forties, du Maurier's life-changing love affair with Ellen Doubleday caused her to read much into her dreams and believe that she had a "radar apparatus" which

allowed her to pick up signals of distress from Ellen (see letters to Ellen Doubleday, December 30, 1948 and April 2, 1949).

11. Furthermore Mrs. Stoll's touch confers a more primitive, dark and ancient persona on Grey: she infects him, in fact, with a sexual dis-ease. An uncanny eroticism and an ability to uncover the disturbing sexual natures of others is an aspect of the sense-disabled woman to which du Maurier is repeatedly drawn.

12. Du Maurier revisits the Gothic trope of the double or twin, along with the Gothic landscape of Venice's dank cloisters, labyrinthine passages and crumbling buildings. She skillfully uses these tropes to underpin the Gothic threat posed by her disabled women. (Horner and Zlosnik, Nina Auerbach and Richard Kelly have written at length on the Gothic nature of Venice in "Don't Look Now," a fascinating topic, but one which falls beyond the scope of this essay. See Horner and Zlosnik, 173–187; Kelly, 131–5; and Auerbach, 151–7.)

13. Horner and Zlosnik read the blindness of the psychic sister as the symbolic demonstration of the "fear of castration." (9)

14. This is hardly a reading that is overtly shared by du Maurier, who often presents her disabled woman with repulsion, as an evil source of horror, an unsettling reflection of her personal sense of incompletion. We can take this further and read her characterization of disability as representing female acceptance of limiting, disabling social roles. Du Maurier suggests that a woman who accepts society's limited expectations, as she did, literally *de-forms herself.* What resounds in the subtext of the disabled female is the emotional cost to du Maurier of keeping her limited, fractured self in check.

15. Auerbach argues that in punishing women who do not sufficiently love men in her novels, du Maurier is chastising her "deviant" self. The argument is a compelling one.

16. See the letter to Ellen Doubleday, August 23, 1948: "You are a complete woman, and I have never been." Du Maurier also describes herself as "a half-woman."

17. Du Maurier's feelings for Doubleday shaped much of her writing for over twenty years.

18. There are references to "small rations" of lovemaking in du Maurier's letters to Doubleday (see letters dated July 7, 1949; July 21, 1949).

19. Du Maurier tells Doubleday that she wrote "The Apple Tree"—the first of the tales to feature her peculiar disabled Gothic feminist—"to release pent-up energy" fuelled by her feelings of impotency, rage and disappointment (Letter to Ellen Doubleday, October 9, 1951). The tree of the title clearly represents human disability and difference. Not only is it "humped," it is infertile, unable to bear fruit for years: "Somehow, deep in nature, [it had] gone awry and turned a freak" (*Classics* 95). When it comes to the man who owns the garden, the tree only manages to disgust where it tries to please. Clearly there are echoes of du Maurier's own predicament, not to mention self-image, here. When the tree finally blossoms, its blooms and fruit are scorned by the man who is repelled by its warped physicality. It reminds him of his long-suffering, infertile late wife, and he hates it. Deficient, useless, bearing only blighted fruit, the tree is finally felled by the one person it loves. It is painfully clear that the narrative mirrors du Maurier's own situation, or at least her reading of it. But du Maurier writes a violent ending, in which the tree silently triumphs, avenging the neglected, infertile wife, as well as itself. The pathetic "freakish" apple tree catches the foot of the arrogant man who has felled her in the stump of her trunk so that he is helplessly, ingloriously frozen to death in the snow. Du Maurier thus empowers the tree, and the reader simultaneously experiences repulsion and joy. Because du Maurier referred to this tale as a "little piece of fantasy" which she needed to get "off [her] chest," it is certainly plausible to read it as an exercise in self-empowerment and self-assertion.

Soon after completing "The Apple Tree" and therefore quite plausibly in the same frame of mind du Maurier wrote "Monte Verita." The story was written two months after du Maurier heard a piece of gossip about Doubleday's romantic life. Du Maurier wrote (with unconvincing humor) "I got into one of my most monastic moods, and have been writing a long macabre story ... which ... has relieved my feelings, and worked off a lot of suppressed steam" (Letter to Ellen Doubleday, December 6, 1951). In the story, a young married woman is mesmerized by a secret sect of women who live inside a mountain — the pointedly-named Mountain of Truth — and disappears to join them. When a man who admired her beauty seeks her there several years later he is horrified to find that she is a leper. Du Maurier's British publisher was disconcerted by the tale which implies that heterosexual sex is poisonous and that for special women, independent women, self-fulfillment cannot be found in marriage. The story and the response to it are significant when read in the light of du Maurier's feelings concerning Ellen Doubleday who had rejected her in favor of a continued heterosexual existence. Importantly, and marking her apart from the romantic heroines of the novels, the woman's disease does not make her unhappy; she is utterly at peace with herself. The leprosy is an uncanny transfiguration, the epiphany of the true (deviant and thereby independent) persona. In rejecting the world and its heterosexual norms, the young wife has released her true self. Du Maurier suggests that the grotesque deviance that requires a veil is actually empowering because it necessitates withdrawal from the world: an immensely positive thing because it enables self-discovery. For the young woman in the story, the physical beauty which drew men to her, was the real disability. It kept her from the (Mountain of) truth, from discovering herself through isolation. This is another tale which allows deviance to triumph, indeed in which deviance is celebrated. The tale reflects du Maurier's own psychological transformation at the time. Unrequited passion and unexpressed sexuality forced her to turn inward, to explore psychology, seeking "a new understanding of dreams" (Letter to Ellen Doubleday, January 23, 1953). Her new-found fascination with and reliance on the subconscious clearly influenced the motif of enhanced perception and second sight which runs throughout her macabre.

    20. Du Maurier wrote to Doubleday that she was "[leading] the life of a recluse."

WORKS CITED

Auerbach, Nina. *Daphne du Maurier, Haunted Heiress*. Philadelphia: University of Pennsylvania Press, 2000.

Du Maurier, Daphne. "A Border Line Case." *Don't Look Now*. By Daphne du Maurier. New York: Doubleday, 1971.

_____. "Don't Look Now." *Daphne du Maurier's Classics of the Macabre*. London: Victor Gollancz, 1987.

_____. *Jamaica Inn*. London: Victor Gollancz, 1978.

_____. *Kiss Me Again, Stranger*. New York: Doubleday, 1952.

_____. Letters. *Ellen McCarter Doubleday Papers, circa 1930s–1978*. Princeton University Library, Department of Rare Books and Special Collections.

_____. "Not after Midnight." *Daphne du Maurier's Classics of the Macabre*. London: Victor Gollancz, 1987.

Forster, Margaret. *Daphne du Maurier*. London: Chatto & Windus, 1993.

Hoeveler, Diane. *Gothic Feminism: The Professionalization of Gender from Charlotte Smith to the Brontës*. University Park: Pennsylvania State University Press, 1998.

Horner, Avril, and Sue Zlosnik. *Daphne du Maurier: Writing, Identity and the Gothic Imagination*. New York: St. Martin's Press, 1998.

Kellaway, Kate. "Daphne's Unruly Passions." *The Observer*. 15 April 2007.

Kelly, Richard. *Daphne du Maurier*. Boston: Twayne, 1987.

Deviled Eggs: Teratogenesis and the Gynecological Gothic in the Cinema of Monstrous Birth

Andrew Scahill

Cells fuse, split and proliferate; volumes grow, tissues stretch, and body fluids change rhythm, speeding up or slowing down. Within the body, growing as a graft, indomitable, there is an other. And no one is present within that simultaneously dual and alien space to signify what is going on. "It happens, but I'm not there." "I cannot realize it, but it goes on." Motherhood's impossible syllogism [Julia Kristeva "Desire in Language" 301].

There's this thing growing inside of me. It's not my baby. There's something wrong with the child. They don't belong to us anymore. They're using us, they're using our bodies. They're eating us alive [*The Unborn* 1981].

In 1968, Roman Polanski released his sixth film, a hugely successful adaptation of Ira Levin's modern Gothic novel *Rosemary's Baby*, to a mixed critical response. In the film, young mother Rosemary (Mia Farrow) slowly discovers that she has been impregnated by a Satanic cult, and will bear the son of the devil. Notable for its extreme paranoia and claustrophobia, the film offers Rosemary no reprieve as her husband, her neighbors, her friends, and even her doctors seem involved in a vast conspiracy to circumscribe her autonomy. The film closes with Rosemary staring at her demonic child, noting the inhuman qualities of its body ("What have you done to him? What have you done to his eyes, you maniacs!"), and slowly acceding to maternal responsibility as she cradles her deformed and demonic offspring. Reviewers for the film honed in on Mia Farrow's portrayal of Rosemary, praising her acting talents and simultaneously abhorring her infantile, suffering character. Writing for *The New Yorker*, Penelope Gilliat referred to the film derisively as a base exercise in exploitation that wasted Polanski's skill and sophistication on what she deemed "[a]n exercise in Gynecological Gothic" ("Anguish under the Skin" 87–89).

Conception: The Gynecological Gothic

Indeed, *Rosemary's Baby* calls to mind any number of endangered Gothic heroines who have been ensnared by patriarchal authority. Most notably, the film recalls the protagonist of Charlotte Perkins Gilman's "The Yellow Wallpaper,"[1] infantilized by her husband and driven to fits of madness by a patriarchal medical establishment that deems her "hysterical." In the cinema of the Gynecological Gothic, inaugurated by Polanski's film, the womb is a contested terrain, and the pregnant female is beset both from without and from within. She finds herself alone against a conspiratorial establishment which seeks to control the reproductive function of her body, and she is simultaneously convinced that her unborn child is somehow not her own, its monstrosity apparent by the manner in which it displays a sentience independent and opposed to her own.

Rosemary's Baby is certainly not the first film to play upon parental anxieties or to figure the child as a site of alienation. The child as Other has a long history in cinema,[2] dating back to the maternal melodrama of *The Bad Seed* (1956), wherein an evil young girl commits a series of murders, and covers her crimes by presenting a veneer of performative childhood innocence. There is even a case of village-wide alien impregnation in the 1960 British film *Village of the Damned* which gives rise to a cabal of eerie psychic children out to conquer the Earth. This film, however, represents older children, who are autonomous human beings. The monstrous infant or fetus as a preoccupation of the horror genre seems to emerge in the cinematic landscape with the 1968 release of *Rosemary's Baby* and following *It's Alive!* (1974), other films continued to explore the Gynecological Gothic: *I Don't Want to Be Born* (1975), *Embryo* (1976), *Eraserhead* (1977), *Demon Seed* (1977), *The Manitou* (1977), *Progeny* (1979), *The Brood* (1979), *Alien* (1979), *Humanoids from the Deep* (1980), *Inseminoid* (1981), *Xtro* (1983), *The Fly* (1986), and *The Unborn* (1991). In these films, the unnatural conception and birth is generally attributed to supernatural or fantastic causes: rape by demonic forces (*Rosemary's Baby*), artificial intelligence (*Demon Seed*), or inhuman/alien entities (*Alien, Humanoids from the Deep, Inseminoid, Xtro, The Fly*); possession by ghosts (*The Manitou, I Don't Want to Be Born*); or mad science run amok (*Embryo, The Brood, The Unborn*).

The political ideologies of these films vary wildly; however, what remains consistent is the manner in which the female body has been in some way invaded or corrupted by external forces to create an unnatural monstrosity. In keeping with the syntactic structure of the invasion genre, the witness/mother is often dismissed by the arbiters of medical, legal, and familial authority, deemed as "hysterical" and prone to fantasy or paranoia.[3] In the vast majority of these films, the pregnant Gothic heroine is witness to her own bodily invasion and yet quelled into self-doubt by patriarchal authority. Indeed, forces are continually at work to immobilize the mother, hyperbolizing the methods of modern obstetrics that favor docile, inert bodies, thus mirroring the shift from midwifery to medical surveillance in field of natal care. This formation finds its most exaggerated form in *Demon Seed*, wherein Susan (Julie Christie) is raped and impregnated by Proteus, an artificial intelligence that traps her within her home until the cyborg fetus comes to term. Isolated and infantilized, the beleaguered heroine also finds herself at the mercy of her unborn child whose survivalism will supersede her desire to sever the parasitic bond between them. When the female body is not invaded from the outside, in the Gynecological Gothic, the unborn child itself is a symptomatic manifestation of societal ills — in which the child, socially overdetermined as the harbinger of a better, brighter future — is refigured as the manifestation of a devolving, polluted futurity.

Taken as a whole, monstrous birth in cinema has been critically regarded as intensely regressive pro-life fables, a revenge-of-the-unborn tale delivering punitive remittance for women's increasingly democratized access to birth control. The terrorized female body is deemed arcane and monstrous. In Barbara Creed's ruminations on the "monstrous-feminine," she argues that the Gynecological Gothic portrays the female body as an arcane site of monstrous regeneration. For Creed, who draws heavily upon Julia Kristeva's notion of "abjection," the fecund/regenerative body becomes a spectacle-laden site of horror that encourages the audience to project fascination and repulsion onto reproduction and female sexuality. In these films, says Creed, the pregnant body is an abject site of incoherence, incongruous with the category-obeying self and the societal structures that demand facile identifications.

Certainly, the critical attention focused upon the pregnant female body, made monstrous by the secrets within, is important and productive. Yet the horrible fetus and baby also merit attention in order to consider the cultural discourses that give birth to the image of fetus-as-monster. The cinema of monstrous birth, roughly from 1968 to 1981,[4] provides much material for analysis, including a consideration of how this cinema exploits and negotiates the unprecedented presence of the fetus in the public sphere during this period. More a structured polysemy than a coherent statement, these films evidence an extreme anxiety in reference to changes in reproductive technologies, images, and definitions. The cinema of the Gynecological Gothic stands at the liminal juncture of motherhood's impossible syllogism — competing discourses marking the mother/fetus as simultaneously part and whole and the fetal body as both anthropomorphic and yet inhumanly alien. The Gynecological Gothic is a mode that is remarkably permeable in its interplay between the fictional and the actual, a horror Lucy Fischer calls "an allegory of the real" in her work on parturition anxiety (Fischer 413). Thus, while the representation of monstrous birth within the horror genre is shaped by the social and juridical discourses and ideological battles in the public sphere, the fictional aspect provides a lingua franca to articulate anxieties about these same shifting renegotiations.

Teratogenesis and Fetal Monstrosity

Monstrosity and infancy have a long and intimate history, linked most succinctly in the study of abnormal and deformed bodies. Teratology, or the "science of monsters," has been a consistent preoccupation of medical, religious, and legal sectors since antiquity. Indeed, the study of birth defects and their causes, called "teratogenesis"[5] by the contemporary medical establishment, literally means "monster birth." The categorization of non-normative bodies, like attached twins and hermaphrodites,[6] was part of popular seventeenth-century scientific inquiry, which sought to order the natural world according to emerging scientific technologies for knowing and documenting what once the purview of folklore and magic.[7]

In her essay "Signs of Wonder and Traces of Doubt: On Teratology and Embodied Differences," Rosi Braidotti notes that monstrous childbirth, as a preoccupation of both folklore and scientific discourse, has a long cultural history of expressing anxiety over the reproductive power of the maternal body, including the power to produce non-normative bodies. Indeed, Mary Douglas's *Purity and Danger* has noted the ways in which the pregnant body conjures up archetypal fears of contagion and of "the unborn child with capricious ill will which makes it a danger towards others" (118–9).[8] The deformed child, for its part, has traditionally functioned as a potent symbol that represents, and literally embodies, the danger of taboo-breaking. Recalling etymological origins of teratogenesis, the non-normative infantile body is awe-inspiring and dangerous in its liminality and supposed impurity. Even in contemporary cultural discourse, the non-normative infant body indicates the terrors of taboo sexual practices such as incest and inbreeding, the drama of parental neglect and ignorance (fetal alcohol syndrome, "crack babies"), or the reaffirmation of the primacy of industrialized nations over impoverished "primitive" or "Third World" nations.

In twentieth-century medical and juridical discourse, however, we find teratology and teratogenesis less concerned with confirming the ascendance of normative adult bodies than it is about the reduction of potential abnormal bodies and the suitability of certain adult bodies for reproduction. Indeed, eugenics underlies much of the institutional rhetoric of childrearing, particularly in terms of pregnancy and pre-natal care. Even infant euthanasia has a long-standing, and not always secretive history in America for the healthy maintenance of the national body. As Martin S. Pelnick chronicles in *Black Stork: Eugenics and the Death of "Defective" Babies in American Medicine and Film Since 1915*, the euthanasia of physically deformed babies in the 1910s and 1920s made Dr. Harry J. Haiselden a national hero. His cause, bolstered by the reigning theories of eugenics that had swept the nation, was so well received that parents of handicapped children from across the nation wrote letters of support to Haiselden and requested his help in allowing their children to die. In fact, Haiselden was commemorated in a 1917 film called *The Black Stork*, which detailed his bravery in euthanizing his most well-known charge, a child with multiple congenital deformities dubbed "The Bollinger Baby." As Pernick notes, these debates about euthanasia, eugenics, and "unfit" infants were not specific to the early twentieth century. Indeed, the language of eugenics, and its insistence upon eliminating physical, mental, and sexual "deformity" and "abnormality,"[9] works to form a constitutive base for a complex and contradictory web of discourse that informs the emergence of the Gynecological Gothic during the 1970s.

In this genre, children, who represent futurity, stand in for the future of the (white) race and as synedoches for the national body. This is particularly true of fetuses or infants, whose lack of cognitive development indicates that their physical status becomes the primary means of determining normalcy. The absence of precise marks for identifying the abnormal, especially the mentally abnormal, leads to the possibility that the abnormal will infiltrate the normal. Thus the baby or fetus who might be invisibly deformed conjures the specter of doubt as to the forward progress of the species. Within the Gynecological Gothic, the monstrous fetus, a newly-birthed being halfway between marvel and monster is appropriately unrepresentable and unrepresented. The films continually tease and disappoint our desire to have the infant revealed. In *Rosemary's Baby*, for instance, the child is never shown and barely described, save Rosemary's piteous cry: "What have you done with its eyes?" Other monstrous infants appear only at the end of the narrative — as is the case with *Demon Seed, The Manitou, I Don't Want to Be Born,* and *Inseminoid.* In the majority of the films, the birthing scene is presented as the climax of the film.[10]

These teratological infants exist in the liminal space of what Elizabeth Grosz calls "intolerable ambiguity": so abject and category-defying that their very conception and representability can warrant a complete narrative arc. A 1975 television advertisement for *It's Alive*, fascinates desire by withholding any representation of the infant monster, showing only a bassinette[11] with a claw-like hand protruding. "The Davis's have had a baby," the announcer begins. "But they're not sending out announcements. Most new parents are a little scared when they have a baby. The Davis's are terrified. You see, there's only one thing wrong with the Davis baby. It's alive." The revelation of the distorted physiognomy of the monstrous infants thus stands as undeniable evidence of their inner monstrosity. As the advertising campaign makes clear, it is not the claw of the child which marks it as somehow terrifying: this minor physical abnormality must stand in for a more totalizing, unrepresentable "wrongness" of the child. Indeed, the children of the Gynecological Gothic are so intolerable in their ambiguity that they even resist the moment of gender designation, that first act of proclaiming, and imposing, identity at birth. What J. L. Austin or Judith Butler might call a "performative utterance," the traditional announcement — "it's a boy" or "it's a girl" — chronicles a progression through the speech act from non-personhood (it) to personhood (boy/girl). Consequently, in *It's Alive*, it's an *It*.

When the monstrous infants of the Gynecological Gothic are fully represented, often not until the film is well underway, they invariably present an animalistic reversion. In a nod to recapitulation theory,[12] the deformed and monstrous infants typically represent a previous evolutionary state, a eugenic nightmare of negative futurity. The nightmare sequence in *The Fly* presents a miscegenated larva wriggling out of the birth canal of its unwilling mother (Geena Davis). In *The Brood*, Nola (Samantha Eggar) parthenogenically births a litter of faceless, grunting youths in her external wombs sacs. *The Manitou* conjures up a racist version of this trend by impregnating Karen (Susan Strasberg) with a 400-year old Native American spirit, (re)born as savage pygmy warrior. *It's Alive* presents its infant monster, created by make-up and special effects designer Rick Baker (*The Howling, An American Werewolf in Paris, The Nutty Professor*), nearly an hour into the 91-minute film. The eponymous monstrosity brandishes two animalistic claws, an encephalitic head reminiscent of alien invaders from 1950s science fiction, and a set of vampiric fangs. The alien child of *Inseminoid* looks not unlike a hairless warthog, huffing and grunting its way into the world. These are offspring that directly oppose the doughy, cherubic frame of an Anne Geddes infant, the soft, weak body whose singular defining quality is complete helplessness. In their savage physicality, the monstrous infants suggest an arrested, even regressive, phylogeny.

Fetus as Explorer

D. W. Winnicott once provocatively remarked that "there's no such thing as a baby" (88) by which he meant that a child never exists independently. To speak of a child, he claimed, is always to speak of a child *and* someone, usually a mother. During the 1970s, however, the fetus became increasingly dislocated from the mother. In medical, juridical, and popular discourse, the fetus began to take on a life of its own, with an independent ontology and teleology. The Gynecological Gothic mode reflects the emerging cultural narratives of fetal development: the parent/child roles become inverted so that the emancipated fetus dominates its mother's body in every possible way. In particular, the cinema of monstrous birth hyperbolizes the construction of the fetus in abortion rhetoric and emerging fetal imaging technology.

As several feminist scholars have noted, the ideological battle over a woman's right to choose is not limited to the legal or political spheres, but rather functions within a matrix of competing power relations. One of these battles is rhetorical, grounded in the ability to control the terms, if not the content, of the debate. Indeed, many feminist scholars have noted the emergence and impact of "fetal personhood" discourse in the debate over abortion.[13] Through the debate over abortion rights, the female body served as a "transfer point for relations of power" (Foucault 103). Through these ideological battles, "the fetus" began to take on the persona of a voiceless, endangered proto-citizen. As Sarah Franklin notes in "Fetal Fascinations: New Dimensions to the Medical-Scientific Construction of Fetal Personhood," the idea of the fetus as a separate and distinct body deserving of legal protection and scientific inquiry mobilized the anti-abortion movement to embrace more "medicalized" rhetoric within the 1970s. Evidentiary claims increasingly abandoned religious arguments (the fetus has a soul) in favor of biological and teleological arguments (the fetus is fully formed; the fetus contains its future self in genetic material). "The construction of the fetus as separate, as an individual in its own right, deserving of state protection and medical attention," says Franklin, "has been a central component in the 'biologization' of anti-abortion rhetoric" (191).

Thus the rhetoric of the 1970's tended to shift the image of the fetus from parasite to person. Supplementing this shift in rhetorical constructions, was the contemporaneous advent of "fetal visualization" (Stabile 180) through obstetric technologies such as ultrasound.[14] Cinema representation is hardly independent from these changes. Through the grotesquerie of the Gothic, the films give embodiment to both the neoteric strains of fetal personhood and the anxieties that they engender. In particular, two strains of discourse inform the figurations, which I will call "fetus as explorer" and "fetus as survivor."

As early as the 1960s, existing notions of fetus/mother cohesion were being challenged by the increasing presence of the independent fetus, both through the changes in language, but also in the field of visual rhetoric. One of the most significant and arresting uses of fetal imaging was found in the April 30, 1965 issue of *Life* magazine, where readers were offered an unprecedented view of the actual and "realistic" development of a fetus within the womb.[15] Featuring images by noted photojournalist Leonard Nilsson, the macro images portrayed the fetus as a free-floating form against the blackness of open space. Titled the "Drama of Life Before Birth," Nilsson's photo essay walks readers through the stages of embryonic and fetal development, particularly noting the emergence of features that marked the fetus as "human" according to a subset of normative physical characteristics. From the captions "Adrift in a Salty Sac" to "Pushed Out into a Hostile World," readers were given unprecedented access to the inner working of the developmental process. Thus, in the pages of *Life* magazine, the embryo emerges as an explorer, an astronaut, or even as an extraterrestrial visitor. It should come as no surprise, then, that this infant-cum-interspace traveler finds its apotheosis in Stanley Kubrick's 1968 film *2001: A Space Odyssey*.[16] The film closes famously with the presence of a "Star Child" in a glowing amniotic sac, as it floats freely in space and meditates, Buddha-like, over the image of the Earth. As in *2001*, the photo essay in *Life* presents the child as an independent organism, both angelic and alien, developing freely and without intervention in the inky lacuna of non-uterine space.[17] The mother thus becomes an absolute non-presence. Through fetal imaging, the mother becomes a spectator to the developmental drama within her own body. Indeed, if a constitutive feature of the Gynecological Gothic is the absence of the mother as an agent during the course of her pregnancy, then the visual field of fetal imaging has already charted the narrative.[18] As Stabile notes, "in order for the embryo/fetus to emerge as autonomous — as a person, patient, or individual in its own right — all traces of the female body (as well as the embryo's presence as a parasite within that body) must disappear" (180).

Indeed, this relationship is reciprocal: as the fetus is given personhood, the maternal body is reduced, dehumanized, and erased: to make the fetus a *person* means to make the mother a *thing*. If, as Donna Haraway notes, women have always had a hard time registering as complete, coherent citizens because of the troubling propensity of their bodies to become two, then the fetus is afforded a personhood unavailable to the maternal body. Further, the personhood of the fetus comes at the detriment of the mother, who becomes incomplete in the battle to give the fetus coherence and embodiment — in the Gothic cinematic imagination she becomes a holy vessel, a sacrificial conduit, or a polluted container. Indeed, the Gynecological Gothic witnesses this very act: chronicling the evacuation of the female from the site of her own pregnancy. In *It's Alive*, Lenore begs her doctors to halt the delivery of her infant, claiming, "It's going to kill me!" From the hospital bed, she tries to reason with the doctors and nurses, saying, "Something's wrong — it's just different." Her obstetrician patronizingly silences her: "You've done your share, let us do ours now."

At most, the mother's body is a vacant house haunted by specters and ancient evils that threaten to emerge. Or, her body is an invaded, possessed, host, barely containing the feral presence that dominates her will and erupts from her body, caring little for the woman who has carried it to term. In *The Unborn*, Virginia gives birth to her monstrous, deformed child and confronts her obstetrician only to discover his plot to create a new race of genetically-altered beings. "What am I?" she asks. "A goddamn incubator?!" The mad doctor responds by showing her the next phase of monstrous gestation — a warehouse of test tube babies — and states simply "We don't need mothers anymore."[19]

Fetus as Survivor Warrior

The second set of images surrounding the fetus — the narratives of fetal survival — work to demonize the mother and the maternal site of the woman. The emergence of the fetus itself as the subject of medical discourse, and the recognition of environmental and genetic teratogens popularized the notion of the hyper-endangered fetus. Rachel Carson's 1962 book *Silent Spring*, for instance, was one of several ecocritical works that detailed the teratogenic perils presented by a modern polluted world. The 1970s also witnessed a growing awareness about teratogenic dangers such as Fetal Alcohol Syndrome, identified by Kenneth Lyons Jones and David W. Smith in 1973. Here the deformed child emerges as a complex symbol, able to embody any number of eugenic, environmental, and behavioral dangers that become increasingly synonymous with a polluted futurity.

Perhaps epitomizing this shift, the book *Is My Baby All Right? A Guide to Birth Defects* was written by Virginia Apgar, M.D., M.P.H., and Joan Beck in 1972 and reprinted in *Parents' Magazine* in 1975 as "A Perfect Baby." The title itself is thick with eugenic anxiety, yet as the introduction of the article says, "[m]odern science has given us the tools to greatly increase every couple's chance of having... A Perfect Baby" (55). The article collects a litany of possible genetic and behavioral teratogenic cautions, including the age of the mother, the age of the father, the proximity of conception to a previous pregnancy, the time and frequency of intercourse. These warnings do not delve into the topic of environmental dangers, which are listed in stultifying detail: nutritional deficiencies, nutritional excesses, radiation, rubella, toxoplasmosis, nose drops, laxatives, mineral oil, douches, baking soda, and insecticides, to name a few. The article would be better titled "What You Couldn't Possibly Expect to Expect When You're Expecting," as its promise of a "perfect baby" is inconceivable within the minefield of abnormality-producing agents. In *It's Alive*, a group of expectant fathers opine in the waiting room about the dangerous world in which they live, and how they're "slowly poisoning [them]selves." The teratogens they discuss — among them pesticides, radiation, birth control pills, exterminator chemicals, smog, and lead contamination — offer possible causes to the monstrosity about to be born, echoing the uncertainty and anxiety of the period.

The discourse of teratogenesis within this cultural moment constructs the maternal body as either already-polluted, one mistaken act away from transmitting a mutagenetic legacy of disease or deformity, or as an intensely permeable body, endangered at every turn by polluting invasion from a perilous environment. As Bradiotti notes, the medical and juridical discourse constructs a notion of a maternal body that has to be controlled in order to contain female desires and to limit the possible transmission of the consequences of those dangerous desires to the unborn child. Bradiotti notes:

> [t]he female, pregnant body is posited *both* as a protective filter and as a conductor or highly sensitive conveyor of impressions, shocks and emotions. It is both a "neutral" and somewhat "electrical body." There is an insidious assimilation of the pregnant woman to an unstable, potentially sick subject, vulnerable to uncontrollable emotions [149].

In *The Brood*, Nola's mute, murderous offspring are literally fashioned as her repressed rage become flesh — extending the teratogenic anxiety of the period into the psychological realm.

In the pages of *Life*, the author waxes poetically on "The Marvels of the Placenta," noting that the mother's biological acceptance of her child is a mere matter of suppressing the mother's immunological system, her protection against the invasion of foreign bodies: "the baby is a parasite. From the first day of fertilization, the embryo becomes foreign material. The woman's body does not reject the embryo because of the mediations of the placenta. She tolerates it only because of the placenta's unique ability to subvert her immunological desires." The developing fetus, as an explorer or a survivor, is often thus couched within heroic and masculinist rhetoric. Gestation becomes a war of the vigilant fetus and his trusty shield, the placenta, against the arcane and hostile body of the mother.[20] As Stabile notes, the objectification of the maternal body ushers in "ideological transformation of the female body from a benevolent, maternal environment to an inhospitable wasteland, at war with the 'innocent person' within" (Stabile 178). Within the inhuman emptiness of uterine space, the fetus is not only an explorer, but a warrior-like frontiersman — his goal is to survive a hostile and inhuman female environment and to dominate it.[21]

The Gynecological Gothic diverges from the greater cultural rhetoric in that it is more reluctant to divest itself of previous representations of gestation and birth. As such, the genre evidences an acute anxiety regarding the becoming-personness of the fetus, and an uneasiness with the complete abandonment of parasitic models of pregnancy. A vestigial formation, the monstrous fetus is an alien survivor, drawing life out of its human host. It is within the imagination of horror that these roles become inverted: the attendant struggle between maternal body and fetal survivor remains, but the fetus has shifted from endangered subject to horrific invader.

Gynecological Gothic reconstitutes the haunted space of the Gothic house as the even more feminine enclosed space of the maternal body from which the newly-subjectified alien fetus must escape. Less hostile, and nominally more human than the imprisoning haunted house, the impregnated women typically scrape and gouge at their bellies, desperate to expel the foreign presence inside. *The Unborn* opens with a now-standard Nilsson image of a fetus set against the ominous strains of a science-fiction film score. Defamiliarized through unnatural coloration, extreme close-ups and unusual framing, the representation of the fetus in the credit sequence works against our desire to anthropomorphize the unborn baby. A case of "fetal depersonalization," the film employs the same rhetorical strategy as the Nilsson photographs to emphasize the non-personhood of the fetus: its alienness, its unnaturalness, its thing-ness. In the cinematic imagination, the monstrous fetus gains not so much personhood as it does *monsterhood.*[22]

Fetus as Monster

The Gynecological Gothic thus reverses the parasitic relationship between mother and child, the fetus no longer seeks to invade and colonize the maternal host. Instead the fetus wishes to escape the dangerous prison of the maternal body. In the rhetoric of this period, "[T]he fetus is defined as an individual agent who is separate from the mother and has its own distinct interests of which it is both aware and capable of acting on" (Franklin 193). In *The Unborn* and *Inseminoid*, the monstrous fetus takes over the mother's personality completely. Svengali-like, it bends her will towards its own ends and commands her body to perform hideously uncharacteristic activities. The feral powers of her soon-to-be infant (*The Unborn*) force Virginia (Brook Adams) to become savage and inhuman, rummaging through her refrigerator in a trance to find food that will appease the creature insider her. In this, the film revisits the comical "pickles and ice cream" lore of pregnancy and renders it monstrous, as Virginia eats raw, reddened meat to appease the fetus's presumed bloodlust. Virginia also claws at her husband during sex, marring his body as a result of her newly-acquired insatiable libido. In the culture of the film, the notion is that the convergence of female sexual aggressiveness and pregnancy is a clear sign of serious abnormality. Another pregnant mother murders her lesbian partner, stating "I can't love you both — baby needs all my love." In *Inseminoid*, the alien impregnation gives its host inhuman strength, and she is able to dispatch her male companions with ease. Her physiology is transformed as well: like her unborn monstrous child, she is now able to breathe the alien atmosphere. In these films then, the invading baby possesses the pregnant mother, recalling the earlier types of demonic possession of the body as a way to account for strangely non-normative, and non-female behavior.

As a trope, the monstrous infant crystallizes questions that dominate Gothic discourse: What is human? Can a single definition of humanity subsume the threats of human difference? Are multiple perspectives and narratives necessary to provide multiple answers to these questions? The convergence of multiple discursive forms — fetus as an independent life form, in control of its mother's bodily functions; fetus as infinitely endangered by a hostile pre-natal environment, besieged on all sides by teratogenic threats; fetus as a parasitic organism — is a reminder of past formations. Different aspects of the monstrous fetal narrative respond to the different anxieties generated by the various perspectives. The fetus emerges as a misshapen and vengeful presence — he possesses the body of his innocent mother; he survives the imprisonment of the hostile womb; he seeks to wreak havoc on the outside world. The infantile beast haunts the mother from the catacombs of her anatomy, and when it reaches the surface it learns to hate the world that hates it for its ugliness, for its intolerable ambiguity, and for the "wrongness" of its existence. It is within the Gothic imagination that these discursive strains precariously co-exist, and monstrosity, evidenced by bodily difference, becomes the site of their convergence.

It's Alive *and Paternal Redemption*

Interestingly, only one film within the subgenre does not resort to the conceit of bodily invasion or ecological pollution to produce its monstrous baby. In Larry Cohen's *It's Alive* (1974), the issue of causality is never resolved, which leaves the child's monstrous origins (or teratogenesis) a lingering question. Additionally, *It's Alive* is the only film within this cycle that begins with the monstrous birth that the other films reserve for their climactic finales. As such, we may say that the film concerns itself less with the teratogenic production of the non-normative, but rather with parental accountability for monstrosity that is the inevitable product of a polluted present state.

In the film, Frank Davies (John P. Ryan) and his wife Lenore (Sharon Farrell), a bland suburban white couple, await the arrival of their second child. Upon birth, the monstrous infant kills the doctors and nurses in the delivery room before escaping into the city, where he commits a number of murders in the name of survival. Frank rejects his child as an inhuman monster, and even actively seeks out the infant for extermination. At his wife's urging, however, Frank welcomes the child back into their home and even attempts to protect the infant from authorities before the baby is ultimately gunned down by a battalion of police officers. The film ends with a radio report that another monstrous child has been born, suggesting a boundless (re)generation of monstrosity.

This final section of *It's Alive* is significant because here is where the film courageously challenges the abject construction of fetal monstrosity, and instead considers physical monstrosity as central and co-existent with the discourses of normality. Ultimately, it argues that monstrosity exists at the heart of the American family, and that this frightening futurity must be accepted and integrated as a deformed exemplar of modernity. Several film critics[23] have argued that this film epitomizes a shift towards "progressive horror" in the post–Watergate era. Vivian Sobchack's essay "Bringing It All Back Home: Family Economy and Generic Exchange," argues that the horror genre, along with the science fiction and television melodrama, all begin to critique the normative family structure in the 1970s. Sobchack asserts that this shift towards domestic horror[24] (and science fiction) occurs because of various social movements (women's liberation, youth rebellion) that transformed the bourgeois family, and the patriarchal authority that underpins it, from a site of refuge to one of critique. Ultimately, all three genres — horror, science fiction, and melodrama — "attempt to narratively contain, work out, and in some fashion resolve the contemporary weakening of patriarchal authority ... condensed and represented in the problematic figure of the child" (147). In the sequels that follow,[25] the *It's Alive* series becomes more complex in its treatment of monstrosity, ultimately centralizing the infants as misunderstood freaks in a world bent upon their annihilation. However, the designation of the film *It's Alive* as unambiguously "progressive" is problematized by its abject treatment of the maternal body. This instance of "progressive horror" is figured as a struggle within and through the paternal, and the acceptance of monstrosity at the heart of the family, while still casting a suspicious eye at the polluted, porous body of the female.

As the narrative of *It's Alive* plays upon the Frankenstein mythos,[26] the question of acceptance and/or rejection of monstrosity as paternal plight suppresses the maternal body completely. Frank's paternal narrative echoes the sentiment of the doctor in the delivery room who tells Lenore that she "had done her share" in gestating the embryo. Indeed, the "women's work" of this film seems to entail impregnation and gestation — after that, the delivery and management of the child become the responsibility of the patriarch and the patriarchal state. Indeed, the film tellingly absents the viewer from the actual delivery scene, lingering instead with Frank and the other expectant fathers in the waiting room, where they discuss the polluted and teratogenic world in which they live. "What a fine world to bring a kid into," one father says, sarcastically. The baby's "delivery" (and its subsequent murder of the medical personnel) takes place off-screen. Our introduction to the scene of carnage comes through the eyes of Frank, clearly established as our protagonist, as he descends on the scene. As he surveys the carnage, he seems to avoid his wife strapped to the gurney, who is wildly calling out "What does my baby look like? What's wrong with my baby?" Indeed, he seems horrified at his wife — she seems but an extension of her monstrous infant. This is underlined later when he hesitates to embrace her; she says "You're not afraid of me, are you?" He laughs nervously, and deflects the question by saying "I've always been afraid of you, especially those eyes." But the point is made: after the discussion of pollution and contamination in the waiting room, it is evident that the maternal Lenore, like "mother" earth, is a carrier of pollution, if not infected herself. Later in the film, Frank strikes Lenore on the face after their infant kills Frank's brother Charles. His voice thick with disavowal, Frank screams, "See what your baby did to Charles?!"

It's Alive also draws fairly tacit links between the parasitic presence of the fetus within the mother's womb and the father's fear that the child will become a parasitic presence after its birth. Beneath the placid surface of heteronormative domesticity lies Frank's paternal anxiety about the impending birth, and a suggested resentment towards the couple's previous child, Chris. In the labor room, Lenore says to Frank, "I'm glad we decided to have the baby. It's not going to tie you down, is it sweetheart? You're not going to feel trapped like you did last time, are you?" In *It's Alive*, the child is also parasitic in that it threatens to take over its father's life, and Frank must learn to accept a mixture of love and hatred that characterizes his relationship with both children: the abject child and the "normal" child as well. As Patricia Brett Ehrens and Vivian Sobchack note, the turn towards "progressive" horror saw a proliferation of just this type of patriarchal critique.[27] As a critique of the heteronormative family, the film details the father's acknowledgement of his own murderous intent towards his own offspring — in effect locating the family as a hotbed of repressed pedophobic rage.[28]

If, in the broader discourse, fetal personhood rhetoric and obstetric imaging technology gave the pre-natal child greater prominence and autonomy than ever before, divergent discourses were at work as well. The Gynecological Gothic, and *It's Alive* in particular, seems to rest in an ambivalent space in between — presenting an autonomous but familial being, menaced but menacing, uncannily domestic and yet alien to the normative family structure. For this reason, its designation as progressive horror seems troublesome — even as a progressive example of the Gynecological Gothic. In the rest of the Gynecological Gothic, the mother is cast as an innocent vessel carrying to term a perverse alien presence. *It's Alive* offers no such remove to deny the humanity of the monstrous infant. Interestingly, though *It's Alive* is largely progressive in its treatment of monstrosity and the futility of abjection, it ultimately demonizes the mother as an absorbent receptacle of worldly teratogens. As for the child, the bodily difference of the monstrous child stands in as a synecdoche for the bleak future of the species, in which the eugenic degradation of human form stands as the only defense against a polluted environment.

Afterbirth: Sexual Teratogenesis

Thus the frequent contemporary use made of the semiotic utility of the deformed infant, as a site of monstrous dehumanization, indicates that the easy equation between the non-normative body and inhuman evil continues to influence popular culture and the popular imagination. Bodily difference is especially material in the determination of a child's present and future normalcy; as such, mothers and fathers are encouraged by an entire industry of parental anxiety to monitor the minute developments of their child according to a map of normative growth. In the twenty-first century, we have reached a point in which this monitoring can extend beyond the physical, and indeed beyond the bodily, to bring eugenics to bear on other forms of difference.

In the domestic melodrama *The Twilight of the Golds* (1997), a heterosexual couple awaits the birth of their first child, only to discover through genetic testing that the child carries the genetic propensity for queerness.[29] Unsure whether they would want to raise a gay or lesbian child, Suzanne (Jennifer Beals) and her husband consider aborting the fetus. The issue is complicated by the fact that Suzanne's brother, David (Brendan Frazier), is gay, and during the course of the film he learns that his parents would have aborted him had they known of his potential sexuality. This revelation fractures the tense family structure, and though the family reunites at the film's conclusion, it is clear that David remains a genetic failure in his parents' eyes.

No doubt *The Twilight of the Golds* is a secular humanist fable of issue-driven import. Well within the classic "problem picture" formula, it asks for complete spectatorial allegiance with Suzanne and her decision to keep or terminate her "abnormal" pregnancy. The crisis, however, is figured as maternal and extraparental as the unborn fetus doubles as the past self of the abject adult queer body. Instead of literally possessing sentience and desires as in the Gynecological Gothic, *The Twilight of the Golds* employs the adult David as an emotional doppelganger; at one point he even confronts his father about the proposed abortion, screaming "You're letting her kill me! You're killing me!" Like *It's Alive*, the film ultimately calls for the integration of the infantile Other into its ranks, but only through abjecting the perceived source of its sexual teratogenesis. The rejection of the adult David parallels that of the gestating queer subject — he is, in a sense, aborted from the familial structure as a stand-in for the voiceless fetus. As such, monstrosity is transferred from the maternal body and placed upon the queer subject, a manifestation of teratogenic abnormality that has been transferred, nonsensically, from an imaginary avuncular bond.

From this it becomes clear that the Gynecological Gothic consists not just of generic formula, but is a set of cultural discourses, investments, and anxieties coalesced around the body of the non-normative child. Be it horror, science fiction, or domestic drama, the abnormal or monstrous infant functions in cinema as a constantly renegotiated trope in a complicated discursive terrain. Intensely overdetermined, the child functions as the prescient symbol of our future selves, the nostalgic reminder of our lost history, or something in between — a foreign but familiar presence who will inevitably inherit the world we have created. As an allegory of the real — the political, the psychological, the sociological — the cinema of monstrous birth mobilizes our fears about the future moment that is, right now, gestating as an invisible presence within the present, that is waiting, perhaps not so patiently, to be born.

NOTES

1. In a course I taught at Ohio State on Gothic literature, I found that pairing these two texts works very well to talk about the Gothic and monstrous patriarchy, and the juridical and medical discourses that upend these power relations.

2. The figure of the monstrous child in Gothic/horror literature is even more present and prolific. For an excellent consideration of the shift in child representation from victim to aggressor in fiction, see Sabine Bussing, *Aliens in the Home*. Ann Douglas does

similar work, though focused largely on the late 1970s, in her essay "The Dream of the Wise Child."

3. In the alien invasion cycle of the 1950s, for instance, the first witness to invasion is often a child, a member of a lower socioeconomic class, or a woman. The police or military, therefore, dismiss their claims as over-emotional or uneducated exaggeration.

4. A notable exception outside of this time frame is the 1991 film *The Unborn*, which emerges almost a decade after this trope seems to die out. I include it, however, for its reiterative quality — it seems, in many ways, to plumb the unconscious of the other texts, reproducing the narrative of the previous films with a more pedaphobic agenda, perhaps owing to its B-movie direct-to-video status.

5. Teratology, in contemporary medical discourse, refers to the study of biological defects and abnormal bodies. Teratogenesis specifically refers to the study of birth defects and the discovery of teratogens, or the etiologic causes (often of environmental origin) of birth defects.

6. For a fascinating study of both of these teratological subcategories, see Elizabeth Grosz's "Intolerable Ambiguity: Freaks as/at the Limit."

7. This study gave way to the nineteenth-century freak-show, where curiosities and medical abnormalities were put on display to reinforce the primacy of the normal, abled, white body. In her introduction to *Freakery: Cultural Spectacles of the Extraordinary Body*, Rosemarie Garland Thomson aligns the function of the freak show with that of democracy and mercantilism — indeed, she notes fascinating links between the rise of industrialized standardization in production to an increased valorization of the standardized *body* through eugenic discourse. Freak shows, medical journals, teratology, and sensational media all asked readers and spectators to compare themselves to the defined abnormalities in order to confirm their normative gender, racial, and bodily identities, while at the same time offering group membership through what Thomson calls "a public ritual that bond[s] a sundering polity together in the collective act of looking" (4).

8. Further, the etiology of fetal deformity has long been co-existent with surreptitious moral restrictions and punishments directed towards the female body. One of the most fascinating examples is the case of Puritan religious leader Ann Hutchinson, whose Antinomian teachings brought about the ire of religious officials. After her heresy trial in 1637, Hutchinson was accused of causing the "monstrous pregnancy" of one of her followers, Mary Dyer. The fetus was exhumed and displayed publicly for the parishioners to witness of the horror of Hutchinson's dangerous theology and the results of her teratogenic miscreance.

9. Judith Butler investigates the social politics of infant gender assignment in "Doing Justice to Someone: Sex Reassignment and Allegories of Transsexuality." She notes that the medical discourse concerning hermaphroditic or intersexual children presupposes heterosexual "normality" as a rationale for eliminating male sexual organs.

10. Alexis Carriero, a colleague of mine who works in television studies mentioned that this is also the case with TV shows about pregnancy (for example, "A Baby Story"), cheekily referring to the scene of bodily expulsion as "the mommie shot."

11. The bassinette, one might remember, served as a compelling symbol for the advertising campaign of Rosemary's Baby, only a few years previous. In that image, the baby carriage appears against an oversized portrait of Rosemary, where the bassinette is placed literally "inside" Rosemary's mind. Combined with the tagline "Pray for Rosemary's baby," the deceptive marketing no doubt played on Polanski's past forays into films about women and madness.

12. Published in 1866, Ernst Haeckel's theory of recapitulation (commonly distilled as "ontology recapitulates phylogeny") holds that the evolutionary history of the human species (phylogeny) can be witnessed in the ontological growth of the fetus. Though debunked in modern times, this body of theory has continuing impact on eugenics and

theories of racial superiority, particularly when racial dominance is cast in terms of child/adult developmental stages.

13. For an extended discussion of fetal personhood and reproductive rights, see Franklin 1991, Hartouni 1992, Stabile 1992.

14. As Valerie Hartouni notes in "Fetal Exposures: Abortion Politics and the Optics of Allusion," the demystification of pregnancy through visual technology signaled a major change in how the fetal body, and thus the maternal body, was perceived. As Hartouni says, "[t]he circulation of fetal images by anti-abortion forces, the routine use of ultrasonography in monitoring pregnancy and labor, the development of widely publicized, culturally valorized, medical techniques in the area of fetal therapy and repair have worked together to shift the terms in which abortion is now framed, understood, experienced, and spoken even by those who champion 'choice'" (131).

15. See Hartouni for an extended discussion of this practice.

16. Adapted from Arthur C. Clarke's 1968 novel of the same name. The novel is clearer in its designation of the Star Child as an immortal deity able to destroy and rebuild the galaxy.

17. One of the more macabre and ironic elements of the Nilsson photographs is that though they purport to demonstrate "how life begins," all of the embryos and fetuses pictured were, in fact, post-mortem autopsy photos. Several were also manipulated (embryonic sacs removed, placentas peeled back) and backlit in order to achieve a more aesthetically appealing photograph. Pictures of the "drama of life," were, in fact, memento mori, photographs of deceased infants.

18. This recalls the recurring trope of the absent mother in the traditional Gothic text.

19. Thus, the mother is erased in the Gynecological Gothic, as she is erased in the conventional Gothic novel, since Horace Walpole's *The Castle of Otranto* and Ann Radcliffe's *The Sicilian Romance* in the eighteenth century.

20. In *Life* magazine, the author marveled at the suppressive power of the placenta, as if it were the fetus's original suit of armor against the ravenous maternal body. In extremis, the infant emerges hardened and feral. As their deformed and animalistic physiognomy suggests, the Quasimodic children of cinema have been genetically primed for battle, be it global or simply gestational. Indeed, these monstrous infants are self-sufficient, savage survivors. They emerge from the womb as seasoned warriors, ready to conquer a hostile post-natal environment as they have already conquered an infinitely more treacherous pre-natal terrain. This is explicitly apparent in *Demon Seed*'s infanta ex machina, a fusion of a woman and a sentient computer, who is born clad in literal bronze armor, like St. George emerging victoriously from a monstrous uterus.

21. It is fairly common in the horror and science fiction genre for the mise-en-scène of an alien environment to be characterized as uterine, or feminized in its grotesque (super)nature. For a historically-grounded investigation of this trope in 1950s science fiction, see Peter Biskind's *Seeing is Believing: Or, How Hollywood Taught Us to Stop Worrying and Love the Fifties*. For a more contemporary psychoanalytic perspective, see Barbara Creed's *Monstrous-Feminine: Film, Feminism, Psychoanalysis*.

22. To be sure, the fetus gains separateness and distinctness from the maternal body, but the films do not go so far as to dub this humanity. Indeed, the films recapitulate a fairly strong undercurrent of pedaphobic de-anthropomorphizing of the infant that characterized the period. Folklorist Alan Dundes has argued, for instance, that the proliferation of "dead baby jokes" during this era evidenced a thinly-masked cultural rage towards the parasitic nature of children and moral anxiety concerning abortion amid the discourse of fetal personhood. (The "dead baby joke cycle," which emerges in the late 1960s, is an exercise in sick humor which is intended to shock and scandalize, for example: Q: What is pink and red and sits in a corner? A: A baby chewing on razor blades.)

23. See Wood's *Hollywood from Vietnam to Reagan ... And Beyond*, and Williams's *Hearths of Darkness*.

24. A shift that echoes the domestication of the Gothic by the Sensation novel of the late nineteenth century.

25. This includes two sequels, both by director Larry Cohen: *It Lives Again* (1978), and *It's Alive III: Island of the Alive* (1987). In the first sequel, Frank returns as an impassioned advocate for the teratogenic infants, pleading for their asylum in open court and traveling around the country to educate expectant parents.

26. Besides the allusion in the title, evoking a line from the 1931 film adaptation of Mary Shelley's novel, *It's Alive* presents a soliloquy midway through the film in which "Frank" questions the permeable boundaries between normality and abnormality, monster and non-monster: "When I was a kid, I always thought that the monster was Frankenstein. You know, Karloff walking about in those big shoes grunting. I thought he was Frankenstein. Then I went to high school and read the book and I realized that Frankenstein was the doctor who created him.... Somehow the identities get all mixed up, don't they?"

27. See Ehrens, "Stepfather: Father as Monster in Contemporary Horror Film," and Sobchack, "Bringing It All Back Home: Family Economy and Generic Exchange."

28. Interestingly, this era witnessed a growing skepticism concerning the efficacy of the compulsory reproductive economy. In a March 1979 *Time* article entitled "Wondering If Children Are Necessary," Lance Morrow chronicles what he sees as a new wave of non-parental/non-familial heterosexual adulthood. Indeed, in conjunction with the advent of the "dead baby" joke cycle, one can see a counter-discourse of (at times virulent) anger directed at the cultural imperative of heterosexual fecundity.

29. Though set in an alternative or possibly near-future reality where this technology is available, many actual research studies have been conducted to map a genetic propensity for queerness, as in the work of Simon LeVay.

WORKS CITED

Apgar, Virginia, and Joan Beck. "A Perfect Baby." *Parents' Magazine and Better Homemaking.* Nov. 1975: 55–59.

Betterton, Rosemary. "Promising Monsters: Pregnant Bodies, Artistic Subjectivity, and Maternal Imagination." *Hypatia* 21.1 (Winter 2006): 80–100.

Bussing, Sabine. *Aliens in the Home: The Child in Horror Fiction.* Westport, CT: Greenwood, 1987.

Butler, Judith. *Bodies That Matter: On the Discursive Limits of "Sex."* New York: Routledge, 1993.

_____."Doing Justice to Someone: Sex Reassignment and Allegories of Transsexuality." *GLQ: A Journal of Lesbian and Gay Studies* 7 (4): 621–36.

Carroll, Noel. *The Philosophy of Horror: Or, Paradoxes of the Heart.* New York: Routledge, 1990.

Creed, Barbara. "The Dream of the Wise Child: Freud's 'Family Romance' Revisited in Contemporary Narratives of Horror." *Prospects* 9 (1984): 293–348.

_____. "Horror and the Monstrous-Feminine: An Imaginary Abjection." *The Dread of Difference: Gender and the Horror Film.* Ed. Barry Keith Grant. Austin: University of Texas Press, 1996

Douglas, Mary. *Purity and Danger: An Analysis of Concept of Pollution and Taboo.* London: Routledge and Kegan Paul, 1966.

Dundes, Alan. "The Dead Baby Joke Cycle." *Western Folklore* 38.3 (Jul 1979): 145–157.

Ehrens, Patricia Brett. "Stepfather: Father as Monster in Contemporary Horror Film."

Dread of Difference: Gender and the Horror Film. Ed. Barry Keith Grant. Austin: University of Texas Press, 1996.

Fischer, Lucy. "Birth Traumas: Parturition and Horror in *Rosemary's Baby.*" *Dread of Difference: Gender and the Horror Film.* Ed. Barry Keith Grant. Austin: University of Texas Press, 1996.

Foucault, Michel. *The History of Sexuality: An Introduction.* Vol. 1. New York: Vintage, 1990.

Franklin, Sarah. "Fetal Fascinations: New Dimensions to the Medical-Scientific Construction of Fetal Personhood." *Off Centre: Feminism and Cultural Studies.* Eds. Sarah Franklin, Celia Lury, and Jackie Stacey. London: Harper Collins, 1991.

Gilliat, Penelope. "Anguish Under the Skin." *New Yorker* 15 June 1968: 87–89.

Grosz, Elizabeth. "Intolerable Ambiguity: Freaks as/at the Limit." *Freakery: Cultural Spectacles of the Extraordinary Body.* Ed. Rosemarie Garland Thomson. New York: New York University Press, 1996. 55–68.

Hartouni, Valerie. "Fetal Exposures: Abortion Politics and the Optics of Allusion." *Camera Obscura* 29 (1992): 131–151.

Kristeva, Julia. "Desire in Language." *The Portable Kristeva.* New York: Columbia University Press, 1997.

Morrow, Lance. "Wondering If Children Are Necessary." *Time* 5 March 1979: 42, 47.

Paul, William. *Laughing Screaming: Modern Hollywood Horror and Comedy.* New York: Columbia University Press, 1994.

Pernick, Martin S. *Black Stork: Eugenics and the Death of "Defective" Babies in American Medicine and Film since 1915.* Oxford: Oxford University Press, 1999.

Rosenfeld, Albert. "The Drama of Life before Birth." Photographer Leonard Nilsson. *Life* 30 April 1965: 54–71.

Sobchack, Vivian. "Bringing It All Back Home: Family Economy and Generic Exchange." *Dread of Difference: Gender and the Horror Film.* Ed. Barry Keith Grant. Austin: University of Texas Press, 1996.

Stabile, Carol A. "Shooting the Mother: Fetal Photography and the Politics of Disappearance." *Camera Obscura* 28 (1992): 179–206.

Thomson, Rosemarie Garland. "Introduction: From Wonder to Error — A Genealogy of Freak Discourse in Modernity." *Freakery: Cultural Spectacles of the Extraordinary Body.* Ed. Rosemarie Garland Thomson. New York: New York University Press, 1996.

Williams, Tony. *Hearths of Darkness: The Family in the American Horror Film.* Madison, NJ: Fairleigh Dickinson University Press, 1996.

Winnicott, D. W. *The Child, the Family, and the Outside World.* Harmondsworth: Pelican, 1964.

Wood, Robin. *Hollywood from Vietnam to Reagan ... And Beyond.* New York: Columbia University Press, 2003.

_____. "An Introduction to the American Horror Film." *Movies and Methods,* Vol. 2. Ed. Bill Nichols. Berkeley: University of California Press, 1985.

"Journeys into Lands of Silence": The Wasp Factory and Mental Disorder

MARTYN COLEBROOK

> He reminded me of a hologram, shattered; with the whole image contained within one spear-like shard, at once splinter and entirety [Banks *The Wasp Factory* 184].

Iain Banks, a contemporary Scottish novelist whose work transgresses ideas of genre and form, publishes two different styles of novel, under two separate names. As Iain Banks, he writes popular, commercial fictions that often focus on postmodern Gothic transformations of the thriller genre. Under his second authorial name, Iain (M.) Banks, he writes works of scientific or speculative fiction, set in his critical Utopia, The Culture. Although these two different outputs are published under different names, the differentiation between the two personae is overcome by the frequent overlaps and inter-textual references in the different novels. Thus Banks is a novelist who has created his own double, an author for whom the ideas of a split writing persona and the sense of splintering and fragmentation are key.[1] He is a wildly innovative, imaginative, popular and subversive novelist, whose novels are infused with dark elements that give them a forbidden, cultish, underground status; he is also a writer who creates fictions that are perceived as being more conventional and less evidently speculative. Banks's doubled writing persona, which resists a location within a singular genre or form, promotes his status as a non-canonical author of subversive novels, including the notorious novel, *The Wasp Factory* (1990), a Gothic novel that fuses the darkly comic with the shocking and the provocative.[2]

Scottish Gothic

Writing in *The Scottish Novel since the Seventies*, Gavin Wallace makes the shrewd observation that "the literary revival of the 1970s succeeded in the compellingly imaginative depiction of Scotland as the one country best designed to drive anyone with the faintest glimmer of imagination quietly insane" (218). Wallace's essay, "Voices in Empty Houses: The Novel of Damaged Identity," deals with the trope of the "damaged mind" as a recurrent feature in contemporary Scottish literature. Mental damage, whether it be through alcohol-abuse as in Ron Butlin's *The Sound of My Voice* (1987) or Alasdair Gray's *1982 Janine* (1984), or through sexual obsession, as found in Duncan Maclean's *Bunker Man* (1997), is a recurrent theme in the contemporary Scottish novel, as it is in all of Gothic literature. These contemporary novels are linked further with the Gothic by their affinity for considerations of the unknown Other.

The related tropes of the Other and the doubled character are deployed by earlier Scottish writers to heighten the Gothic horror of their texts. Robert Louis Stevenson presents these tropes in *The Strange Case of Dr. Jekyll and Mr. Hyde* (1886) and *The Master of Ballantrae* (1889), as does James Hogg in *Private Confessions and Memoirs of a Justified Sinner* (1824). Moreover, the Gothic convention of fracturing and doubling identity, and the related convention of the unreliable narrator are connected to important aspects of Scottish culture. As Angela Wright notes, "Like all Gothic fiction, Scottish Gothic is intimately concerned with the process of telling a tale. But through its minutely detailed attention to the artifacts which give rise to narratives, Scottish Gothic debates the process of uncovering histories" (76). Additionally, the strategies of the Gothic narrative echo the Caledonian *antysyzygy*, "the characteristic yoking together of realism with fantasy in Scottish textual practice" (Middleton 20). This term was originally applied by C. Gregory Smith to highlight the integration of realism and fantasy in the Scottish literary tradition, particularly the narrative strategies of Hogg and Stevenson.

Contemporary Scottish literature continues to reveal an affinity for the Gothic. Angus Calder observes that "the Scotland of recent fiction has been a grim and dangerous place" (237). For Duncan Petrie, "such a preoccupation with a darker and more destructive side of the human condition ... asserts a distance from the respectability and refinement of bourgeois Anglo-centric high culture" (115). As Wallace notes, "there is a new cultural identity celebrated in recent Scottish fiction, but an identity whose instability and claustrophobic intimacy with psychological maiming writers inevitably deplore, yet appear incapable of forsaking" (218). The cultural identity that Wallace identifies seems to be riddled with the ambiguity or contrary values that typically besiege the Gothic. Like the Gothic these texts revel in their own fascination with the carnivalesque and transgressive, grappling with the stability of identity.

Yet there is a sense of frustration and despair with those who display a destabilized identity, a sense that to write about such individuals and their "instability" and "psychological maiming" has become an obligation rather than a choice, given that this topic is firmly embedded in the Scottish culture. As Wallace notes, "such motifs have become entrenched as readily identifiable and assimilable literary tropes which, despite their continued creative appeal, may not have only outlived their function, but also become the internalised submission to a condition in which the Scottish imagination will eventually colonise itself" (220). Essentially the argument is that the trope has become too familiar and is in danger of being exhausted. By defining the problem with the image of the Scottish imagination "colonising itself," Wallace astutely implies that the origins of the "damaged voice" and the recurrent presence of mentally and gender-disturbed characters have taken on a politicized significance. That is, authors attempting to construct or propagate a national mythology tend to appropriate these tropes. The use of the word "colonise" contextualizes this strategy with those of dominant English structures of literary London. Thus the Scottish and the Gothic are both located in the margins of canonic literature.

The Wasp Factory as Scottish Gothic

Concerns of Gothic colonization arise in the critical response to *The Wasp Factory*. Duncan Petrie suggests that the novel can be "positioned as a fable about the need to move beyond the self-defeating myths rooted in masculine hardness and violence" (121). Petrie also notes a number of Gothic tendencies in *Factory*: the Scottish trope of the isolated island, echoing the typically isolated Gothic setting, is "a recurring emblematic feature in representations of Scotland concerned to stress Otherness through distance — geographical, social, moral — from metropolitan certainties, conventions and rules" (121). Although Petrie highlights the example of the "hard man" as a Scottish myth that needs to be abandoned, his emphasis on Otherness further evidences the projection of the culturally marginalized, outsider voice onto the individual, in this case the brothers, Frank and Eric Cauldhame. Thus Banks deploys the capacities of the Gothic and the more regionally specific "Scottish Gothic" as a mode for exploring mental illness and as a representation for cultural marginality. In this case, the sense of cultural difference, of otherness, is displaced onto the mentally different individual. Banks accomplishes this switch by deploying the trope of the double. The exchange of the psychological for the cultural is easily accomplished as the individual Other, Frank, mirrors the national Other, Scotland. Banks also capitalizes on the connection between the Gothic interest in matters of fixed identity — including questions of the unified mind as opposed to the disintegrated mad mind — and the splitting of Scottish national identity, as defined by Petrie: "an internal anxiety that renders the national subject split and incapable of achieving self-identity" (116). Thus in *The Wasp Factory*, Banks taps into the shared concerns of the Gothic text and Scottish culture to consider the consequences of the social and psychological pressures that result in the marginalized and split self. In doing so, Banks projects fear and horror onto the brothers, Frank Cauldhame and Eric Cauldhame.

The Damaged Mind

Readings of *The Wasp Factory* often focus upon Frank Cauldhame's gender performance and the novel's conclusion that unmasks him as "Frances," a girl whose father has led her to believe she is a castrated male. However, attention should also be paid to other aspects of mental illness that are present throughout this text. Iain Banks deploys a combination of humor and Gothic horror to portray the concerns of identity and mental stability. Through the use of the double Banks creates a persistent debate throughout the text: are the characters mentally disturbed or do their actions performance and simulation, challenge clinical and social constructions of mental illness.[3] That is; is the flaw located within the diseased self or within the society that insists on diagnosing pathology?

A story of estrangement, excision, absence, loss and dislocation, *The Wasp Factory* represents a provocative and edgy analysis of contemporary masculinities and mental disability. Regarded as a startling, visceral and disturbing debut, the novel provoked astonishment, repulsion, praise, and, significantly, a notably uneven critical response. Re-staging the typical Gothic encounter with mysterious otherness, the excessive and the abject, *Factory* is structured around the first-person narrative of Frank Cauldhame, an adolescent with a penchant for torturing animals, who lives with his father, Angus, on a remote Scottish island. Frank is an obsessive and a fantastist, who thinks that his social function is to defend his dwelling from the threat posed by outsiders, especially his brother, Eric, the most apparent source of outside danger. Banks's use of the monologue form allows Frank to assume authorship of his own story, gaining a degree of narrative power over the reader and over those in his community who judge him by the actions of his psychotic brother,

Eric. Having recently escaped from an institution for the insane, Eric has returned to his island, a return that Banks suggests represents his search for self.

Madness Visible: Diagnosis as Reality

From his authoritative narrative stance, Frank takes care to inform his reader of his brother's non-normative status. By revealing Eric's "escape," Frank alerts the reader to the potentially criminal status of his brother; his confinement suggests that he has committed a transgression although Frank does not reveal details of any actual crime. Yet gradually we come to understand that despite Frank's insinuations, and Eric's incarceration, he is not a dangerous criminal. In fact, Eric has been institutionalized as a consequence of his heightened sensitivity, or to put it into the terms of the eighteenth-century Gothic, his excessive sensibility. As Frank eventually reveals, Eric's mental distress dates back to his early twenties, when he was at University training to be a doctor. While working on a hospital ward, he stumbled upon a child whose brain had become infested with maggots. In fact, the scene that Eric witnesses, and his response to it, comes directly from the Gothic tradition, most notably the episode in which the heroine of Ann Radcliffe's *The Mysteries of Udolpho* (1794) becomes unhinged after coming upon a figure of a maggot infested corpse, that turns out to be a wax figure, a penitential aid of sort. Emily responds by fainting, but is not sanctioned for her response because it is gender-appropriate; Eric, a male twentieth-century character, a scientist, no less, is diagnosed with mental illness and institutionalized because of his similarly sensitive response. Once officially diagnosed, his madness becomes a social reality, an unquestionable quality of his identity.

Madness Invisible

Just as Frank exploits his narrative power to exaggerate his brother's Otherness, suggesting criminality as well as insanity, so does he withhold crucial information from the reader in an attempt to define himself in opposition to his insane brother. The opening chapter, "The Sacrifice Poles," introduces the reader to the world of Frank Cauldhame: "I had been making the rounds of the Sacrifice Poles the day we heard my brother had escaped. I already knew something was going to happen; the Factory told me" (1). As this passage indicates, Frank's world-view is unusual. The word "rounds" suggests a ritualized existence, a need for habit and regulation in his patterns.[4] This word also echoes the word for the scientific movement of physicians within a hospital — suggesting another doubling with his brother. Such an existence, characterized by the need for order, repetition and control, could, as in the case of the physician, indicate a rationally structured life. However, Frank's intense and excessive application of order points strongly to his placement on the autistic spectrum.

The island setting also provides some subtle clues to his mental condition. It is the domain that he controls, as he controls the narrative, the only link to the mainland is "a little suspension bridge"; posted is a sign that reads "Keep Out — Private Property" (2).[5] The island is thus an exclusive space in which Frank operates, a location that simultaneously reflects his physical and mental isolation and his power.[6] As Frank tells Eric "I don't like leaving this island for that long, Eric. I'm sorry, but I get this horrible feeling in my stomach, as though there's a great big knot in it. I can't just go that far away, not overnight or ... I just can't" (16). David Punter highlights the condition between Frank's disorder and his situation on the island. The island is "akin to the fortress of an autistic child, into which nothing must be allowed to intrude, and out from which Frank himself can barely venture" (168). Frank's agoraphobia, his refusal or inability to leave, indicates an obsessive need for familiarity, for routine and for finding safety in the location he defines as his territory.[7]

These early clues suggest that Frank's presentation of the stability of his own mental state may not be entirely accurate, and that Frank's name is an ironic red herring. In fact, the name does lend itself to misinterpretation. In her unpublished doctoral thesis, *Spectral Ambiguities: The Tradition of Psychosomatic Supernaturalism in Scottish Fiction*, Kirsty Macdonald suggests that the name Frank "underlies the sincerity of, and therefore lack of conscious control over his warped beliefs" (120). In fact, this is only partly correct. While his understanding of his own logic is indeed frank and rational, his presentation of his narrative is far from frank. He neglects to mention that his actions are self-justified acts of vengeance performed by a self-appointed avenging angel fighting a moral crusade, based on his own idiosyncratic beliefs about gender and retribution. Frank thus adopts the characteristic Gothic narrative stance of the unreliable narrator, who gains his audience's complicity by withholding information, eventually implicating the audience in his actions through the macabre simplicity of his logic. Thus is appears that the family surname, Cauldhame, translated loosely as "cold home," is a much more reliable indicator to the reader of what is to come than is Frank's given name. The surname suggests a home that is not warm and "heimlich," to adopt Freud's terms, but is instead uncannily cold and "unheimlich."

Eventually, as the reader comes to read Frank's narrative more skeptically, we begin to realize that Frank is, in fact, much more insane and horrifying, than the officially diagnosed and institutionalized Eric. Frank's spaces, the Factory that initially suggests a comforting tool of communication and prophecy, and the Sacrifice Poles, whose name also could suggest a sort of commemoration, are revealed as the outposts and markers of the animals and human beings that Frank has killed or maimed. They are the sacrifices that he offers to the Wasp Factory, in return for the cryptic predictions that it provides. As the novel progresses, we also hear about such sites as "The Snake Park," "The Bomb Circle" and "The Skull Ground," all commemorative of Frank's killings and representing territory that Frank has claimed.

The Terrifying Double: Madness Visible, Madness Invisible

Through these atrocities and Frank's justifications for them, Banks makes it clear that Frank is actually Eric's double in his mental illness; in fact, Frank's insanity far exceeds his brother's. As MacDonald notes, "the most potent figure of Scottish Gothic [is] the diabolic and uncanny figure of the double, or doppelgänger" (118). Eric and Frank are, in fact, mirrored reflections. Eric has been diagnosed and institutionalized for a breach in normative decorum (in accordance with Foucault's observation that deviant behavior calls for social isolation).[8] On the other hand, Frank's homicidal madness remains invisible; he remains undiagnosed, uncategorized, and thus is free to roam transgressively through his space.

Throughout the novel, Franks attempts to distance himself from Eric and his confining diagnosis. He proclaims to his off-island neighbors: "I'm not Eric; I'm me and I'm here and that's all there is to it.... The people in the town may say 'Oh, he's not all there you know,' but that's just their little joke" (10). Of course, Frank's attempt to create distance is an attempt to create distinction because Eric, as the reflecting double highlights Frank's insecure and hidden, mental situation. Frank tries to sustain the boundaries between himself and his brother, in order to maintain his alignment with sanity. Yet Banks's narrative indicates the erasure of such boundaries, thereby suggesting that the category of sanity is not inviolably distinct from insanity. Public sanity may only indicate insanity that is not yet visible, that has not yet been diagnosed.

During the most significant exchange between Eric and Frank, Banks shows the tenuous nature of the boundary between the officially insane brother and the unofficially insane brother in a dialogue that is simultaneously comic and horrifying:

> "Porteneil 531," said Eric. I thought it was Eric, at least.
> "Yes." I said.

"Yes, this is Porteneil 531."

"But I thought this was Porteneil 531."

"This is. Who is that? Is that you–"

"It's me. Is that Porteneil 531?"

"Yes!" I shouted.

"And who's that?"

"Frank Cauldhame," I said, trying to be calm. "Who's that?"

"Frank Cauldhame," Eric said [126].

This dialogue demonstrates the overlaps and interchangeability of the two voices, alerting the audience to the possibility that Eric (or Frank?) has descended into a hallucination that he is Frank or that Frank may in fact be Eric. This use of "exaggeration and pastiche" (118), Macdonald suggests, projects mental illness onto both Eric and Frank. Banks's use of comic confusions thus disrupts the reader's perception of unified character and subverts the diagnosis of mental instability by suggesting that superficial performance alone determines the diagnosis.

Mental illness, or sanity, thus becomes an unstable binary of identity, rather than a fixed category. Following his murder of a woman, the calculating mentality of Frank comes to the fore: "I knew that three deaths in my immediate vicinity within four years had to look suspicious, and I had already planned my reaction carefully" (119). Frank spends a week performing varying states of hysteria and catatonia, effectively pretending he has been mentally disturbed by the death of three people close to him in an effort to deflect the attentions of those who may suspect him of the killings. Thus, paradoxically, in Frank's world the signs of insanity indicate normative, or at least non-homicidal, behavior. When discussing Eric's return, Frank suggests that "maybe he's not crazy after all. Perhaps he just got fed up of acting normal and decided to act crazy instead, and they locked him up because he went too far" (145). Banks thus unsettles the entire question of how mental disturbance is perceived and diagnosed.

At the end of *The Wasp Factory*, then, the reader is left with disturbing questions. Since Frank's invisible insanity is even more dangerous than Eric's visible insanity, how can we be confident about the social dependence on the accuracy of scientific diagnosis? The traditional Gothic is famously concerned with making the Other visible, in order to sustain a clear distinction between the Other and the Self. Thus in the conventional Gothic, the category of madness is easily identifiable. No one could possibly ignore the madness of Bertha Rochester, for example. But Banks's text posits a far more troubling possibility. The mad Other might be horrifyingly invisible, free to transgress the boundaries that separate madness from sanity, deviance from the norm, the Other from the Self. In fact, the mad Other may actually be the Self. Here Banks taps into a central anxiety of the Gothic, the fear that the boundaries between Self and Other will dissolve. The doubled brothers of Banks's *The Wasp Factory* succeed in reviving this ancient fear.

NOTES

1. In terms of his background and its relevance to the thematic engagements of this essay, Banks studied for an undergraduate degree in English, Philosophy and Psychology at the University of Stirling. This provided him with a particularly keen interest in issues pertaining to the complexities of the mind and identity, two issues that are also at the forefront of later novels such as *Complicity, Walking on Glass* and *The Bridge.*

2. The major influences for *The Wasp Factory* (and, indeed, the novels that *The Wasp Factory* has influenced) are drawn from a range of texts that vary considerably in their critical reception and the status they have been ascribed, in the same way as Banks's work is persistently overlooked. Günther Grass's *The Tin Drum* (1962) has been cited by Banks as a seminal influence for his own particular fusion of realism and surrealism. Russell Hoban's *Riddley Walker* (1980) set in an apocalyptic landscape presents a young male protagonist whose hyperactive but highly rational voice is suggestive of Frank Cauldhame's. Patrick McCabe's influential Irish Gothic text, *The Butcher Boy* (1992), focuses on mental disturbance and its eventual manifestation in extreme violence through the protagonist, Francie Brady, a figure of fear and estrangement who finds himself ostracized from the community and witnesses his family's incarceration for suspected insanity.

3. Although *The Wasp Factory* was Banks's first published novel, it was not the first novel he had written. In sequence of publication, it was his seventh manuscript and the editorial relationship upon which much of Banks's success has been built reveals that this novel had a significant influence upon his later authorial practices. The themes of Banks's book — the presence of a mentally disturbed teenager, with the propensity to become a serial killer, who sets about killing a group of people located within a specifically domestic space — also clearly influences the works of others.

4. According to David Punter, "he lives his life entirely according to what he calls symbolism — every part of the island, every movement he makes, every part and exudation of his body forms part of this symbolism — but which would psychologically be more recognisable as a version of infant ritualism" (168).

5. This in important for a multitude of reasons and connects *The Wasp Factory* with a later Banks novel, *Complicity* (1993), which is also a narrative of doubles.

6. The sign also identifies Eric as the potential Gothic invader of the domestic.

7. Frank's need for control and power, for the safety in repetition and ability to exclude people from his society is at odds with the incursion of the natural elements. His building of dams in the early part of the novel evidences this; he identifies the sea as one of his enemies because of its destructive "female" qualities. As Duncan Petrie asserts, the "essential fluidity of the sea and its elemental ability to erase boundaries represent the antithesis of Frank's obsessive need to control and micromanage his world" (121).

8. Since the otherness of madness leads to repression behind walls, as Foucault asserts, Eric's escape represents the return of the repressed, the imprisoned, displaced and marginalized brother who comes back to haunt the family.

WORKS CITED

Banks, Iain. *The Bridge*. London: Abacus Books, 1995.
_____. *Complicity*. London: Abacus Books, 1994.
_____. *A Song of Stone*. London: Abacus Books, 1998.
_____. *The Wasp Factory*. London: Abacus Books, 1990.
Butlin, Ron. *The Sound of My Voice*. London: Serpent's Tail, 1987.
Calder, Angus. "By the Water of Leith I Sat: Reflections on Scottish Identity." *New Scottish Writing*. Ed. Harry Ritchie. London: Bloomsbury, 1996.
Grass, Günther. *The Tin Drum*. London: Secker and Warburg, 1962.
Hoban, Russell. *Riddley Walker*. London: Cape, 1980.
Hogg, James. *The Private Memoirs and Confessions of a Justified Sinner*. London: Oxford University Press, 1969.
Macdonald, Kirsty A. *Spectral Ambiguities: The Tradition of Psychosomatic Supernaturalism in Scottish Fiction*. Diss. University of Glasgow, 2005.
McCabe, Patrick. *The Butcher Boy*, London: Picador, 1992.
Middleton, Tim. "Constructing the Contemporary Self: The Works of Iain Banks." *Contemporary Fiction and National Identity*. Eds. Tracey Hill and William Hughes. Bath: Sulis Press, 1995.
Miller, Karl. *Doubles: Studies in Literary History*. Oxford: Oxford University Press, 1985.
Petrie, Duncan. *Contemporary Scottish Literature and Television*. Edinburgh: Edinburgh University Press, 2004.
Punter, David. *The Literature of Terror: A History of Gothic Fictions from 1765 to the Present Day*. Vol. 2: *The Modern Gothic* London: Longman, 1996.
Smith, C. Gregory. *Scottish Literature: Character and Influence*. London: MacMillan, 1919.
Stevenson, Robert Louis. *The Master of Ballantrae*. London: Cassell, 1889.
_____. *The Strange Case of Dr. Jekyll and Mr. Hyde*. London: Oxford University Press, 1997.
Wallace, Gavin. "Voices in Empty Houses: The Novel of Damaged Identity." *The Scottish Novel Since the Seventies: New Visions, Old Dreams*. Eds. Gavin Wallace and Randall Stevenson. Edinburgh: Edinburgh University Press, 1993.

Contributors

Ruth Bienstock Anolik teaches at Villanova University. She has a special interest in the interplay between Gothic literature and social and cultural structures. She has published essays in *Modern Language Studies, Legal Studies Forum, Partial Answers* and *Studies in American Jewish Literature.* She has edited two previous collections of essays, *The Gothic Other: Racial and Social Constructions in the Literary Imagination* (with coeditor Douglas L. Howard; McFarland, 2004) and *Horrifying Sex: Essays on Sexual Difference in the Gothic Imagination* (McFarland, 2007).

Martyn Colebrook is a final-year doctoral student at the University of Hull with a dissertation on the fiction of Iain Banks in relation to contemporary British literature. He completed his BA and MA at the University of Hull, writing on the novels of Don Delillo. He has published the article "To the Insane; I Owe Them Everything": J.G. Ballard and the Subversion of Dominant Literary Forms" and has co-organized conferences examining the work of Iain Banks, Michael Moorcock, Angela Carter, and the representation of 9/11 in contemporary narratives. He regularly reviews for *Literary London* and *Critical Engagements.*

Christine M. Crockett teaches in the department of English at Chaffey College. Her research and teaching interests include eighteenth- and nineteenth-century literature and culture, the Gothic, and studies in gender and sexuality. She is currently working on a study of autoerotic discourse and the British novel.

Catherine Delyfer is an associate professor of English at the University of Montpellier, France, and assistant editor of the journal *Cahiers Victoriens et Edouardiens.* She has published several articles on late nineteenth-century British culture and literature, in particular on the art magazine *The Studio,* the art of Aubrey Beardsley and James Whistler, and the works of women writers of the period such as Vernon Lee, Marie Corelli, Victoria Cross and Lucas Malet.

Elizabeth Hale lectures in English literature and writing at the University of New England, in New South Wales, Australia. She has published articles on nineteenth- and twentieth-century children's literature and classical reception studies. With Sarah Winters, she is the editor of *Marvelous Codes: The Fiction of Margaret Mahy.*

Cynthia Hall earned her PhD from University of California at Riverside and is an assistant professor at Abraham Baldwin State College in Georgia. Her dissertation, "The American Backbone: Curved Spines, Social Reform, and Nineteenth-Century Fiction," was the inspiration for her essay. Her research on spinal deformity has grown out of her own experience as a person with scoliosis whose adolescence was spent physically encased in a plastic and metal body brace.

Lisa M. Hermsen is an associate professor and the director of Institute Writing at Rochester Institute of Technology. She is completing a book entitled *Manic Minds: A Mad History of Psychiatry and Its Neuro-Future*. She teaches courses in science writing, the rhetoric of science, and the history of madness.

Carla T. Kungl teaches British literature and technical and developmental writing at Shippensburg University in Pennsylvania. She is the author of *Creating the Fictional Female Detective: The Sleuth Heroines of British Women Writers 1890–1940* (McFarland, 2006) and editor of *Vampires: Myths and Metaphors of Enduring Evil* (Inter-Disciplinary Press, 2004). She wrote "'Long Live Stardoe!' Can a Female Starbuck Survive?" for *Cylons in America: Critical Studies in Battlestar Galactica* (Continuum, 2007).

Paul Marchbanks teaches nineteenth- and twentieth-century British and Irish literature at California Polytechnic State University, where he is an assistant professor of English. He has published articles on Robert Browning, Charles Dickens, Liam O'Flaherty, and Charlotte Brontë in such journals as *Dickens Quarterly*, *The Victorian Institute Journal*, and the *Journal of Literary and Cultural Disability Studies*. His current research explores fictional renderings of intellectual disability within the cult of sensibility recreated (and transformed) by George Eliot's novels and novellas.

Maria Purves is a fellow of Lucy Cavendish College, University of Cambridge. She is the author of *The Gothic and Catholicism: Religion, Cultural Exchange and the Popular Novel, 1785–1829* (University of Chicago Press, 2009).

Andrew Scahill is a PhD candidate at the University of Texas at Austin in the radio-television-film program. His work, focusing on the place of the child as a rhetorical figure in cinema, combines work in genre studies, queer theory, and discourse analysis. His dissertation "Malice in Wonderland: The Perverse Pleasure of the Revolting Child" examines the child-as-monster in horror cinema as a site of pleasurable and transgressive spectatorship.

Tara Surry earned a PhD with distinction from the University of Western Australia. Her dissertation examined Virginia Woolf's essays and forms of urban space. She has presented numerous conference papers, some of which are in the process of being published. Her scholarly interests include modernism, the city, the Gothic, nineteenth-century studies, surrealism, and feminist and postcolonial theory. After living in New York and London, she has returned to Western Australia and is currently working on future writing projects.

Tamara S. Wagner obtained her PhD from Cambridge University. Recent books include *Longing: Narratives of Nostalgia in the British Novel, 1740–1890* (2004) and *Financial Speculation in Victorian Fiction: Plotting Money and the Novel Genre, 1815–1901* (forthcoming, 2010) and an edited collection on *Antifeminism and the Victorian Novel: Rereading Nineteenth-Century Women Writers* (2009). She is editing a special issue on Charlotte Yonge for *Women's Writing*.

Melissa Wehler is a doctoral candidate at Duquesne University with a dissertation directed by Laura Engel about dramatic representations of madness in the long eighteenth century. She has presented papers about Joanna Baillie at the South Central Society for Eighteenth-Century Studies and the East Coast Society for Eighteenth-Century Studies.

Simon J. White is a senior lecturer in romantic literature at Oxford Brookes University, Oxford, England. He wrote *Robert Bloomfield: Romanticism and the Poetry of Community* (Ashgate, 2007) and, with Bridget Keegan and John Goodridge, edited *Robert Bloomfield: Lyric, Class and the Romantic Canon* (Bucknell University Press, 2006). He has published articles on John Clare and Walter Scott, and is currently working on a book-length study of the representation of the rural community in the political polemic and poetry of the Romantic period.

Carolyn D. Williams is a senior lecturer in English and American literature at the University of Reading in Berkshire. Active in the British Society for Eighteenth-Century Studies, and a founding member of the London Women's Studies Group, 1500–1837, she is the author of *Pope, Homer, and Manliness* (1993) and *Boudica and Her Stories* (2009), and has published widely on gender, scientific history and links between English literature and the Greek and Roman classics. She is currently working on resuscitation in literature from Shakespeare to Dickens.

Index

aesthetics of the body, non-normative (ugliness) *see* Collins, Wilkie; dwarf; *Frankenstein*; giant; Hardy, Thomas; Lippard, George; Malet, Lucas; obesity; Shelley, Mary; Woolf, Virginia

aesthetics of the body, normative (beauty, perfection) 23, 31, 33*n*1, 131, 138, 140*n*13, 205–206; *see also* Malet, Lucas

African Americans 45*n*2, 145–146

age as disability 32, 54, 63, 106*n*3, 116–117, 194*n*9

AIDS 17*n*12

albino 183–184

aristocrats 29–30, 48–49, 57*n*4, 123, 168*n*15, 184; *see also* Lippard, George; Poe, Edgar Allan

Aristotle 25, 125–126, 127*n*4

babies, deformed *see* fetuses and babies, monstrous

Baillie, Joanna 114; *Orra* 13, 115–116; *Witchcraft* 13, 116-7

Banks, Iain: *The Wasp Factory* 15, 217–226

beauty *see* aesthetics of the body, normative

blindness 24–25, 27–29, 102, 190, 195*n*13

Braddon, Mary Elizabeth 170–171; *Lady Audley's Secret* 14, 171–173; *Thou Art the Man* 14, 176–177

Brontë, Charlotte: *Jane Eyre* 117

Byron, Lord 118*n*5

cancer 182

The Castle of Otranto 83, 181

Chinese 153*n*6

class, social and economic 57*n*8, 98, 100, 116–117, 140*n*11; *see also* aristocrats; Lippard, George

Cleland, John: *Memoirs of a Coxcomb* 13, 122–128

Cohen, Larry: *It's Alive* 208–211

Collins, Wilkie 47–60; *The Law and the Lady* 11, 51–54, 85; *The Legacy of Cain* 11, 55–56; *The Woman in White* 11, 48–51

Crete 187–88

curse as cause of disability 75–76; *see also* Malet, Lucas

Daniel Deronda 94*n*25

Darwin, Charles 92

Davis, Lennard 45*n*1, 86, 94*n*15, 94*n*20

deafness 186–190

deformity, physical *see* aesthetics of the body, non-normative

detection 47, 51

developmental disability 25–26, 33*n*3

diagnosis 4–8, 12, 13–14, 17*n*9, 35, 38–39, 41, 88, 94*n*18, 126, 129, 137, 147–150, 158, 163, 172–173, 175–176, 220–225; *see also* detection; Duganne, A.J.H.; the gaze; Hardy, Thomas; surveillance

Disability Rights movement 4–5, 8

disease *see* illness

doctors *see* physicians

"Don't Look Now" 185, 190–191

double 102–103, 122, 124, 187, 194*n*9, 212, 217, 220, 222–225, 225*n*5

Duganne, A.J.H.: *Knights of the Seal* 14, 157–169

du Maurier, Daphne 14, 181–196; "Don't

"The Little Photographer" 184–185
London 113; *see also* Woolf, Virginia

madness *see* mental illness
Male Gothic *see* Female and Male Gothic
Malet, Lucas: *The History of Sir Richard Calmady* 12, 80–96
"The Masque of the Red Death" 13, 147–153
masturbation 13, 129–141
Matilda 23
medical technology *see* Enlightenment medicine
medicine *see* Enlightenment medicine; folk medicine; physicians
Memoirs of a Coxcomb 13, 122–128
mental illness 12–13, 55–56, 58n15, 157–169, 213n11; *see also* Baillie, Joanna; Banks, Iain; Braddon, Mary Elizabeth; Duganne, A.J.H.; Foucault, Michel; Shakespeare, William
Middlemarch 11, 61–67
Modernism *see* Woolf, Virginia
monsters 7–10, 12, 51–52, 63–66, 76–77, 147; *see also* aesthetics of the body, non-normative
Morrison, Toni 145–146, 154n9

The Narrative of Arthur Gordon Pym 146
Native Americans 142–156; Kiowa tribe 142–144
New Woman 177–178; *see also The History of Sir Richard Calmady*; Malet, Lucas
norm 86, 94n20
"Not After Midnight" 186–190

obesity 48–51, 58n14, 155n18
Orra 13, 115–116

patriarch and patriarchy 66n4, 113, 137, 186, 209–210; *see also* husband, Gothic; Malet, Lucas; physicians; scientists and science
Philadelphia and Philadelphia Gothic 17n15; *see also* Duganne, A.J.H.; Lippard, George; Poe, Edgar Allan
physical deformity *see* aesthetics of the body, non-normative
physicians 13 55, 129–130, 139n1–2; 139n5, 139n7, 140n12, 172, 205, 209; *see also* diagnosis; the gaze; surveillance

plague *see* illness, contagious
Poe, Edgar Allan 145; "Hop Frog" 152; "The Masque of the Red Death" 13, 147–153; *The Narrative of Arthur Gordon Pym* 146
Polanski, Roman: *Rosemary's Baby* 197–198, 201
Pope, Alexander 121
postpartum depression 179n4, 198; *see also* pregnancy
pregnancy 198–199
Punter, David 4–6, 15, 17n9, 222

The Quaker City, or The Monks of Monk Hall 11, 35–46, 157, 166n3

race *see* African Americans; Chinese; Native Americans
Radcliffe, Ann 8–9, 81, 181, 221
rape 199
Rebecca 17n12, 182–183
religion/ethnicity 10; *see also* Italians; Jews
Richard III 84, 122
Rome 62
Rosemary's Baby 197–198, 201

Satan 10, 39, 59n18, 117, 121, 164–165, 197
scholars *see* scientists and science
scientists and science 18n17 134–135, 140n7–8, 186–189; *see also* diagnosis; Eliot, George; *Frankenstein*; *Middlemarch*; physicians; Shelley, Mary
Scotland and Scottish Gothic 53; *see also* Baillie, Joanna; Banks, Iain
Scott, Sir Walter 116–117
Sensation novel 18n16, 215n24; *see also* Braddon, Mary Elizabeth; Collins, Wilkie; Malet, Lucas
sense disability *see* blindness; deafness; du Maurier, Daphne
sexual "deviance" *see* gender and sexuality, non-normative
Shakespeare, William 114; *Hamlet* 13, 111; *Richard III* 84, 122
Shelley, Mary 23; *Frankenstein* 1, 5, 11, 13, 24–29, 84–85, 129–141, 210, 215n26; *The Last Man* 11, 29–34; *Matilda* 23
size, non-normative *see* dwarf; giant; obesity